Families in Changing Urban America

Mishpokhe

A Study of New York City
Jewish Family Clubs

WILLIAM E. MITCHELL
University of Vermont

New Preface to the Paperback Edition
WALTER P. ZENNER

Foreword by
MARSHALL SKLARE

AN ALDINE PAPERBACK

Mouton Pu'
The Hague · Pari

To Rhoda Métraux

First published by Mouton Publishers

1980 Paperback Edition published by
Aldine Publishing Company
200 Saw Mill River Road
Hawthorne, New York 10532

ISBN: 0-202-01166-6 Paper-Aldine
90-279-7695-3 Cloth-Mouton

Preface
to the Paperback Edition

An increasingly rare event in the social sciences is the publication of a significant research monograph which can be read profitably by students and members of the general public alike. *Mishpokhe* is such a book. It is a contribution to several specialties within anthropology and sociology: urban studies, the family and kinship, Judaic studies, and voluntary organizations. There are several issues of great import for which this study serves as an apt illustration. The first and most central issue is the question of the role of kinship, especially those relatives who are not members of one's nuclear family, in modern societies. Morton Fried wrote of this in recommending this book:

> If any demise has been announced more prematurely than that of "the family," it is the alleged passing of kinship as a basis for association in modern society. William Mitchell is modest enough to claim no predictive knowledge of the future with regard to the health of kinship in times yet to come, but his study of Jewish "cousin clubs," formed in what is sometimes referred to as the most urban city in the world, is stunning proof of the viability of kinship under the most atomizing circumstances. Indeed, it is not surprising that precisely the forces of social atomization produce a major stimulus for the active pursuit of extended relations of kin.

Mishpokhe describes the continuation and development of such extended kinship through an unusual form of voluntary organizations.

Academic and popular sociology have both implied that kinship beyond the family has become irrelevant for modern people and that family life in cities is impoverished. In this view, whereas formerly people could rely on grandparents, siblings, and cousins, now they must derive their material and emotional satisfaction from the fragile nuclear family. There is a basis in experience for such generalization. Country-folk who come to the city find that they come from a place of kith and kin to one inhabited by strangers. In a highly mobile society one has only short-term relations with most people, who thus remain acquaintances rather than becoming life-long friends or kin. When one wants a job or a loan, one must seek out strangers. At the local supermarket, one no longer encounters familiar faces behind the cash register, but people who change from one week to the next.

But this is only one side of modern society. Upper class and elite solidarity appears to have some roots in kinship and deep friendships formed in prep schools, first-rate colleges, and exclusive clubs. In other classes, "the forces of social atomization," as Fried puts it, are themselves causes for finding refuges through the formation of close personal ties, including those of kind. Contact with kinfolk is one of these havens. People turn to their kin for credit, for influence in getting jobs, for information and advice, and for reconstructing their genealogies. In the process, they may run into difficulties. Mitchell and his colleague, Hope Leichter, reported on some of these problems in their book *Kinship and Casework* (N.Y.: Teachers College Press, 1978). For instance, family businesses among New York City Jews were often the sources of conflict within the family as emotional ties among relatives were strained by the economics of small enterprises. Still, ties with extended kin are strong. Not only family businesses and cousin clubs, but a whole variety of kin ties and assemblages are found in this community.

What Mitchell and Leichter found to be true in New York City has been found among other modern urban groups around the world. Even formal kin-based organizations comparable to the cousin clubs are present in Lebanon and among Overseas Chinese. Of course, in both cases the form is not identical to that of Jews in the United States.

The argument against the conventional view of the modern family can be attacked from another side, too. The weaknesses of the extensions of kin and family relations have been traced by historians back in time to the period before the Industrial Revolution. In Europe, for example, households tended to be small in pre-modern times. Thus, the presumed connection between the decline of the family and industrialization can be questioned.

In a less direct way, the family club phenomenon can be seen as an example of ethnic survival through cultural transformation. While ethnic groups often maintain their separate identity on the basis of particular cultural symbols, the nature of the cultural traits which define the group may change over time and in different places. Thus, certain foods and food habits may distinguish the group in one place and other food habits in another locale. To use Jews, the subjects of this book as an example, traditional European Jewry was distinguished by its disdain for non-kosher foods, especially pork, as well as a freer use of garlic and onions than was common among their European neighbors. Jewish neighborhoods in New York City and Chicago are often notable for having a large number of Chinese restaurants. This taste for Chinese food by non-orthodox Jews may be traced to maintaining a distaste for pork, except thoroughly disguised, plus a desire to follow the middle-class fashion of eating exotic foods.

The family clubs Mitchell discusses are also part of this process of acculturation which has marked Jews in America, especially New York City. For many, the most significant Jewish reference group has become the family. Those religious rituals which have become most central are connected to the family and kin, including Bar Mitzvahs, weddings, funerals, saying the *Kaddish* (a special prayer connected to mourning for a parent), exchanging presents at Hanukkah, and having a Seder meal on Passover. Even on Yom Kipper, the Day of Atonement, observed by more Jews than any other holiday, one finds the synagogue more crowded at the time of the Yizker (Memorial) prayer than at any other time of the day. In fact, for many Jewish-Americans religion and ethnic loyalty have been reduced to those customs revolving around the family. It is not surprising that such a "familistic" group should also produce formally organized family clubs.

As Mitchell points out, however, family clubs are not the sole form of voluntary organization of American Jewry. Indeed, American Jews have a rich variety of such organizations and clubs, even though there is no over-arching government of the community as such. Jews participate in many interdenominational associations organized on purely secular lines, as well as forming their own groups.

The family clubs which span the ideological chasms dividing Jews bear some resemblance to the /landsmanshaftn, or hometown associations of an earlier period. New types of organizations along these lines continue to appear. I have heard of a group of New Yorkers who meet in a Texas city over lox and bagels every Sunday morning. Whether this group is composed solely of Jews or not, it certainly has a Jewish ambience. In the suburbs of one Northeastern city, two Jewish girls found that they were of similar origin, causing their parents to found a club. The meetings of this club, like those of the cousin clubs Mitchell studies, were occasions for eating together.

These processes of cultural transformation and voluntary organization to meet the demands of a new society are not limited to Jews, but can be found in all ethnic groups, whether West Indians, Italians, Lebanese, Chinese, or Greeks. Still, the differing conditions which they find in the new environment, their own original culture, and the groups they imitate may result in unique formations, of which the clubs described by Mitchell are an example. The family clubs in *Mishpokhe* thus provide an example of how values and forms taken from the Jewish tradition have been adapted to the circumstances of the American metropolis.

A third issue illustrated by this book is the nature of anthropological field research in a metropolitan area. In the Appendices, Mitchell describes his use of participation-observation, questionnaires, and documents. In this way, he shows how anthropologist must bridge the social sciences and history. For instance, he makes good use of data found in an earlier WPA study.

The personal factor also comes into play. For decades anthropologists have, perhaps self-servingly, argued that outsiders have advantages in studying a culture. They assert that the stranger can bring an objectivity which insiders lack, since they do not take the culture itself for granted, and can reveal what is hidden to members of the society. Of late, the "natives" whom we have observed have revolted against such an "ideology" of participation-observation and stressed the bias of the outsider.

Mitchell, referred to by Fried in his recommendation as a "freckled faced *goy* from the midwest," was an outsider to the Jews of East European origin whom he studied. He writes that he originally underestimated Jewish-Gentile animosity, but that the members of the cousins clubs confronted him directly about their suspicions. In the social sciences, we have tended to diminish the significance of the identity of the investigator as a factor in the study, whether it be North American, Latino, black, white, Jew, Christian or Muslim. Importantly, Mitchell does not do this. But, at the same time, his study of Jewish family clubs reveals the advantages available to the outsider. In *Mishpokhe,* Mitchell has successfully uncovered a facet of American Jewish life which was obscure even to the Jews themselves. He has made the most of the outsider's advantage.

SUNY   Walter P. Zenner
Albany
September, 1980

Foreword

The paucity of treatments of the American-Jewish family from the perspective of the social sciences stands in sharp contrast to the large number of treatments of the subject by writers of fiction. Doubtless our image of the Jewish family has been strongly affected by works of fiction, particularly by the works of American-Jewish novelists. And if the fictional literature on the Jewish family has impressed itself upon the classes the routines of Jewish comedians appear to have impressed themselves upon the masses. The Jewish comedians have educated Americans about Jewish family relationships, especially in respect to the interaction of family members.

The contribution of novelists and comedians should not be denigrated — their material frequently contains insights unavailable elsewhere. But it is apparent that their work covers a limited range. It concentrates on the relationship between parents and children, the interaction of siblings, and the question of awakening sexuality. Occasionally the relationship of grandparents to grandchildren is discussed. In any case the emphasis is on childhood experience. Even when the protagonists are adult the source of their response is seen as having its origin in childhood.

It appears that both Jewish novelists and Jewish comedians have minimal ties with extended kin. Thus it is not surprising that few of them have had anything to say about the subject of Prof. Mitchell's concern: the family club. If the subject matter of Prof. Mitchell's investigation is rarely treated by humorists or writers of fiction, it also appears to have escaped the notice of scholars. The only study of Jewish family clubs other than Prof. Mitchell's was published in 1939 in Yiddish. The study was the result of a W.P.A. project which included both *landsmanshaftn* (voluntary associations of individuals from the same village or region in Europe) as well as family clubs. While the project unearthed valuable material it did not have the advantage of being directed by a trained anthropologist. Thus the value of Prof. Mitchell's work is magnified by virtue of the fact that for the first time disciplined scholarship has been brought to bear on the understanding of the important but neglected phenomenon of Jewish family clubs.

Is Mitchell's work a contribution to contemporary Jewish studies or is it primarily a contribution to the study of the family? It is obviously a contribution to both. If we look at it as a contribution to the study of the family it is clear that his work serves as a contribution to the growing literature which seeks to modify the conclusions of an earlier generation of social scientists.

Scholars of an earlier era concentrated upon the view that the family was undergoing a crisis. They highlighted the limited functions of the contemporary family, especially the fact that the family was no longer an economic unit. As they saw it only the nuclear family could persist; social forces would inevitably destroy relationships with extended kin. In their view the extended family was not viable in modern society. How, they asked, could extended kinship relationships survive in a society which was not organized around kinship?

Kinship relationships were, for example, challenged by social mobility. One of the effects of social mobility was that the rate of social mobility would not be uniform among members of an extended family. Thus the extended family would include individuals on different class levels. The same would be true for education — not everyone in the extended family would achieve the same educational level. The end result would be that members of an extended family would come to occupy very different statuses, with the result that it would be difficult if not impossible to maintain family cohesion. The drift away from ties to the extended family was seen as inevitable — modern economic organization was viewed as rewarding individuals who were capable of freeing themselves from the restrictions which come with strong kinship involvement.

If this were not enough it was apparent that the extended family was threatened by geographical mobility. Relatives would no longer live in the same street, neighborhood, or city. Furthermore, given the individuation which occurs in modern society even when relatives were accessible, interaction with them would be supplanted by the growth of clique groups and the efflorescence of interaction between individuals who shared common interests rather than a common lineage.

All of these developments suggested that traditional bonds of kinship would be replaced by newer bonds centering around congeniality and common interests. Such developments were seen as centered in the city; urbanism as a way of life would inevitably loosen and ultimately destroy kinship networks. As regards the Jews, since the great majority of them had concentrated themselves in a dozen of the nation's largest cities, their traditional relationships with extended kin were seen as particularly vulnerable. The common view, then, was that the kinship principle — namely that the closest bonds and the most fulfilling relationships are those which exist among kin — was seen as a phenomenon which would inevitably wither away.

The more we learn about actual social interaction in modern society (in contrast to theories about such interaction) the clearer it becomes that kinship persists to an extent previously unimagined. And despite the forces which were supposed to undermine the solidarity of the Jewish family, the more we learn about the Jewish family the more we see that bonds with extended kin also persist. Prof. Mitchell's work is especially valuable because its focus is on the unexpected; it emphasizes the prevalence of kinship interaction rather than its absence.

It can be argued that Prof. Mitchell's work, which emphasizes the shift from older informal bonds which served to maintain family cohesion to a newer form which is essentially a voluntary association, is itself testimony to a sharp decline in family loyalty. Along the same line it can be asserted that the family club represents an intermediate stage in the inevitable dissolution of the bonds with extended kin. However, the formation of Jewish family clubs can, with equal cogency, be viewed from the perspective that the extended family is responsive to the threat to its viability and acts to combat the forces which endanger its survival. That the extended family forms itself into a kind of voluntary association can be interpreted as a survival mechanism which demonstrates an abiding desire to continue kinship bonds. Furthermore this desire to continue kinship bonds can be looked upon sympathetically in terms of a justifiable fear of replacing kinship bonds with social relationships which are by their nature highly ephemeral.

If Mitchell's work is a contribution to the understanding of the family in modern society it is at the same time a significant contribution to contemporary Jewish studies. Jewish identity in the Diaspora is closely intertwined with the nature of the Jewish family. Thus Mitchell presents an analysis of an important aspect of the changing Jewish community. To be sure there are any number of other developments in the American Jewish community which can offset the cohesive effect of the family club. They include a low birth rate, the sharp rise in divorce, the escalating rate of intermarriage, the impact of the rise in the level of secular education and the entrance of Jews into new occupations, the movement from Northern cities to the "Sun Belt", and, most recently, the rise of a new feminism which is frequently contemptuous of traditional Jewish family life. The new feminism is complemented in some cases by the desire of Jewish men to remain unencumbered by the obligations of marriage and the rearing of children.

It is by no means clear at the present time how the Jewish family can maintain itself in the face of such changes. Whatever the eventual fate of the Jewish family, Prof. Mitchell's study of family clubs advances our knowledge of a little-known phenomenon. His analysis serves as a corrective to the over-simplifications about the family in modern society which we have inherited from an earlier generation of social scientists. It also serves to alert us to new social arrangements which come into being in order to preserve age-old traditions. In its millennial history the Jewish community has proven to be unusually resilient to challenges which would defeat its desire for continuity and survival. Such resiliency has frequently rested upon the elaboration of innovations necessary to meet challenges unknown in previous generations. Prof. Mitchell is to be commended for the painstaking research which he has undertaken in respect to one such innovation.

Brandeis University   Marshall Sklare
Waltham, Mass.
January, 1978

Author's preface

How can Jewish relatives who range in residence and occupation from a Scarsdale doctor to a Brooklyn butcher and who diverge in religiosity from an Orthodox cantor to a ham-eating atheist maintain close family ties? It is a social truism that families with conflicting life styles scattered over a sprawling urban area fall apart. Even those families with a strong sense of duty to stay together will begin to lose their cohesiveness as members' contacts become increasingly erratic and highly preferential.

This book is about *family circles* and *cousins' clubs*, two remarkable social innovations by New York City Jews of Eastern European background, that attempt to keep relatives, the *mishpokhe* (Yid.), together even as the indomitable forces of urbanization and industrialization continue to rend them apart.

The family circle first appears on the New York City Jewish scene in the early 1900's as an adaptive response to preserve, both in principle and action, the social integrity of the immigrant Jewish family. It consists of a group of relatives with common ancestors organized like a lodge or club with elected officers, dues, regular meetings, and committees. But as the younger members became more Americanized than their immigrant parents and grandparents, the generation gap widened. By the 1930's a new type of family club was invented. The cousins' club excludes the older generations from membership, although they are included in some of the club's social activities. Today family circles and cousins' clubs continue to exist as important variant types of family structure in contemporary New York Jewish society. One out of five married couples in our questionnaire survey belongs to a family club.

The principal data on which this book is based are the product of the social science research project, "Studies in Family Inter-action", directed by Hope Jensen Leichter and sponsored under the joint auspices of the Jewish Family Service of New York City and the Russell Sage Foundation. The project's first volume, *Kinship and Casework* (Leichter and Mitchell, 1967), reports on the kinship patterns of New York Jews and on the role caseworkers play in altering or redefining contacts with relatives.

When the research team began its study of the Jewish family, we had no prior knowledge of the existence of family circles and cousins' clubs. But as we interviewed families about their ties to relatives, spontaneous references to family clubs freqently were made. Then, as we began to ask more about them, we became increasingly intrigued. Here was a form of the American family — a family club — that was not reported in the social science litera-ture. To understand urban Jewish kinship patterns, it was obvious we would have to know much more about these family clubs as social systems and their place in Jewish culture. This book is one outcome of our research.

The origins of most types of kin groups studied by anthropo-logists are lost in time. The fact that we can closely approximate the temporal beginning of Jewish family clubs is very unusual. And whereas the historic origins of specific clans found in tribal societies are usually unknown or explained by myth, a Jewish family club may present one with the minutes of its organizing meeting.

In this and many other ways, the family circle and cousins' club are more closely related to the "formal organizations" char-acteristic of an urban-industrial society than to the traditional types of kin groups found among less technologically developed societies of the world. Still, by using a rule of descent as a primary structuring principle, the family circle and cousins' club are cor-porate kin groups. So, from a strictly typological perspective, these family clubs do not fit neatly into the established conceptual schemes of social organization and their existence raises a number of theoretical questions. Consequently, my analysis of these family clubs is not of a conventional tidiness. In order to under-stand the ethnographic facts about the family circle and cousins' club, I have used a range of relevant concepts derived from studies about descent groups, voluntary associations, and formal organi-zations. My own notions about how best to classify these typo-logically maverick groups are discussed in Chapter eight.

The basic research data for this study were collected between 1960 and 1962. According to informants with whom I maintain contact and students' papers on Jewish family clubs sent to me by colleagues teaching in the New York City area, no important changes in the structure of family circles and cousins' clubs have occurred since that time. However, when I began this study the idea that large corporate kin groups could exist in New York City seemed preposterous to many social scientists. Some with whom I corresponded or talked were initially adamant that the family circle and cousins' club were not kin groups at all but urban associations with kinship an incidental or even accidental matter. Their skepticism is understandable when considered within the context of the then prevailing social science theories about the nature of kinship in urban-industrialized societies discussed by Professor Sklare in the Foreword.

One basic assumption was that large-scale kin groups were structurally and functionally incompatible with the occupational requirements of an urban-industrial society. It was further assumed that the existence of descent groups of any kind was incompatible with the social and geographic mobility required of a population in a highly urbanized and industrialized society. There were no ethnographic examples to contradict these assumptions, and they appeared to be valid. For example, in those instances where industrialization and descent groups did coexist, the descent groups were breaking up under the pressures of a rapidly advancing process of urbanization and industrialization (cf. Goode 1963b: 369). Certainly no one would have argued with Zelditch's (1955: 340) statement that "... in our society the nuclear family is a clearly stronger solidarity than any other kinship-based group, and no corporate descent group exists". But the "discovery" of the Jewish family circle and cousins' club has provided new data that modify these earlier assumptions as Zelditch (1964a:712–728) among others, has noted.

The major part of the book describes how these intimate, spirited, and often contentious family clubs are organized and how they function. The two concluding chapters deal with the challenging problems of how Jewish family clubs happened to emerge in American society and their theoretical implications for contemporary kinship studies. The research methods used in the study – a combination of intensive informant interviews, participant observation, and respondent questionnaires – and problems of doing field-oriented research in an urban setting, are presented in Appendix A. Questionnaire items, examples of club documents, and genealogies appear in successive appendices.

All of the names of family clubs and members appearing in these pages are fictitious as confidentiality of identifying data was promised to my informants as a condition of their cooperation in the study. Exceptions are the names of those family clubs and their members quoted from or cited in published sources; these appear unaltered.

The standard authority for the romanization of Yiddish terms is Uriel Weinreich's English-Yiddish Yiddish-English dictionary and is the source for the transliterations used throughout the text. See Weinreich (1968:xiii xxxix) for a discussion of this system.

The data gathering stage for the research was supported by the Jewish Family Service of New York City and the Russell Sage Foundation and the analysis and write-up stages by the Hope Foundation and the University of Vermont. My project colleagues were Fred Davis, Hope Jensen Leichter, Judith Lieb, Candace Rogers, Alice Liu Szema and Diana Tendler. All enthusiastically shared with me their materials and ideas on the family clubs.

I am especially grateful to Hope Leichter for working with me on the theoretical implications of these unusual groups, to Max Wall for translating from the Yiddish the historically crucial WPA study on the New York City Jewish family, and to Joyce Slayton Mitchell for her special reports on family club meetings. Marshall Sklare, the acknowledged expert on the sociology of American Jewry, has been an encouraging colleague and graciously contributed the Foreword. Other friends and colleagues who offered advice or assistance at strategic phases of the research include May Ebihara, Raymond Firth, Marvin Gelfand, Walter Karp, Fred Lief, Roger Peranio, David Schneider and Claire Taschdjian. It is with sadness that I cannot thank Nathan Ackerman, Millicent Ayoub, Maurice Freedman and Natalie Joffe; I can only acknowledge their memory. The book is dedicated to Rhoda Métraux who as fellow anthropologist, wise mentor and friend has facilitated in countless ways my field work studies from the streets of New York to the jungles of New Guinea.

Three of my Columbia University professors had an important influence on the study. Margaret Mead, whose writings originally helped lead me into anthropology from philosophy, closely followed my research on the family clubs and made detailed comments on an early manuscript draft. Morton Fried, whose lectures first excited my curiosity about the complexities of kinship behavior, offered many helpful suggestions as did Conrad Arensberg whose emphasis on the multiple determinants of behavior is reflected in Chapter Seven.

The initial draft of this monograph titled *Cognatic Descent Groups in an Urban Industrial Society* was submitted in 1969 in partial fulfillment of the requirements for a doctoral degree from Columbia University. In 1970, I went to Papua New Guinea on a three-year grant to study culturally contrasting therapeutic systems and upon its completion began to revise the manuscript for publication. Those helping in the technical preparation of the manuscript include Kathy Greer, Peggy Derby, Laura Tonseth, Jeanne Thibault and Marjory Walton.

Although it is my informants who provided the principal material for this book, they must remain nameless here. Their intelligent responsiveness and unencumbered immediacy were gratifying stimulants to my work. They humored me, fed me, challenged me, and praised me. But my greatest acknowledgement is to their trust in me, for without this precious ingredient there can be no ethnography nor the ultimate attainment of an encompassing science of human behavior.

Contents

List of tables and figures

1. The Jews of New York City

Who invented the idea of Jewish family clubs? We simply don't know. But a lot is known about the New York City Jewish community during the years of immigration and settlement when the clubs were first formed. It is important information not only as cultural background data for this study but directly pertains to later discussions about how these clubs came into existence and the models within the Jewish community on which they are based.

Today in New York City there is no "Jewish community" in the sense that it is represented in the larger community by a single organization as its spokesman. The Jews of New York are not a unified group but are heterogeneous both culturally and physically and have a multitude of often competing political, social, economic, and religious organizations.[1] There are also some Jews who, although maintaining a Jewish identity, are less interested in things "Jewish" and have affiliated with community associations that are not based on Jewish ethnicity. The only "Jewish" factor that all New York City Jews have in common today is that they are descendants of individuals called "Jews" and by a rule of descent are also "Jews". But it was not always this way.[2]

From the middle of the seventeenth century until the nineteenth, the Congregation Shearith Israel was New York's only synagogue and the accepted spokesman for a united Jewish community. But the unity was broken beyond repair with the establishment of a rival synagogue, the Congregation Bnai Jeshurun, in 1825, and a subsequent rash of other new synagogues established by successionist groups. Since this date no single organization has been able to speak with unanimity and authority for all New York Jews. As the cultural diversity among them became more marked and their numbers within the city increased, so did the number and types of organizations increase to meet their changing social and economic needs in a rapidly changing urban society. The family circle and cousins' club are but two of the more recently established organizations to meet these needs.

NEW YORK'S FIRST JEWS: THE SEPHARDIM AND ASHKENAZIM

The Jews of New York City have a long and often rousing history. The first Jew to settle in New York, then the Dutch colony of New Amsterdam, was Jacob Barsimon, an Ashkenazic Jew who arrived in 1654. He was followed later in the same year by 23 Sephardic Jews who were expelled from the Dutch colony of Pernambuco in Brazil when it was retaken by the Portuguese. A few Jews arrived from London and the West Indies soon after England took over the colony in 1664, and a few French Jews are reported to have immigrated by way of England in 1696. But the bulk of the early population, although small was comprised mainly of the descendants of the Sephardic Jews (sometimes referred to as "Portuguese" or "Spanish" Jews) who had earlier lived in Portugal and Spain, and the descendants of the commonly named Ashkenazic Jews who had earlier lived in Germany. However, most of the early Ashkenazic Jews who settled in New York came from Holland and England.

The Ashkenazim and Sephardim are two important subcultures of international Jewry and joined together to make New York's first Jewish community. It was an unusual union for the Sephardic and Ashkenazic communities were rigidly separate in the contemporary European cities. For one thing the Sephardim considered themselves to be the Jewish aristocracy and encouraged endogamy. But the two groups were different in other ways, too; they differed in language (the Sephardim spoke Portuguese, the Ashkenazim German), pronunciation of Hebrew, synagogue customs, and in their style of dress and food preferences.

For the first 50 years of New York Jewish history the Sephardim were the more numerous and the acknowledged leaders of the Jewish community. During this period New York was little more than an overgrown trading post and the Jewish community was not yet a hundred strong. Shearith Israel, the only synagogue and Sephardic in ritual, was the place of worship for Sephardim and Ashkenazim alike. By 1695 the Jewish population had finally reached 100 in a city of about 4,000 (See Table 1). By this time the Jews were fairly evenly divided between Sephardim and Ashkenazim, but by 1729 the Ashkenazim were in the majority, a majority that would continue to grow until they, in turn, were outnumbered by the great migration of Eastern European Jews to New York's Lower East Side in the late nineteenth century.

In the seventeenth and eighteenth centuries, however, the Jewish population of New York remained relatively small. Although only a hundred Jews lived in New York in 1695, 100 years later there were only 350 although the city had become the largest in the United States with 33,000 inhabitants. It took until 1825 for the population to reach an even 500.

The Jews who immigrated to New York during the colonial era appear to have been poor. Grinstein (1945:24) writes:

The Ashkenazim from Germany, Poland, and Holland came to America, for the most part, because they wanted to raise their standard of living. It was the lower rather than the upper classes among the Jews who joined the immigrant group. Few of the Jews of early New York knew Hebrew; a Jewish scholar was a rarity. Most of the immigrants seem to have been poor, many actually penniless. Save for the Marranos, who may have possessed some wealth, no rich Jews came or seemed to want to come to America.

There are also indications that these early Jewish immigrants of the seventeenth and eighteenth centuries came alone and that the tradition of families immigrating together did not develop until the nineteenth century.

Perhaps both of these factors helped Jews to assimilate quickly to the pattern of the broader community while maintaining a Jewish religious identity. According to the statement of a German officer at the time of the Revolutionary War, (Glanz 1947:20) New York Jews were indistinguishable from other citizens and this probably applies equally to an even earlier date. And Weinryb (1958:9) has documented how the early Jews, at least linguistically, were moving away from their traditional languages to the exclusive adoption of English:

In this connection it is significant to note that the minutes of Congregation Shearith Israel of New York City are written in Portuguese up to 1741, and later in a mixture of that language and English. However, by the end of the eighteenth century, English is employed exclusively. In 1757 the Congregation demands a cantor "who will be able to teach the children Hebrew with translation into English and Spanish", but five years later only Hebrew and English are required. Furthermore, the leadership was rapidly losing all contact with Hebrew. In 1728, of the 17 people signing the regulations of Shearith Israel, only three (all having Ashkenazic names) employed Hebrew script. By 1746 it was only one out of 47. In 1761 the first English translation of the holiday prayer book (*machzor*) was published in America. In the preface to the 1766 edition it is stated that many understand very little Hebrew, others none at all. . . . In short, American Jews of the second half of the eighteenth century seem to have had much in common with the non-Jews with whom they frequently congregated and with whom they did business.

During the period of Dutch rule in New York the Jews were required by law to live in a separate section of the city, but

Table 1. *The early Jewish population of New York City* *

Year	Number of Jews in New York City	General population of New York City	Percentage
1695	100	4,000	2.5
1750	300	13,000	2.3
1794	350	33,000	1.1
1809	450	96,000	0.5
1815	350	. . . .	. . . .
1820	450	123,000	0.4
1825	500	166,000	0.3
1836	2,000	270,000	0.7
1840	7,000	312,000	2.2
1842	10,000	. . . .	. . . .
1846	12,000	371,000	3.2
1850	16,000	515,000	3.1
1855	30,000	629,000	4.7

* From Grinstein (1945:469). These Jewish population estimates are based variously on the number of seats in the synagogues, the consumption of matzoh, and other data. The general population figures for New York City are given in round numbers. For a discussion of the problems inherent in Jewish demography, see Seligman (1958).

Grinstein (1945:30) indicates that the law was never really en-
forced. He does say, however, that "the earliest Jewish neighborhood was on Whitehall Street, probably near the tip of Manhattan Island". When the British took the colony in 1664, the
Jewish ghetto law was not reinstituted and the Jews of New York
have never been forced to live in legalized ghettos. They have
tended, however, just as other large ethnic groups in New York
have done, to group themselves in separate neighborhoods. During
the colonial period of New York, the Jews clustered in close
proximity to their synagogue on Mill Street. In the eighteenth
century as the city grew in population and economic strength, its
boundaries expanded and some Jews began moving "uptown". But
even as late as 1818 when the old synagogue was rebuilt, its location was unchanged, for the center of the Jewish population was
still in the Mill Street neighborhood.

The Sephardim of New York were able to maintain firm control
of Shearith Israel throughout the eighteenth century, but because
of their small numbers it was inevitable that they should inter-
marry with the Ashkenazim who continued to immigrate to the
city. The choice was often that of marrying either a Christian or a
Tedesco, the Sephardic pejorative term for an Ashkenazic Jew. As
Grinstein (1945:167) has noted, "One after another chose the
latter alternative, and thus family after family of Sephardim became associated with Ashkenazim until there were virtually no
real Portuguese left". By the beginning of the nineteenth century
most of the earlier Sephardic families were assimilated through
intermarriage. The resulting population was a highly Americanized
mixture of Polish, German, and Sephardic Jews sometimes referred to as neo-Portuguese. They considered themselves as a native
American group and superior to the new immigrants.

The exclusiveness of the Americanized group forced the immigrant Ashkenazim in each period to form a temporary coterie
which was socially outside the pale of the native group. The
immigrant Jew in New York had to undergo a long process of
Americanization before he was admitted to the so-called
Portuguese and neo-Portuguese group (Grinstein 1945:167).
By 1825, when a group of recently-arrived Ashkenazim broke
away from Shearith Israel to found their own synagogue, the neo-
Portuguese Jews were an established Jewish sub-culture and they
remained the elite of New York Jewry throughout the nineteenth

century. They constituted an exclusive group of cultured American Jews marrying among themselves and with their own religious, educational, and social organizations. According to Grinstein (1945:169) they "lived a self-contained life, with many non-Jewish friends and contacts, but with few social contacts among the German, Polish, or Russian Jews".

CULTURAL PLURALISM: THE 1800'S

In 1825 the Jewish community was still small and accounted for only .3 per cent of the total New York population. But looking at Table 1, the 500 Jews of 1825 increased to 2,000 by 1836 and in 1855 to 30,000, or 4.7 per cent of the city's total population. By 1859 the Jews further increased to approximately 40,000 (Grinstein 1945:29). This amazingly fast growth in the immigration rates of Jews during the first part of the nineteenth century was due primarily to the influx of Ashkenazim from England, Holland, Poland, and Germany.

The Ashkenazic English Jews were a small group compared with the German and Polish Jews. They immigrated to New York early in the 1800's, speaking both Yiddish and English, and adapted easily to the life of the city. In terms of group status they ranked just below the native American neo-Portuguese group. The English Jews had their closest social contacts with the small group of Dutch Jews, and the two groups made up the body of the Hebrew Mutual Benefit Society.

A much larger group were the Polish Jews, who by 1860 comprised one-third of the New York Jews. Most of the earlier immigrants came from the province of Posen, originally a Polish province that was incorporated into Prussia at the end of the eighteenth century. They had their own mutual aid societies but joined with the English and Dutch Jews on communal projects. They apparently had not acculturated to the Prussian culture before immigration and had little in common with the German Jews of New York. But when hundred of thousands of low status Eastern European Jews poured into New York in the 1880's and later, these earlier Polish Jews were careful to distinguish themselves from the new Jewish immigrants from Poland and Russia.

The largest of the four groups were the Jews from Germany,

who accounted for almost half of the New York Jews in 1860. The first of these immigrants arrived as the country was expanding and became peddlers in the cities and the countryside. They were generally poor and ignorant in comparison with the native Jews who were firmly established in the mercantile class. But immediately after the unsuccessful German Revolution of 1848 – a revolution with both nationalistic and liberal goals – there was a rush of German Jewish intellectuals and persons of wealth to New York. Weinryb (1958:13) writes that:

> These people were steeped in German culture and thought. They served as intermediaries here between the Germans and the German-Jewish Group, "representing" the latter in German clubs and associations, voicing their sympathy with Germany and German culture, and celebrating the founding of the Reich at the beginning of the 1870's.

At this time Americans had great respect for German learning and culture, and scholars and scientists travelled to the prestigious German universities for their training.

The educated German Jews brought with them a belief in Reform Judaism, which had its greatest impetus in Germany. Supporters of Reform Judaism as a movement within Judaism were trying to modernize Judaism by emphasizing its religious spirit instead of its behaviorally confining laws. The laws and customs of Orthodox Jewry demanded rigid behavioral conformity to ritual ordinances that went far beyond the Western concepts of morality and good citizenship. Reform Jewish leaders also looked upon the traditional Ashkenazic service as an incongruous anachronism in the modern world. As Glazer (1957:27) has noted:

> "Reform" Judaism began [in Germany] as a movement of Jews of high social status who wished to dignify Jewish religious services and make them decorous. They did not like the idea that the traditional Jewish service was ... a rather cacophonous Hebrew outpouring by the congregation, dressed in hats and prayer shawls led by a cantor ... using a decidedly un-Western and un-Germanic mode of singing, or rather chanting. And then too there was nothing that might be understood as edification in this service, for there was no sermon; twice a year the [visiting] rabbi ... would deliver a barely intelligible discussion of some Talmudic problem.

But even before the German revolution of 1848, an interest in

Reform Judaism was growing in New York. In 1844 a small group of German Jews had called for the formation of what they termed a "Cultus Verein". According to Grinstein (1945:355), "The sponsors of this call advocated a change in Jewish worship; among the reasons given were these: to permit the Jews to occupy a position of greater respect among our fellow citizens, to enable the Jews to worship with greater devotion, and, finally, to attach to themselves the rising generation of young people." They formed the Congregation Emanu-El the following year. At first the "temple's" only real innovation was a choir but more radical changes were gradually instituted, and it grew rapidly in influence and power. By 1860 it had almost reached the prestigious pinnacle occupied by Shearith Israel.

In the 1920's the Jewish neighborhood began to move uptown along Broadway, richer Jews mostly to the west and poorer Jews to the east. The very poorest continued to live in the old quarter. But as Grinstein (1945:32) reports: "It wasn't until the 1830's and early 1840's that Jews began to move over into the Lower East Side and establish neighborhoods based on kinship and country of origin, in addition to distinctions of wealth." These neighborhood patterns changed with the rate of immigration and the more Americanized or native-born Jews moved out of the Jewish quarter to "go West" and "uptown".

Toward the end of the nineteenth century a pattern of Jewish life was well established. Sharing in the economic progress brought on by industrial centralization and encouraged by the "openness" of American society, New York Jews advanced materially and geographically. Although they were never as rigidly divided into clusters of national groups as the London Jews, there were strong differences among them determined by national origin, wealth, and religious orientation.[3] It was never a completely united community of Jews. From the first, distinctions existed between Sephardim and Ashkenazim, native and immigrant, poor and rich.

The so-called Portuguese Jews, who considered themselves descendants of the poets and philosophers who had inhabited the Iberian peninsula, felt superior to and disliked the Ashkenazim. These, in turn, looked on the neo-Portuguese as ignorant folk who were dreaming of a lost glory. The German Jew considered the Pole a boor; the Pole thought of the German as Jewishly un-lettered. The English Jew, because he spoke

English, considered himself closer to the native Jew than to any
other Jewish group (Grinstein 1945:166).

These were not the kinds of difference that could be reconciled
easily.

Although the New York Jews were factionalized into irrecon-
cilable groups, they were alike in undergoing a process of secularization. In this connection Grinstein (1945:15) tells us that,
"the Jew in the European ghetto had God constantly before his
mind; the Jew of New York was aware of God only on certain
occasions and in certain times and seasons". The ancient custom
of Jewish men engaged in Hebrew scholarship for its own sake was
almost nonexistent, traditional religious observances were ignored,
and the celebration of the Sabbath as a day of rest and of prayer
was neglected. It is no wonder that the newly-arriving Eastern
European Jews found it difficult to tell the Jews and the Christians
apart. As for the Americanized Jews of the 1880's, many viewed
the intense poverty and piety of the new immigrants with mixed
feelings and attempted to discourage their coming. But just as the
Chief Rabbi of England was unsuccessful in keeping the Eastern
European Jew from his shores, so were the Jews of New York
(cf. Gartner 1960:24). By the outbreak of World War 1, over two
million — one-third of Eastern Europe's Jews — had come to
America and most of them to New York. Among them were those
who invented the family circle.

THE EASTERN EUROPEAN JEWISH EXODUS: 1880—1920

At the invitation of the Polish king, Boleslav the Pious (1227-
1279), the Jews of Europe began to migrate to Poland in large
numbers. There they were needed to bolster an economy de-
ficient in tradesmen and quickly "... found places as money
lenders, tax collectors, innkeepers, whiskey distillers, grain merchants, factors, stewards, artisans, and general middlemen"
(Rischin 1962:22). By the late eighteenth century Poland's empire
and power had gradually withered away, and with a series of
partitions in 1772, 1793, and 1795, most of the country was
taken by Prussia, Russia, and Austria. The Congress of Vienna
(1814—1815), held after Napoleon's downfall, set up a nominally
independent kingdom of Poland but in close alliance with the

Russian Tsar. When the Poles, encouraged by the French Revolution, revolted in 1830–1831, they were crushed by the Russian Army. The Polish constitution was suspended, and the kingdom became virtually a part of Russia. In 1863 the Poles attempted another revolt, but this was put down and led to even more humiliating measures. One account (Miller 1903:184) tells us that:

> The name Kingdom of Poland indeed remains, but all the autonomic institutions of the country have been swept away, and the whole country is being rapidly Russified. The Polish language has been entirely superseded by Russian in all courts of law, educational establishments and public offices, and all official correspondence must be in Russian.

Until the first partition of Poland, the Polish Jews for the most part were unmolested and valued as important to the economy. Under partition, a minority of the Polish Jews came under the rule of Austria with the annexation of Galicia and under Prussia with the annexation of Posen. But the greatest number of Jews came under Russian domination. It was the beginning of a bitter time. Almost immediately the Russians limited the residence rights of the newly-annexed Jews. They could live only in the area tacitly left to Poland and in the provinces of Lithuania, Byelorussia, and Ukraine. This area eventually was called the Jewish Pale of Settlement, and all but one-twentieth of Russia's Jews lived within its confines.

After Spain's expulsion of professing Jews in 1492, leadership in Jewish learning and thought passed to the Jews of Eastern Europe. Here Talmudic scholarship was an end in itself and the avenue for great esteem. And the Talmudic Law was such that all members of the community, men and women, the young and the old, were guided by its ideals and rules.

> Religious practice and observance, lightened by a sense of religious uniqueness, constituted the Jewish life. Divine thanksgiving hallowed each daily task so that the spiritual intertwined with the mundane. . . . The Giver of the Law in all his prescience and wisdom, supervised work and rest, dress and deportment, reading and writing, food and drink, cleanliness and health. . . . To deviate even in detail was heresy and invited ostracism (Rischin 1962:35).

Zborowski and Herzog (1952) have created a vivid portrait of this culture as lived in the small towns and villages of Eastern

Fig. 1 *Map of Eastern Europe and the Jewish pale of settlement*
Reprinted from M. Rischin, *The Promised City*, 1962, p. 21.
With kind permission of Harvard University Press.

Europe. But as they also tell us (1952:34), it was a culture that in the late nineteenth century was beginning to undergo radical changes, especially in the cities where many Jews were rebelling against the pervasive authority of the Torah.[4] This challenge to the traditional religiosity was stimulated by modern Western influences championed by those few with an advanced secular education, who wanted the Jews of Eastern Europe to find a secure place as equals to non-Jews.

The Haskala, or Jewish enlightenment, spread throughout the Pale and with it went the disruptive notions of Zionism, Socialism, and trade unionism. An eroding skepticism was threatening the structure of Eastern European Jewry:

> Young men who had pored over the Law turned to Haskala literature and Gentile knowledge. The sensitive at first were shocked, then intoxicated, by the imminence of worlds only dimly comprehended (Rischin 1962:40).

In some industrial sections of the Pale the new ideas inspired strikes, but the tsarist regime ruthlessly struck back.

Throughout the nineteenth century, the Russians subjected their Jewish subjects to a continual series of despotic edicts and humiliations. Many of these were attempts to drive the Jew from his established middle-class occupations in commerce and trade. In 1863, when the Russian serfs were emancipated, the forces of industrialization were well under way. But few of the Jews had the capital, training, or privilege necessary for successful participation in the increasingly complex economy. Instead, their economic position worsened. In the 1800's the "May Laws" denied Jews the right of owning or renting land outside of towns and cities. There were quotas on Jews entering the gymnasia and universities. Then:

> In 1891 thousands of privileged Jews were expelled without warning from Moscow, St. Petersburg, and Kiev. Thousands more were deprived of their livelihoods as innkeepers and restauranteurs in 1897 when the liquor traffic became a government monopoly. Finally, coercion culminated in violence. The "spontaneous" outbreaks of 1881, the massacre at Kishinev in 1903, the pogroms that followed, and the revolution of 1905 obliterated hope. The accompanying economic crisis reduced Russia's Jews to penury (Rischin 1962:24).

In 1868 there was a cholera epidemic and the following year a famine in Poland. In 1871 there was an organized massacre or "pogrom" of Jews in Odessa. The Jews began looking towards the United States, and during the 1870's, 40,000 emigrated, compared to the 7,500 who had left since 1800.

Thereafter the flow, steady and strong, generated its own momentum. In the 1880's over 200,000 crossed the ocean to the United States; in the 1890's another 300,000 followed. From 1900 to the outbreak of World War 1, the pioneers were joined by 1,500,000 of their kin as young men sent steamship tickets to their wives, children, and fellow townsmen; with the tide of families on the move, the number of emigrant women rose appreciably. During the Russo-Japanese War of 1904–1905, thousands of army reservists earmarked for slaughter in Siberian wastes stole across the frontier into Germany and struck out for America (Rischin 1962:20).

Jews were emigrating not only from Russia but also from Galicia with its primitive economy and poverty, and from Rumania where Jews, although materially better off, were politically and socially discriminated against. Throughout Eastern Europe pressures from within and from without were convincing Jews – poth the pious and the rebels – that New York was the promised city. In all it was to be New York City's greatest influx of a single cultural people. Those who left Eastern Europe were the lucky ones. Most of the Jews who remained and their descendants – some six million – were executed by the Germans in World War II.[5]

These newcomers to New York were sometimes referred to collectively as "Russian Jews", and they made quite an impact on the city as noted by one Jewish observer in 1905:

The Russian Jewish Element defies analysis. With its Lithuanian, Volhynian, Bessarabian, and other constituents, and its Galician, Polish, and Rumanian tributary streams, it is more complex than either of the other two [i.e., the earlier Sephardic and Ashkenazic Jews]. Besides, we are still caught in the eddies and currents of the Russian migration, and we are being thrown hither and thither by it (Szold 1905:14).

Not only did they arrive in tremendous numbers with a variety of Yiddish dialects and political views, but those who were ill or without funds put a demanding burden on the Jewish philanthropic and service institutions. They crowded into the Lower East Side pushing the Gentile communities of Germans and Irish further up-town. There within the Great Ghetto with the greatest population density in the city, they established their separate Jewish quarters. The Hungarians lived in the northernmost quarter and just below them the Galicians with the Rumanians to the west. The southern part "... was the preserve of the Russians – those from Russian Poland, Lithuania, Byelorussia, and the Ukraine – the most numerous and heterogeneous of the Jewries of Eastern Europe" (Rischin 1962:78).

Here the new immigrants were crowded into the notorious "double decker", or "dumbbell" tenement houses that were part of a much larger proliferating economic and political pattern. As Arensberg notes (1955:1157), these slum buildings of the in-dustrial cities were "... congruent and coincident with the mone-tarization and the commercialization of the cultural age of the free market and the *laissez-faire* capitalism they represent".

Many of the immigrants found work as peddlers or jobs in the garment industry that would eventually be controlled and mana-ged by the Eastern Europeans. Rischin (1962:59) writes that an estimated 66 per cent of the employed Jewish immigrants between 1899 and 1914 had industrial skills:

> Jews ranked first in 26 out of 47 trades tabulated by the Immigration Commission. They constituted 80 per cent of the hat and cap makers, 75 per cent of the furriers, 68 per cent of the tailors and bookbinders, 60 per cent of the watchmakers and milliners, and 55 per cent of the cigar makers and tinsmiths ... 30 to 50 per cent of the immigrants classified as tanners, turners, undergarment makers, jewelers, painters, glaziers, dress-makers, photographers, saddlemakers, locksmiths, butchers, and metal workers in other than iron and steel.

Although the hours were long, the pay low, and the working conditions bad, the labor market of the city was able to absorb most of the new immigrants. The Jews had arrived at a time when New York City was quickly becoming an industrial center as well as a center of trade and commerce, and cheap labor was a highly desirable commodity.

The patterns of secularism that originated in the Pale grew in size and importance in the New York Ghetto. Intellectual debate among workmen and educated alike in the "coffee and cake parlors" of the Lower East Side continued far into the night on the topics of Socialism, Communism, Anarchism, the Yiddish theatre, a new production at the Metropolitan Opera, or the outcome of a chess game. Women, too, especially the younger ones, had found a new kind of freedom in the ghetto, and some were joining the men in their exploratory movement of dissent. But their emancipated behavior struck some contemporary observers as unseemly.

> And where the cigarette smoke is thickest and denunciation of the present forms of government loudest, there you find women! One wishes he could write these women down gently. But to none would gentle words sound more strange than to the women of the radical coffee "parlor", who listen to strongest language and loudest voices nor fail to make themselves heard in the heat of the discussion. Yet it is hard to criticise them. . . . Unromatic perhaps, and yet we hear of them toiling, slaving, denying themselves until some man has won a degree and an entry into one of the professions. But as they sit there in an atmosphere of tea steam and cigarette smoke, one who does not know sees them only as unwomanly women, pallid, tired, thin-lipped, flat-chested and angular, wearing men's hats and shoes, without a hint of color or finery (Fromenson 1905:225).

The close crowding and generally unsanitary conditions of the ghetto created health problems and also accelerated the process of secularization.

> . . . the street becomes the common meeting place for man and maid . . . such young people soon become inoculated with the shallow cynicism of the ignorant. The Jewish faith as they know it, with its ceremonies and restrictions, is to them ridiculous and contemptible (Reizenstein 1905:48).

And also for the first time in the history of New York Jews, adult crime, prostitution, and juvenile delinquency became a part, although a relatively small part, of the ghetto scene. In 1904 there were 262 Jewish children under 16 in the juvenile Asylum committed for various misdemeanors. But even with its multiple problems, the ghetto was an alive, vital place with intellectual traditions. The Eastern European passion for Talmudic learning simply was exchanged for a passion for secular learning as the key to success in America.

Although Eastern European Jews moved into the Brownsville and Williamsburg districts of Brooklyn in the 1890's in great numbers, as the twentieth century wore on, the successful left these early ghetto areas for finer residences in Washington Heights, the East Bronx, Borough Park, and the West Side of Manhattan. Thousands of others left New York to establish large Jewish communities in every great American city. The Lower East Side began to lose its now fabled picturesqueness and to fade into the rest of the city.

The peak years of Eastern European immigration were 1906 and 1907, and a new, even bigger wave was assuming shape when the outbreak of World War I put a stop to all immigration. Americans were beginning to fear for the purity of the "Anglo-Saxon" stock, and the Chinese already were excluded. The restricting Immigration Law of 1917 and successive legislation put an end to the mass immigration of Eastern European Jews.

THE URBAN DISPERSAL: 1940—

By the time this study was made, most of the children and grand-children of the Eastern European immigrants had attained middle-class status and, according to Glazer (1958:138),

> ... were more or less to the level previously achieved by the German Jews. These changes have wiped out most of the economic and occupational distinctions between the two elements and along with other developments have in large measure merged the two formerly distinct elements into a single community.

For example, Reform Judaism, once wholly identified with German Jews, has lost this exclusiveness as both the rabbi and members are likely as not to be of Eastern European descent.

The first generation of Eastern Europeans is now dead or aged, and the younger generations, with a traditional emphasis on enterprise and education, are primarily business and professional men. As a group, their occupational achievements have been exceedingly impressive. Two-thirds of New York Jews are engaged in non-manual work compared to the non-Jews of the city with only one-half or even less in non-manual work.[6]

One of the most profound changes — and with important implications for this study — is the continued urban dispersal of the Eastern Europeans, their children, and grandchildren. As national

Table 2. *The Jewish population of Greater New York, 1960**

New York City

    Manhattan 293,000
    Bronx 432,000
    Brooklyn 794,000
    Queens 408,000
    Staten Island 10,000
    Total 1,937,000

Westchester County

    Mt. Vernon 11,800
    New Rochelle 22,500
    White Plains 9,700
    Yonkers 23,000
    Southern Sect 41,700
    Northern Sect 7,700
    Total 116,400

Nassau County

    Hempstead 218,300
    North Hempstead 55,600
    Oyster Bay 55,200
    Total 329,100

Suffolk County

    Eastern Sect 900
    Central Sect 6,800
    Western Sect 12,400
    Total 20,100

Greater New York

    GRAND TOTAL 2,402,600

---

*Compiled from Fine and Himmelfarb (1961:59).
  All figures are rounded to nearest zero.

prosperity increased in the forties, so did the dispersal of Jewish families throughout the metropolitan area. Relatives were scattered from Long Island suburban communities across Brooklyn and Queens, throughout Manhattan and up to the Bronx, Westchester County, and even Connecticut.

At the time this study was made, the *American Jewish Yearbook of 1961* showed the Jewish population of New York City as 1,936,000 and the three suburban counties of Westchester, Nassau, and Suffolk had a combined Jewish population of 465,000. Therefore, the total Jewish population was almost two and one-half million in the Greater New York area. A breakdown of these figures is given in Table 2.

2. The origins of family clubs

As cultural institutions the family circle and cousins' club of New York City are found only among Jews whose ancestors emigrated from Eastern Europe during the great wave of immigration from 1870 to World War I. During this period over two million Jews left their homelands to settle in the United States. But these Jews did not bring the family circle and cousins' club with them from Eastern Europe, and comparable kinship organizations were unknown there.[1] The family circle and cousins' club emerged as cultural institutions only after permanent settlement was made in the United States. Both groups may be interpreted as social innovations for restructuring the traditionally close affective and instrumental kinship ties of Eastern European Jewry — kinship ties that were first disrupted by immigration and then further threatened by the gradual geographic dispersion of relatives throughout the New York City area and the accompanying process of differential social mobility. Only then did *mishpokhe*, the traditional Yiddish term for relatives, begin to organize themselves into corporate family clubs.

Although this study of the Jewish family circle and cousins' club is limited to the New York City area, the organizations have a much wider distribution. They may be found in any big American city where Eastern European Jews settled in large numbers, for example, Chicago, Detroit, Pittsburgh, and Philadelphia. It also appears that Eastern European Jewry is the only American ethnic group to have innovated such highly-organized family clubs that come together regularly throughout the year. While the Old American Protestant family reunion (Ayoub 1966) is in some ways similar to the Jewish family clubs, it frequently is not a corporate organization and it is loosely organized and meets only once a year.

The family circle is historically older than the cousins' club, dating back as it does to the first decade of the 1900's while the cousins' club is of more recent origin. In both types of kin groups, affiliation rights pass through both males and females. The spouses of cognates, whether male or female, may also affiliate. Once an individual joins a group, he enjoys equal rights with all other members. However, a very few groups, especially family circles, exclude in-marrying non-Jews from membership.

A primary structural difference between the two groups is that in a family circle all descendants of the apical ancestor are eligible for affiliation. The cousins' club introduces a limiting generational principle that eliminates the ascending generations of several groups of lineally-related siblings. In this sense a cousins' club restricts membership to a group of first cousins and their descendants. Their parents and the common grandparents from whom descent is reckoned are excluded from affiliation. Cousins' clubs also limit membership to adults, either married or single, who must usually be 21 years old or older.

Both the family circle and the cousins' club are "closed" groups in the Weberian sense that a highly standardized principle of selection is active so that the participation of certain persons is excluded, limited, or subjected to conditions. But for those individuals who are eligible to affiliate, membership is optative. Also there is no restriction on the number of family clubs which an individual may join; some individuals studied belonged to as many as three.

Family clubs are usually led by elected officers and, true to their egalitarian spirit, any member — cognate or affine, male or female — is eligible to hold office. Business meetings are usually held once a month followed by the serving of food and visiting. Organizational records are held in common by the group, and the dues levied on all members along with other monies are kept in a bank in the group's name. There are, however, some family circles and cousins' clubs that meet regularly during the year but do not have elected officers or dues. A very few family circles are incorporated by the State of New York and also a few own cemeteries for the burial of members. Most of the groups, although not all, are primarily concerned with their own family affairs and are not involved in community affairs as a group.

AGE OF CLUBS

The data on the age patterning of the family circle and cousins' club are from the WPA Yiddish Writers' Group questionnaire study (Rontch 1939) and the "Family Research Questionnaire" gixen to a sample of clients of the Jewish Family Service of New York City.[2]

Table 3. *Founding dates of family clubs studied by the WPA Yiddish Writers' Group (N = 112)*

Year founded	Number founded	Year founded	Number founded
1909	1	1927	1
1910	2	1928	7
1912	3	1929	2
1913	2	1930	2
1916	1	1931	6
1919	4	1932	6
1920	3	1933	8
1921	1	1934	13
1923	3	1935	3
1924	2	1936	15
1925	1	1937	10
1926	1	1938	12

Table 3 gives the number of groups organized for each year from the WPA sample. The earliest group known organized was in 1909; this was the Friedman Family Circle. It was organized to: (1) hold the family ties of the separated generations together and (2) to help members when they were in need. It met every second Sunday of the month at the Hotel McAlpine in Manhattan and also had special "greetings meetings" when members or relatives came for a visit from other cities or countries. When the group was organized, it had only 13 members, but in 1938 when the WPA study was made, it had 110, of whom 90 per cent were American-born. The occupations of the members were 10 per cent laborers, 25 per cent professional and civil servants, and 65 per cent business. Unlike many of the earlier groups which held meetings in both English and Yiddish, the Friedman Family Circle used English exclusively for its business meetings, correspondence, and minutes. There is no indication whether the group had a constitution. They did, however, issue a bulletin called the *Friedman News* after each meeting and owned a section of burial plots in a cemetery. Some of the meeting programs featured lecturers on Judaism or Jewish problems relating to municipal and state concerns.

The two other oldest groups in the study were founded in 1910. These were the Moses Family Circle and the Wilfried Family Circle. The purposes of the Moses Family Circle were: (1) to hold family get-togethers, (2) to establish a loan fund for members, and (3) to provide death benefits. When the group was organized it had only ten members, but in 1938 the group had grown to 115, of whom 70 per cent were American-born. The occupations of members were 10 per cent professional, 15 per cent laborers, and 75 per cent business. They met every third Sunday of the month at 257 West 93 Street, presumably in a rented hall. The meetings, correspondence, and minutes were all in English. They had a printed constitution and "issued printed material," the nature of which is not given. They also gave financial support to local institutions and to the "old home"[3] relatives still in Eastern Europe. To help fulfill their "death benefits" purposes, they owned burial plots.

The Wilfried Family Circle is similar to the other two groups. It was organized for: (1) fellowship and get-togethers and (2) relief. It began with four members but had grown to 65 when studied. Sixty per cent of the 65 members were American-born. Percentages are not given for occupations although the data show that members were variously laborers and business and professional men. They met the first Sunday of the month at the home of members. The meetings and minutes utilized both English and Yiddish, but the correspondence was only in English. There was a printed constitution and financial support was given to the "old home".

Similar data are available on each of the 112 groups studied by the WPA Yiddish Writers' Group. These summaries of the three oldest groups in their research sample give an indication of the kind of data they systematically collected. Although there are differences even among these three groups, the most structurally important differences are only apparent when the earliest groups are compared with the ones organized later.

The 112 groups in the WPA sample were founded during the 30 years from 1909 through 1938. Of these only 8 per cent were founded in the initial 10-year period through 1928, and the majority, 69 per cent, in the last 10-year period. All of the groups studied were family circle in type with the exception of the Baron Cousins' Club, founded in 1938.[4] Three of the groups were auxiliary clubs of a larger family circle with either age or sex membership restrictions. Two were clubs for the children of members, viz., the Michael Tenzer Junior League and the Levin Family Club (Junior Group). The other was the Ladies Auxiliary of the True Family Circle.

The Jewish Family Service "Family Research Questionnaire" obtained data on 90 family clubs, but information on the founding date was given on only 38 of the 42 cousins' clubs and 37 of the 48 family circles that made up the sample. These data are compared to the WPA sample in Table 4. Both samples clearly show that the family circle antedates the cousins' club. The family circle, from these figures and those in Table 3, seems to have made a gradual start early in this century and to have reached its greatest popularity in the 1930's. After World War II the figures clearly show that there is a shift in popularity from the family circle to the cousins's club; today fewer family circles are founded compared to cousins' clubs.

These data are only on organizations that were active when the two samples were made. Neither table deals with defunct organi-

Table 4. *Founding dates of family circles and cousins' clubs in two samples**

Founding dates	JFS sample (N = 75)		WPA sample (N = 112)	
	Family circle (N = 38)	Cousins' club (N = 37)	Family circle (N = 111)	Cousins' club (N = 1)
1919 or before	4	0	13	0
1920–1929	1	0	24	0
1930–1939	7	0	74	1
1940–1949	9	3	...	...
1950–1959	17	34	...	...

* The samples are from the Jewish Family Service (JFS) and Works Progress Administration Yiddish Writers' Group (WPA) research projects. The figures for the WPA project are through 1938.

zations, but there is both statistical and interview data indicating that many family clubs are organized but eventually disband. For example, Table 4 shows that there were more groups founded in the ten years previous to when the two samples were made than in earlier decades. This generalization holds for both samples although one was made in 1938 and the other in 1960. Apparently there is a tendency for groups to disband as they grow older, a hypothesis that is supported by the interview data.

This is further supported by data on a question in the "Family Research Questionnaire" that asks, "In the past have there ever been any cousins' clubs or family circles among either your mother's or father's relatives that no longer exist?" Of the 381 respondents who answered this question, 55 said that such a family club existed previously. Table 5 shows that when the respondents' active and defunct groups are grouped together, 38 per cent of the groups founded by their relatives had disbanded. Therefore, out of every ten groups founded, four had disbanded by the time this study was made. There are, unfortunately, no data on how long the defunct groups were organized before they disbanded.

Table 5. *Number and per cent distribution of existing and defunct family clubs reported by Jewish Family Service sample*

Family clubs (N = 145)	Number	Per cent
Existing	90	62
Defunct	55	38

GOALS

The goal or purpose of a formal organization may be examined from several positions. For example, the stated or manifest purpose of an organization as phrased by its members may be different from the social scientist's statement about its purpose in relation to the larger social system or the personal needs of individual members. Here I am concerned only with the manifest purposes of family circles and cousins' clubs as stated by the club members themselves.

The data in Table 6 are abstracted from the brief summaries on family circles and cousins' clubs in Chapter Two of the WPA study. In all but two of the groups studies, the manifest purposes are characterized as promoting family solidarity and/or economic aid.[5] For example, some of the "family solidarity" explanations are: "to hold the family together in close bonds", "for family social get-togethers", "for social fellowship", "to keep the family closely bound together", "to maintain closer family ties", "to unite the family and bring unity and friendship among all of the families", "to remain closely bound in acquaintance", "to keep the family together in America", "attracting and bringing together different generations", and "to hold the family in close bonds through frequent meetings".

Table 6. *Per cent distribution of the organizational goals of family clubs in WPA sample (N = 111)*

Organizational goal	Founding decade		
	1909—1919	1920—1929	1930—1939
Family solidarity	13	14	28
Economic aid	6	18	19
Family solidarity and economic aid	81	68	53
Total per cent	100	100	100
Number of cases	16	22	73

If a group has a constitution, the purpose is usually stated in the first or second article. The Horowitz-Margareten Family Association itemizes four purposes:

(a) To keep the members of the families united,
(b) To have the members cooperate socially and otherwise and to assist in promoting each other's general welfare,
(c) To promote such social functions as will tend to strengthen the bond of true friendship between the relatives, and
(d) To publish a monthly journal containing news of interest to the members only.

The purpose of the Goldfarb Family Circle is stated in less detail: "The object of the organization is to create a closer relationship between the members and to carry into effect programs that will benefit the entire family."

Interview data on the purposes of family circles and cousins' clubs, however, not only stress the social integration of relatives but their integration through time as well. Informants active in groups want their children to know their relatives and especially their cousins. One informant's statement that "the purpose of our family circle is to keep the nieces and nephews together after we are gone" is typical. She continued, saying:

> Well, my husband's family is large and is dispersed, and we thought that since there were 26 grandchildren, or cousins, that they might get together every once in a while and keep in touch with each other because as it was, the only time we saw each other was at funerals or an occasional wedding if we happened to be invited.

The "economic aid" category of purposes is more complex and includes free loans, low interest rate loans, financial and material gifts to needy members and/or to relatives remaining in Europe, burial expenses, and cemetery plots. In the WPA study these purposes are described by some of the groups as follows: "to help members when they are in need", "a loan fund and death benefits", "to provide cemetery rights", "funeral expenses and a free loan society", "to support poor relatives in Europe", "relief, sick, and death benefits", "to provide a cemetery", "to help needy relatives", "to help each other", "a free loan society to help relatives in the old home", and "assisting needy relatives".

The groups organized earlier in this century frequently gave not only economic aid to their own members but also, as some of the statements of purpose above attest, contributed financially to relatives remaining in Eastern Europe. From 1909 to 1919, 31 per cent of the groups founded contributed funds to relatives overseas. In the decade of 1920–1929 the figure was 32 per cent of the new groups, but it dropped to only 17 per cent of the groups organized during 1930–1939. The WPA figures stop at this date. They do show, however, a lessening of interest in family ties to Eastern Europe. What ties did remain at the beginning of World War II were mostly broken by the German annihilation of European Jews. In my interview sample none of the groups founded after the war mentions European kin ties. However, one of the oldest family circles that originally gave help to kin in Eastern Europe now gives interest-free loans to family members in Israel.

In the three decades covered by the WPA study, Table 6 shows that 81 per cent of the earlier groups founded, i.e., from 1909 through 1919, gave equal emphasis to family solidarity and economic functions, but this decreased to 53 per cent of the groups in the 1930–1939 decade. Another indication that groups organized later had fewer and less elaborate economic functions is that 37 per cent of the groups founded in the 1909–1919 decade had burial benefits for their members, but this decreased to 14 per cent for the groups founded in the 1920–1929 decade and finally to only 3 per cent for the 1930–1939 groups. Thus, even before the 1940's and World War II, groups were beginning to be organized with less elaborate economic functions.

From my interview sample of family clubs none of the organizations founded after World War II includes death benefits and only one organization includes a loan fund for its members. This is a small family circle organized in 1955 that allowed a few close friends to join to broaden its economic base.[6] I also know of several family circles that were reorganized after the war as cousins' clubs with nominal dues but without death, loan, and welfare benefits.

Although the data show that there was always a type of family club organized with the exclusive purpose to promote family solidarity, it now appears to be the only type of club formed. And though the old type of family circle with its mutual aid purposes continues to exist, recently organized family circles are, like cousins' clubs, concerned only with keeping the family together. Corporately organized mutual aid is not a club goal.

This de-emphasis on the economic functions of newer groups can be correlated to twentieth century changes in the American social system and the status of family club members within this system. In an increasingly affluent American society with strong private and public economic and service institutions, there is less need for relatives to band together for crisis economic support. And of equal importance is the fact that club members, no longer poor immigrants in a strange land, have found important niches in New York's industrial economy and a share in the city's prosperity. The psychology engendered by low status in a precarious and exploitive economy that brings individuals together in mutual aid organizations is no longer appropriate to most of New York's

Jews. For example, one informant, a young advertising executive, told me the following about his family circle organized after World War II:

> Another small conflict I remember . . . was in reference to the purpose of the club or family circle. Was it primarily social? Were there going to be any benefits to the members of the club and their children? And someone brought up a burial plot . . . but the overall majority . . . [felt] that this was strictly a social club, a club of friendship and fellowship and keeping the family together, and each one should worry about his own burial rights and tomb and burial concerns for his family rather than as a club. . . . I mean, you see, it's more or less a get-together rather than worrying about a burial-together.

FORMING A CLUB

Family circles and cousins' clubs are formed in one of two rather obvious ways, i.e., planned or spontaneous. The planned formation is usually the idea of a single person who begins to talk about the possibility of a family club to his relatives and to sell them on the idea that such a group is necessary to the happiness and/or prosperity of the family members. He will lament the falling off of intra-family contact and appeal to the members' sense of family identity to rectify this loss with a family organization. For example:

> A cousin of mine had the family over and decided it would be a nice thing if we could all get to see one another — set aside a day and make an appointment and know that this would be a day to see one another, to be together and enjoy each other and then perhaps go to a nightclub once a year and celebrate the forming of the club. I guess that's how it all started.
>
> In 1960 this cousin of mine approached me and said, "Why don't we organize a cousins' club? . . . . So he said, "I'll tell you what I'm going to do; I'm going to invite everyone over to my house, and we'll see if we can get something going." So in 1960 he invited all of us over to his house . . . and he took the floor and said that he invited us over there to try to organize a cousins' club in the respect that we would get together, and we wouldn't drift apart, and get to keep in close touch and know

when children are being born, and we can sort of make social activites. Have Hanukah parties and have outings and socialize and be friendly rather than just being relatives and in business. My data indicate that there is no single type of situation that motivates an individual to begin lobbying for a family club but that they may be very diverse. A serious illness, the loss of one's own family by immigration, the perpetuation of a husband's name, a desire to save money, or simply a desire to organize are but five of undoubtedly many motivating circumstances for individuals that can be documented by informants:

One of our cousins' aunts who was very ill, and I guess — she was a very, very old person, very cold and disinterested — she had become ill and all of a sudden she started thinking about her aunts and her cousins, and she realized that she had a family. And she got us all together and she said, "Look, this is terrible! We don't see each other, and we don't know each other, and the children don't know each other. Let's start a group!" So we started one.

Milton, the one who organized this club . . . is a native-born European who married the daughter of Morris and Estelle. . . . Perhaps this was just a carry-over from his European days when he was probably torn away from his family and was sort of lonely and here in the United States. Having married into a nice little family unit, he would like to feel that he is part of a family unit and keep his contemporaries who are again all about the same age, in their early thirties, together.

The grandmother gave $200 to the organization when it started. She was really one of the pivotal people who wanted the organization to come into being, and it was her $200 that swung the group to name it after her husband. They had first thought they would call it the "Good Times Family Circle", but since she was giving the $200, they decided to satisfy her wishes.

We all go on vacations, and we thought if we would all start a savings club, we might save money better. It would be something like a Christmas Club. No one would miss two dollars a week!

There is one cousin in the family who is extremely — I don't know how to put it — but dealt in all these activities and is quite active in his own synagogue and community affairs and just thrives on this sort of thing and likes to be part of something like this. And he was, I should say, the main person who got this [cousins' club] going.

The other source for group formation is a spontaneous suggestion made by someone when relatives are already gathered together. As the following five examples show, these large kin gatherings are usually in relation to a funeral, wedding, or Bar Mitzvah:

So my sister said, "Well, now dad's went" — and everybody loved dad; he was really a great guy, had a wonderful sense of humor — and shortly after his death, we all got together and decided that at least once a month we would have this family circle.

And there was some talk — right after Bob's father died when so many people were together — about forming a cousins' club.

Well, it seems that there was a wedding . . . and, of course, these people got together, and they were very happy to see each other, and they said, "Gee, it seems that the only time we see people is at weddings and funerals. Why don't we get together, at other times?" And so I said, "Why don't you form a cousins' club?" And they decided right then and there they would. And they sent out cards to all the members of the family, you know, even the very distant ones, and most of them responded. Most of them came.

[My mother] talked about [the cousins' club's] formation at Ann's wedding, my cousin whose husband sells the stocks. . . . At her wedding, members who eventually formed the cousins' club were sitting at the same table, and my Aunt Ida or my father's cousin Rose were supposed to have suggested the cousins' club idea . . . and it was unanimous at Ann's wedding. And soon afterwards their cousins' club was formed.

About 17 years ago we had a Bar Mitzvah for one of the sons of a cousin. And one of the cousins said, "The only time we see each other is at three places: weddings, Bar Mitzvahs, or funerals." And he says, "Gee, we ought to start a family circle!" And we all thought this was a very good idea, and so we started one.

The organizational meeting for a family circle or cousins' club is always one of high spirits and high hopes. It is a festive gathering suffused with a feeling of well-being at the prospect of keeping the family together. Although it is impossible to get the undivided attention of all the participants, the group is organized amid the spirited confusion.

A vivid description of the formation of a family circle in 1921 appears in the first issue of the *Horowitz and Margareten Family Journal* with the front page headline "Family Association Organized". It is reported in full below. The excitement generated at this meeting is similar to that reported by informants for recently formed cousins' clubs.

At the height of the "Matzoh" season last April the idea occurred to Uncle Ignatz Margareten that it would be very much worthwhile for the "Mishpochoh" to get together into some kind of family association. The idea met with instant approval, and a call was sent out for a meeting to be held as soon after Passover as practicable. Accordingly, on Rosh Chodesh Iyar, Monday, May 9, everybody, young and old, all the uncles and the aunts, with the children, big and little, with husbands and wives, came trooping to the Margareten home in Borough Park bubbling over with eagerness and enthusiasm for the organization that was about to be formed. In all about one hundred persons were present.

Tante Rebush's ample home could hardly contain all of the guests and from the dining room and parlor and sitting room they overflowed on to the porch. Moreover, due to the congestion and especially to the irrepressible desire of everybody to talk things over with those they hadn't seen since many days, the business meeting was conducted with some difficulty. Furthermore, even those few whose mouths were not filled with words were so busy partaking of the good things set out on tables all over the place that they could not pay much attention to such tasteless matters as the chairman's call for "Order", the motions being proposed, and the discussion that was being attempted up at the front of the room.

However, in spite of these distractions under the patient and good-natured chairmanship of Mr. Joseph Goldstein, the meeting managed to organize itself into the Horowitz-Margareten Family Association and finally to adopt, after much discussion, the name which we now bear. Committees were also appointed to take care of the other details of organization and administration, such as a Constitution committee composed for the most part of our best legal talent, under the capable chairmanship of our editor, Jacob L. Horowitz, Esq.; a Membership committee under the chairmanship of Mr. Julius Weiss, aided by many of our fairest, handsomest juniors, a House committee under the expert chairmanship of one of our leading young housewives — may their number increase — Mrs. Samuel Weiss aided and assisted by a charming array of "junge Weiblich" and marriageables. The date of the next meeting was fixed for June 5th.

As the formal meeting was about to adjourn, Mr. Jacob Weiss, who could not restrain his enthusiasm for the Association, rose up and proposed to contribute some money immediately towards the expense of the organization. This was the signal for a general rush of the women to their men folks for money to do their share, and as usual "Father" paid up. As no dues had yet been fixed, the money was accepted to be applied against future dues.

A word of commendation is in order for the good work done by Miss Rose Weiss and Mr. Jacob Margareten, who served as acting secretaries of the meeting. It was a difficult task, and they acquitted themselves well thereof.

The mighty impulse for just indulging in social "stuff", such as gossiping, eating, drinking, dancing, and kissing "Hello" and "Goodbye" was finally let loose, when the chairman at last declared the business part of the evening "Closed". There was no possible doubt that everybody was having a delightful time. Everybody was talking as fast as he could to as many people as possible at the same time, and one person remarked to your humble reporter that the muscles of her face were getting tired with smiling. It was a terrible strain. Jollity went merrily on, and the hours sped quickly by.

There were so many people to talk to, so many good things to eat and drink, and so much pleasure in just looking on and watching the happy groups here and there that the evening past [sic] all too swiftly. But Borough Park is far from the Bronx and still further from Jersey, and many had far to go, and even as lovers must part, so we had to break away and make for home. With lots of kisses and embraces, good wishes, and handshaking, the party at last broke up vowing that they had never had such a "good time" in their lives and that they would be sure to come very, very early to the next meeting of the association on June the 5th.

And so a family club is born. It is really the easiest part. As in any organization, the principal problem is to maintain viability as a corporate structure through time. At a later point I will examine some of the internal and external vicissitudes that challenge the structural continuity of family clubs. For the present discussion it is important only to know that if a group does become inactive or disbands, it may reorganize at a later date.

RE-FORMATIONS

I did not attempt a systematic inquiry into the disbanding and re-formations of family clubs. However, in the course of collecting interview data on these groups, I sometimes discovered that a group was a re-formation of an earlier organization. Invariably I found that some members of a disbanded family circle had re-organized themselves into a cousins' club. Here is one example.

When one of my informants was a young girl, there was a family circle among her maternal kin, but her parents did not participate. Its potential members were her mother and five siblings and their families. For some reason, she thinks it may have been "personal friction", the group dispersed. Then in 1958 the children of the six siblings, now married with children of their own, organized a cousins' club that met five times a year. Whereas the family circle was a highly structured organization, the cousins' club was unusually informal with no officers or dues although at each gathering ". . . everyone chips in three dollars a couple to pay for the food. It's just a party, that's all. . . . It's just a way to spend an evening together and have a little fun." The members take turns in "making the party" and providing the refreshments.

Another cousins' club was preceded by two abortive family circles. Both were broken up by quarrels among the apical sibling group generated especially by the brothers' wrangles regarding joint business ventures that set the various families against one another. The cousins' club was 15 years old when I studied it, but my informant told me that the club had almost disbanded three different times. Each time the strife was stirred up by the "aunts and uncles". This group was highly organized with a constitution, officers, and dues.

One of the family circles was actively considering the possibility of reorganizing as a cousins' club.

That's why we came to the idea of having a cousins' club and meeting on a Saturday night instead of Sunday afternoon because the children have their own groups, their own friends. You can't force them to get to know each other or to be friendly with each other, especially if they only see each other two or three times a year. So when they got together [at the family circle meeting], our kids would carry on with the children they knew whom they could see any week.

Further interviewing uncovered a family-wide argument over invitations to a wedding that had caused bitterness among the older generation of brothers and sisters. It was the informant's husband who commented, "It was mainly to eliminate the [older] generation that we talked about making a cousins' club."

A third informant explains the history of family clubs in her family in this way:

Well, it happens we had a family club, and it just petered out. And after the war the boys came back, and we started again, and it petered out. And then we decided that perhaps it needed a different approach so we organized a cousins' club. And now the way we meet — we throw everybody's name into a hat, and we draw the names, and the people whose names come out are the ones to give the party.

Another informant shows how deaths of pivotal kin in her family circle led to frequent reorientations and finally to the formation of a cousins' club.

[We] felt that older members of the family were dying off. Of course, like every family when the grandparents are alive, my father's parents, well when they were alive and their brothers and sisters were alive, then everyone came to visit them, you know. The whole family rotated around the grandparents. Then after they died . . . everything rotated around my father. He was the oldest son. Then when my father died, so did the family. That unity broke and though we did have an organized family circle from before when my grandmother was alive yet, but you know it kept on petering out. And then a few members of the family died, and everybody felt that the cousins — though we all knew each other, let's say I and my brothers were the older ones — the younger ones didn't know us well, and the children, our children, didn't know each other. You see [we're] still at the age where everybody is married and has children [at home]. So everybody felt they did want the family to know each other. So we didn't love each other enough to see each other more often than four times a year [at the cousins' club meetings], but four times a year we were very glad to see each other.

I know of no case where a defunct family circle was reorganized in its original format. Nor do I know of a cousins' club that disbanded to reorganize itself as a cousins' club at a later date, although I think this more likely than the previous possibility.

For example, an informant who was giving me data on her family circle said that there had been a cousins' club on her husband's side. It met monthly for about three years then broke up over a monetary argument. Recently she heard talk of reorganizing the group:

Last winter one of our cousins . . . said, "How about getting together? I'll make the start. Come to my house because I have a big home and a basement. We will have the first meeting. Let's get together every three months; maybe once a month was too often. Then let's meet in a restaurant or somewhere where no one will have any fuss or bother." And, of course, some of us felt, "Gee, what's a fuss or bother of coffee and cake. Or a sandwich is so terrible! Your turn will come once in two or three years." But evidently the interest just wasn't there. I don't know what it was, but we were supposed to hear from them in September or October, and I haven't heard from them yet!

In summary, the limited data indicate that members of a kinship network may make repeated attempts to establish themselves as a family club, even when there is strong interpersonal antagonism among the members. But if a defunct family circle attempts to reorganize today, it will choose the more informal and flexible structure of a cousins' club.

NAMING PATTERNS

In the WPA sample of family circles, the most frequent source of a name is the surname of the male apical ancestor, e.g.,

Birman Family Circle,
Littman Family Circle,
Tescher Family Circle,
Greblovsky Family Circle.[7]

Sometimes the group adopts the first and surname of the male apical ancestor, e.g.,

Michael Tenzer Family Circle,
Sam Levitt Family Circle,
Joseph Kreinik Family Circle.

Or just his first initials may be used, e.g.,

D. Boardman Family Circle,
L. S. Bernstein Family Circle.

It is unusual for a family circle to be named after the female apical ancestor, but it does occur, e.g.,

Mary Engel Family Circle,
Pearl Gologorer Family Circle,
Clara Levinsky Family Circle.

The WPA sample lists several family circles that include two or even three surnames, e.g.,

Yakev and Leibush Family Circle,
Frankel Moss Family Circle,
Kowalsky, Gertl, Krow Family Circle,

but there are no data as to how these family names were chosen. Sometimes the choice of genealogical names depends on special circumstances. The

Horowitz-Margareten Family Circle

includes the descendants of Isaac Horowitz, who was born about 1797 and died about 1845. However, there were several early marriages of Horowitz women to Margareten men so the latter name is the source of several large branches and is included in the organization's name (Margareten et al. 1955).

In my interview sample of family circles all are named for the surname of the male apical ancestor with the exception of three named after the male apical ancestor's complete name and two named after the apical pair, e.g.,

Esther and Irving Gelber Family Circle.

Twenty-three per cent of the WPA family circles do not use the term "family circle" in their name but use a wide variety of terms. These include

Family Schonberg Aid Society,

Family Benevolent Society,
Goldfarb Family Club,
Rosenkrantz Family Society,
Letitchever Family Benevolent Association, Inc.,
Yakev Sheinback Family Assoication,
Feit and Auster Benevolent Society,
Mathis Family Harmony Society,
Levin Family Tree, Inc.,
Blatt Social Organization,
Leon Bleecker Sunshine League,
The Goodwill Benevolent Society,
Gitelson-Komaiko Descendants,
Anshei Bnai Chaye Yakev Silber Society,
Association of Descendants of "Rashi".

It is obvious that the names of some of these organizations, by including the term "aid" or "benevolent", emphasize their economic functions. It also shows the close historical relationship of the family circle to the Jewish "mutual aid" and "benevolent" societies and lodges that flourished among the early Eastern European immigrants. This topic will be pursued in greater depth in Chapter Seven.

The naming patterns of cousins' clubs is much less elaborated. In my interview sample all, with the exception of six, are named for the surname of the male apical ancestor to whom all cognatic members can trace descent. One of these used the initials of the first and last names of the ancestral pair, e.g., L.M.N. Cousins' Club, and another chose an English phrase denoting unity but spelled it backwards. Two others called themselves the No Name Cousins' Club, a name I heard for other cousins' clubs not included in my interview sample. Whether this denotes a lack of imagination or patronymic neutrality, I am not sure. The other two had no formal name but were referred to simply as "the cousins' club". This is reflected in the conversational style of members of named family clubs who in common parlance refer to the group only as the "family circle" or "cousins' club".

Apparently there is little controversy of a serious nature in choosing the name for a family circle or cousins' club. Old minutes show that the debate may be lively, but then most decisions of these groups are debated with vigor. Also, once a group is named, it seems to stick. In one of the family circles I studied, there was an attempt to change the group's name, but it was unsuccessful. Two wealthy brothers, members of the group through their mother, wanted to change the name to that of their own.

They said they would subsidize the club. . . . Anything that was needed they would support if the family circle name were changed to Grossman. . . . Well, everyone wanted to know why. Most of them were descended from the chart from this person here [points to kinship chart], and the Grossmans were just one family structure within the grouping. [The name] should come from the main support, the main stream, rather than from one of the lower echelons. And, the group as a whole — even though there were others there than Silvers — felt that they should keep the Silvers' name, and they were voted down overwhelmingly. . . . [The Grossmans] essentially dropped out of the club. They are members, but they rarely come. . . . In other words, if they couldn't own the club, they weren't coming!

According to my informant, the members' attitudes to the two brothers was, "You want to help these circles, start one! This is the Silvers Family Circle, and you either are our member or start your own and be a member of both." It also demonstrates the attitude that any family may have a family club if they just start one; there are, from the informant's viewpoint, no special prerequisites.

3. Membership and leadership

MODES OF LATERALITY AND LINEALITY

In discussions of kinship phenomena the combining terms "lineal" and "lateral" are frequently used interchangeably. Firth (1957: 5–6), however, makes a definite conceptual distinction between them that clarifies their usage. The mode of laterality refers to the way an individual is affiliated to a kinship group. Among the family clubs there are four possible modes of affiliation for an individual, that is *matrilateral, patrilateral, virilateral,* and *uxorilateral.* In other words, an individual may affiliate with a club if his or her mother, father or spouse is a member or is eligible for membership. Or if Ego is interpreted as a married couple, the laterality modes of affiliation may be described as *virimatrilateral, viripatrilateral, uxorimatrilateral* and *uxoripatrilateral* with articulation to the group respectively via the husband's mother (HuMo), husband's father (HuFa), wife's mother (WiMo), and wife's father (WiFa.)

Unlike some kinship groups where only cognates in the network are members of the group, the family clubs include the spouses of cognates as well.[1] This principle is expressed in the constitution of one family circle as, "Any person is eligible for membership who is a descendant of Joseph and Rose Goldfarb according to the family tree on file with this constitution, their offspring, and their spouses." But who can and who does actually join family clubs? All New York City Jewish families of Eastern European background, of course, do not have family clubs. Yet in our random sample of 238 couples completing the "Family Research Questionnaire", 31 per cent indicated they could join a family club if they wished and 19 per cent added that they were members. This means that almost one out of every three couples can join a family club and one out of five couples actually does. Family clubs, then, are a statistically relevant form of Jewish kinship organization in New York City.

Among the couples belonging to family clubs, 68 per cent are affiliated with a single club, 30 per cent with two clubs, and 2 per cent with three clubs. In only a single instance did a couple fail to opt membership in *all* of the groups available to them. This couple joined only two of the three clubs they could affiliate with. Thus, if several family clubs exist among a couple's network of relatives, they evidently feel constrained to belong to all of these rather than to be accused of partiality. This is supported by interview data where informants affiliated with all possible groups or none at all.

The number of couples who can and do affiliate with family clubs and the mode of laterality is shown in Table 7. These data are recombined in Table 8 to show the favored points of articulation among the possible choices. Although the differences certainly aren't impressive, the data disclose that a higher percentage of possible uxorilateral affiliations are chosen over virilateral ones and matrilateral affiliations over patrilateral ones. In other words, a couple more frequently joins the wife's group instead of the husband's, and their mother's groups instead of their fathers', demonstrating a very slight preference for affiliation with

Table 7. *Number of married couples who can and do affiliate to family clubs and the mode of laterality (N = 74)*

Mode of laterality	Number of couples	
	Can affiliate	Do affiliate
WiMo	16	11
HuMo	13	8
WiFa	13	8
HuFa	9	5
WiMo, WiFa	5	3
HuMo, HuFa	5	3
WiMo, HuMo	5	3
HuMo, HuFa	4	2
HuFa, WiMo	2	1
HuMo, HuFa, WiMo	1	1
Multiple, unclear	1	1
Total	74	46

a group through a linking female. But I would emphasize again that these percentage differences are slight indeed.

The mode of lineality refers to the lines along which membership is transmitted from one generation to another. In the family clubs the continuity of the group is maintained by transmitting membership rights "ambilineally" (Firth 1957:6), i.e., through both male and female links from the apical ancestors. In the family circle these rights pass lineally to all of the cognatic descendants of the apical pair regardless of sex. In a cousins' club the lineal transmission is identical to a family circle with the important exception that the apical ancestors are the founding cousins, not their grandparents, although their cognatic kin tie is reckoned from this second ascending generation. In either case the group is then formed by a process of self-selection from the extensive genealogical network or, to use Radcliffe-Brown's term (1950:16), "stock". As affiliation to a group is by choice, it is obvious that not all descendants, as the data show, will opt membership. Some of the extra-genealogical factors involved in individual membership decisions are discussed later.

Table 8. *Number and per cent of couples opting various modes of lateralty for family club affiliations (N = 45)*

Mode of laterality	Number of couples		Per cent
	Can affiliate Number	Do affiliate Number	
Uxorilateral			
WiMo	29	19	66
WiFa	23	14	61
Combined	52	33	64
Virilateral			
HuMo	28	17	61
HuFa	16	9	56
Combined	44	26	59
Matrilateral			
WiMo, HuMo	57	36	63
Patrilateral			
WiFa, HuFa	39	23	59

I know of only one organization where the ancestor for cal-
culating the rights of membership was not born within the past
160 or so years. This is a family circle included in the WPA study
called The Association of the Descendants of "Rashi". This
unusual group was founded in 1933 "to uphold and maintain the
golden chain of Rashi", a famous Jewish scholar and commentator
on the Old Testament and the Talmud. He lived from 1040 to
1105, and he is still a glorious name among seminarians. In 1938
forty-five families were members of the organization, each tracing
its ancestry to the illustrious rabbi.

THE STRUCTURED VARIABILITY OF MEMBERSHIP CRITERIA

The essential genealogical difference then between family circles
and cousins' clubs is that the former count as potential members
all the living descendants of the ancestral pair, while cousins' clubs
include all of the descendants of a group of cousins. In a family
circle all descendants of the apical ancestor may affiliate, but in
a cousins' club ascending generations from the founding cousins
are specifically excluded from membership. For example:

INF:[2]   This cousins' club is open to all cousins, no parents. That
was one of the first things established. They didn't want
any parents around.

WM: Why was that?

INF: Well, because they wanted to keep the authority among
themselves, and once you start dealing on the parent level,
there are pressures and influences brought about by your
mother and your father and your aunts and your uncles.
... These are all first cousins who have mothers and
fathers that are sisters and brothers. So that was actually
one of the first written by-laws of the organization — that
no parents would be allowed in, just cousins. Any sort of
second, third, [and] first cousins, of course.

At the present time cousins' clubs appear to be somewhat age-
graded, but as the cousins' children and grandchildren attain adult-
hood and join, it should become transgenerational in membership
composition and resemble the family circle. This is, of course,
assuming that the cousins' clubs follow this temporal paradigm. It
it also possible that as the apical cousin generation dies off, the

group will dissolve or at least segment into smaller clusters of kin. At the present time it is too early to predict these structural changes with any sense of assurance. The genealogies, however, show that the great majority of the cousins' children are still in school although the married children of the cousins are beginning to come into the clubs.

Most of the groups in my interview sample permitted in-marrying Gentiles to be members. Some family circles still restrict membership to Jews, but Josephy (1967:53) notes that the rigid Jewish endogamy of the Friedman Family Circle is breaking down. My data would suggest that the more formally organized the group and extensive its economic functions, the more likely Gentiles are to be excluded. This is partly related to the fact that Gentiles cannot be buried in family circles' cemeteries that are consecrated exclusively for Jews. Family circles *without* officers and cousins' clubs with their emphasis on sociability tend not to exclude Gentiles. However, in those cousins' clubs where the religiously Orthodox parents of the cousins have an influence on the organization, I was told that a Gentile would not feel completely welcome.

In regard to adopted children and step-children, I know of no case where they are excluded, but I observed in one family circle constitution that they are explicitly included. I have already mentioned that affines who are spouses of cognates, i.e., who are the in-marrying husbands and wives of members, are eligible for membership and are expected by the family to join. Nor is it unusual when there is a remarriage after an affine's spouse dies for the new spouse to be given full membership as well. For example, one woman had joined her husband's family club as a young woman, and the couple and their children had been active in its affairs. When the husband died his widow remarried and her new husband was given membership without question.

There are also instances where the parents of a person who has joined a family club through marriage seek membership. Here an informant refers to her newly-married daughter's husband's parents:

Harvey's parents would love to be with our family circle. I know that, and they've actually told me as much. But I wouldn't even attempt to bring it up because first of all, they're not family — as far as we know it — and I think the rest of them would resent it if I did mention it. But I told them that they were always welcome to come to a meeting socially just for social purposes. They can listen. We have nothing secret. And whenever we have a meeting here, I'll have them over. I'll invite them, and whether the rest will do the same will be up to them. In fact, the custom of inviting cognates of affines is fairly common among most family circles and cousins' clubs. The woman sponsoring the meeting in her home feels free to invite a few of her or her husband's close relatives not eligible for membership or even friends to the gathering.

I know of only one instance where a decision was made by a club to include a parent of an affine as a member. It was an unfortunate mistake. Here an informant tells me about how her sister's son's wife's mother obtained membership in the family club.

They're beginning to resent that she's a member . . . and, of course, actually she was sort of pushed in on us, you could sort of say. . . . That was about a year ago, but they made it an open vote. . . . Well, my sister Dottie put it up on the floor as an open vote whether she should be accepted or not. And with open voting, very few people are going to say, "No", even because they feel that it isn't right. So after she was accepted, we made a new rule to the constitution that if there are any members that have to be voted in, — that is, that aren't part of the family — that it would have to go through a closed vote.

I previously noted that one small family circle became a composite kin and friendship group soon after it was organized. But I think in most groups the idea of including friends may be met with scorn:

This one time there was a discussion whether or not they should take in outsiders because we felt [membership] was dropping, and we didn't want to see it going out of existence. Maybe we should take in friends [but] a few of them like this [uncle] felt it was a very bad thing. [Another uncle] thought it was a bad thing; [my aunt] was very much against it. There was a lot of bitterness there. Then there were others who had very dear friends who wanted to take them in. . . . Bob and Jennie had some friends that they wanted to take. Milton and Harriet had said at one time they wanted to bring some friends, but it was vetoed, and we decided not to. . . . [My uncle] said that if they did [pass it], he was dropping out and a few others [too]. And we decided it wasn't fair to have people drop out of it who were really legitimate members just to take in some outsiders who, after awhile sometimes, like the ones that Milton and Harriet had wanted to take in originally, have turned into bitter enemies. All of the cousins' clubs I studied restricted membership to adults, but the determining age varied between sixteen and twenty-one. In all instances, however, the age criterion was waived if the individual married at an earlier age. The age-grading criterion for membership is explained as necessary because of the night meetings and because the occasion is an adult social occasion, and children are hindrances to the festive atmosphere. Children are neither members nor invited to the regular meetings. In discussing these matters with one informant, she explains:

When my daughter wasn't supposed to come to meetings, she was very indignant.When she was younger, she wasn't eligible. You see, we wanted to have the freedom. You see my father was the oldest so I am the older cousin, and the others are sort of petering down towards thirty, you know. So they wanted to have the freedom of expression and not be hampered by the children. If they want to get silly and make a joke, they should-n't be embarrassed by children. So they said if a child is over twenty-one or married, they can join the club. Now that Sheila is married, she is eligible. So now she's not interested! But before, she carried on something terrible.

In the family circle the situation is somewhat more complex as the family circle is oriented cross-generationally. The meetings are often held earlier in the day so that both the young and old may attend. The emphasis is on *all* of the family. The children of member parents are usually considered members at birth. The WPA study (Rontch 1939:55) makes this observation at a family circle meeting:

The president reminds the audience that according to the law which he as president has instituted, every new-born child is automatically taken into the society, and the president must pay the first dollar. The president immediately hands over a dollar, and the audience applauds. At this point the grandfather of the new-born child gets the floor. He is grateful for the tre-mendous honor which they have given him in taking his grand-son as a member of the society, and he hopes when he grows up, he will do good works with them.

Family circles do, however, restrict voting to adult members, marking the transition at twenty-one, or, less frequently, eighteen. As in the cousins' club, this requirement is waived if a member marries prior to the established voting age.

One other structural point on variations in membership criteria must be discussed, i.e., honorary members. I came across this membership classification in only three of the cousins' clubs I studied, but several informants said they had heard of cousins' clubs with honorary members. The honorary classification refers to the parents of cousins invited to attend meetings but not allowed to hold office or to vote. For example:

> Well, they just decided that [the older generation] cannot have any choice in anything to do or any say in anything the organization does — that they are invited to come to all the meetings, any outings, any parties, or anything that we have, but they cannot have a voice. Just sort of honorary members but pay your own way. [Laughs] I mean they are all people substantial financially.

In this group the honorary members make financial contributions to the club's treasury, and there are several uncles who are very successful businessmen. At another club's annual inaugural dinner-dance which my wife and I attended, she was told by one of the members that a particular uncle, an honorary member, had paid for most of the affair.[3]

Honorary members sometimes sponsor a meeting in their home and supply and serve the refreshments. During my interview there was considerable levity among members and honorary members alike around the fact that honorary members are expected to contribute financially but are precluded from the formal decision-making process. It appeared to me that the honorary members are quite content with this status, so pleased are they that their children meet regularly. It was also obvious from my observations that the most financially benevolent uncle received considerable deference from his nieces and nephews. At one of the regular meetings I attended, the group listened with quiet respect when he spoke. When others spoke, including the president, there was always a certain amount of chattering going on.

In the third cousins' club only one maiden cognatic aunt was voted in as an honorary member. The minutes of the first meeting in the middle 1940's include this item: "Aunt Ida was voted in as an honorary member and is to come to all meetings and get all benefits as the rest of the members." It was explained to me that this was the only aunt who got along well with *all* of her nieces and nephews. The other aunts and uncles quarrelled among themselves, and this was said to have a negative effect upon their children's inter-relationships because they rallied to their parents' defense. Consequently, with the exception of the one aunt, the older generation is excluded both from honorary membership and from attending meetings. The minutes of one meeting read:

The main topic of discussion was whether or not we were to dispand [sic]. After all the pros and cons and everyone laid his cards on the table, we decided to continue as before. We also thought that it would be better that none of the uncles and aunts attend meetings because somehow it started hard feelings among the rest. . . . Meeting ended happily, and I left Elaine's house loaded down like Santa Claus. It's so nice to have such good cousins, God bless all of us.

MEMBERS' RIGHTS AND OBLIGATIONS

The extensiveness of membership rights depends upon the social and economic structure of the group. In a family circle with mutual aid benefits they are greater than in a cousins' club that is organized around the principle of social interaction. In some family circles members enjoy rights to: (1) interest-free loans, (2) a burial plot in the club's cemetery, (3) a cash donation when in dire need, (4) money towards funeral expenses, (5) attend meetings and special gatherings, (6) give one's opinion from the floor, (7) vote on club issues, and (8) hold office. In most other family circles and probably all cousins' clubs, members enjoy all of the above rights except the first four pertaining to various forms of economic aid.

Regardless of the extensiveness of membership rights, there is only one obligation the member must meet to enjoy these rights. He must be a dues-paying member. However, none of the groups I studied had a hard-and-fast rule on whether the individual must be a "paid-up" member. Even if a member is in arrears, as long as he occasionally attends a meeting, he is considered a member and may enjoy the privileges of membership. Or if a members pays his dues but seldom, if ever, attends a meeting, the rights of membership are still his. Finally, if for some reason a member's relationship to the club is severed, his economic rights cease immediately regardless of past monetary contributions. This principle is stated most succinctly in the constitution of one family circle:

> Any member resigning, withdrawing, expelled, or suspended, or severing his or her connection with the Family Circle organization for any cause whatsoever shall not be entitled to refund of any monies paid into the organization during the term of such membership nor to any of the assets of the organization.

There are, nevertheless, a number of informal obligations members should meet. These informal obligations do not affect access to membership rights, but non-performance certainly does affect the member's position within the club. In those groups where meetings rotate among the homes of members, those with sufficient room are expect to sponsor an occasional meeting. If they do not, it becomes a sore spot among the members and open conflict may result. Less clearly defined is the extent to which members should offer aid to each other outside of the family club context. Since these obligations are not at all formally defined, they may also become a point of animosity. Related to these informal obligations are the informal rights. There are always those members who think that their relatives in business should sell to them wholesale or that a relative lawyer or doctor should provide his services at a discount. This is felt as a right, regardless of genealogical propinquity because they are members of the same family circle or cousins' club. If the two members perceive the expectation similarly, there is no problem, but there are considerable data showing this is not always the case. I will discuss some of these problems of disparate kinship expectations among members in Chapter Six on intra-group conflicts.

MEMBERSHIP IN AUXILIARY GROUPS

A very few family circles have auxiliary organizations for children and/or women. In fact, they appear to be very rare. The WPA sample listed only one womens' and two children's auxiliaries. In my interview sample I have only one women's auxiliary. Each of these organizations is affiliated with a family circle. To my knowledge they never exist as extensions of cousins' clubs, and I would think the possibility very unlikely.

The children's groups appear to be organized to facilitate the friendship of the family circle's younger members who are not closely related and otherwise would have little reason to become acquainted. The purpose of the Michael Tenzer Junior League, an affiliate of the Michael Tenzer Family Circle, is "to remain closely bound in acquaintance". According to the WPA study, in 1939 this children's auxiliary had no regular meeting time but met periodically in the homes of members. It had officers, and its activities were listed as "cultural activities, lectures and discussions on various problems". The group was organized in 1929 with a "small number" and had 40 members in 1939, all American-born.

The "Ladies' Auxiliary" in my interview sample is an adjunctive organization of a very large family circle. Any woman who is a member of the family circle can join although not all of them do. The women meet monthly in the daytime for a business meeting and refreshments. Their activities focus on the raising of money for charitable purposes and they do this primarily by selling raffle tickets to the public. These are printed and cost 50 cents. The various gifts are often donated by family businessmen, and the drawing is held in a public hall. Such a raffle, I was told, may raise several hundred dollars. Like the family circles themselves, auxiliaries have no affiliation with larger charitable or social organizations.

RECRUITMENT OF MEMBERS

Regardless of the fact that these kinship clubs and their auxiliary organizations have various limiting criteria for membership, including kinship status, age, and sex, actual membership is voluntary — not prescriptive — and must be validated by formally joining the group and meeting its formal obligations. What are the processes, then, whereby the individuals eligible for membership are recruited? Unlike most urban voluntary associations, the potential recruitment field for the family clubs is greatly restricted because of the imposed limiting criteria of demonstrated kinship ties. This field consists of a network of affective ties behaviorally activated by strong cultural sanctions for the expression of positive family sentiment. This factor considerably lessens the task of member recruitment.

Once a group is formed, new members are brought in primarily by suggestions and/or pressure by the parents of potential members, although other members who have close affective ties with the candidate may also press a young man or woman to join. If the group is a relatively small one and the parents are firm advocates of the club, it is difficult to refuse membership. A young and unmarried adult may balk and complain, but will probably join. By refusing to join, the candidate will create a minor family scandal that reflects negatively upon himself and especially upon his parents. His refusal is perceived by relatives as a denial of his kinship tie and essentially of his Jewishness. It is hard to say which is the more grievous fault. Such an individual will be gossiped about among his relatives, accused of being *goyish*, and of acting "too good for us".

To avoid this embarrassment to his parents, the usual solution is for the diffident candidate to join, pay his dues (most likely his parents will pay for him), but rarely attend a meeting. He may show up at one of the special parties every year at his mother's insistence to keep the relatives from gossiping. Therefore, with some of the younger members it is the external constraints of an active family solidarity more than a personal desire that motivates them to join. But I do not wish to overstate the point for there are always some of the young who are very desirous to join as this letter to a cousins' club indicates:

Dear Cousins,

I am writing to you in regard to my membership in the Cousins' Club.

I am very anxious to join the club, but if agreeable to you, I should like to wait until next January since at present I am too busy with my school work to permit active membership in the club. Of course, I could join and then absent myself from meetings, but I would rather become a member when I feel I can be active and in that way enjoy the full benefits of the club. With cordial regards and hoping you are all in the best health,

   I am,

                              Very sincerely yours,
                              Barbara

In summary, few of the organizations have difficulty in recruiting members. It is easy to join and for most to pay the dues. From my examination of the collected genealogies, few potential members refuse membership unless they live at a great geographic distance from New York City. Even then there may be individuals who are dues-paying members. But the problem is that simply adding names to the membership roll and collecting dues does not obligate the members to take an active role in the group. It is getting *all* of the members to participate regularly that is seen as the major problem of some of the family clubs. This appears to be especially true for those family circles with very large and socially diverse memberships.

SOCIAL DIFFERENCES AMONG MEMBERS

The social differences among members in a club is an important factor in determining the degree of participation within the group.

It is also partly because the members are diverse in educational, occupational, residential, and religious background that the club is organized in the first place as a way to bring the relatives together regularly. Furthermore, the propinquity of kinship statuses and social background may be insufficient in many cases to foster free and easy interaction in other less structured situations. But as members in a common family club, socially disparate kin may meet together in a friendly relationship that fulfills the felt obligation to interact with collateral kin but does not obligate them to further social intercourse.

A study of the club genealogies reveals that the larger the group, the greater are the social differences existing among members and, conversely, the smaller the group, the smaller are the social differences among members. This point is exemplified in Tables 9 and 10 which show the occupations of members in a large family circle and a small cousins' club. These differences appear to be related not to the type of family club, i.e., whether a family circle or a cousins' club, but primarily to size regardless of type. In very large groups it is easier for members to socialize with their own "kin clique" and avoid those members they dislike or with whom they have little in common. But in the small clubs members must socialize with all members at a meeting; not to do so would be

Table 9. *Occupations of employed members of a family circle**

Occupation	Number of members
Drugstore owner	2
Taxi driver	1
Pharmacist	1
Certified public accountant	2
Lawyer	3
Dyeing service owner	1
Clerical	1
Real estate broker	1
Manufacturer of surgical supplies	3
Artist	1
Salesman	1
Candy store owner	1
Fur cutter	1
Fabric cutter	2
Partner in wholesale wool remnant business	1
Saleslady	1
Commercial physicist	1
Doctor	1
Stock broker	1
Total	26

* The total membership of this family circle is 77. Only 34 per cent (26) work, whereas the majority, or 66 per cent, are women and children who are out of the labor force. The occupations were given by one of the members.

Table 10. *Occupations of employed members of a cousins' club**

Occupation	Number of members
Small importer	1
Auto mechanic	1
Store clerk	1
Plumber	1
Salesman	3
Printer	1
Truck driver	1
Watch repairman	1
Milkman	1
Secretary	3
Elementary teacher	1
Bookkeeper	1
Factory operator	1
Total	17

* The total membership of this cousins' club is 23. The majority of the members, 78 per cent (17), including women, work. There are no children members. The occupations were given by one of the members.

perceived as a status insult because of the face-to-face intimacy of the assemblage. Further implications of these social differences are discussed at several points.[4]

ACTIVE MEMBERS

Robert Merton (1957:286–287) has cautioned that to discuss group membership boundaries in terms simply of "member" and "nonmember" is ". . . not fully faithful to the facts, for there appear to be *degrees* of membership which are in part indicated by the rates of social interaction with others in the group". This is certainly true for the family clubs.

Club membership may be conveniently discussed under four classifications, viz., the actives, the inactives, the drop-outs, and the nonmembers. However, the task is rather difficult because apart from their particular relationship to the clubs, the four groups do not exhibit any definite patterning of social characteristics. This is partly because the clubs themselves vary so greatly in detail and emphasis of organization and operation that it is impossible, from my data at least, to make any generalizations about who will be active and inactive members, who will drop out and who won't join. This is sometimes possible within the context of a particular organization, but not comparatively. For example, in one organization there may be a group of professional men who take a very active part in the club while in another club most of the professional men will be inactive or dropouts. But I can discuss some of the relationships between the various classes of membership and the functioning of the group.

In any organization there is always a core of active members who are its nucleus. There are always some who appear at meetings regardless of the rain and snow storms, and it is they who carry the administrative and moral responsibilities of the group. In the family clubs it is the actives who praise the integrative values of the club, extol the family, and exhort the absent to attend regularly. The actives also provide the group's leadership, both formal and informal. In all of the groups I studied, active participation in the group was associated with election to office. The principal function of the actives, i.e., providing leadership, is discussed later in the chapter.

INACTIVE MEMBERS

I have suggested that the major problem of most groups is how to make the inactive members participate more fully. There is always a kind of struggle within the club to keep the actives active and to make the inactives more active. If the inactives begin to attend even less frequently and some of the actives begin to slip into inactive status, the group rightly perceives itself in imminent danger of collapse. When an active member begins to miss meetings with no valid excuse, other actives will exert pressure on him to attend and occasionally the kin group itself may take action. Here is an example from the minutes of a cousins' club:

> Nina said Henry must be a little more considerate to come to meetings, and he will receive a letter from us telling him how we feel about his not attending. We all feel hurt as to how inconsiderate he has been.

Another group passed a resolution stating that if a member misses three consecutive meetings, he will be notified that the next meeting will take place at his home. Both of these examples of negative sanctions regarding attendance are from small cousins's clubs. The very large family circles take a much more passive attitude and the lamentations are not channeled into punishing actions. Also, if the same people must continually assume the leadership roles, they will eventually declare that they have had enough.

> Again I was elected president ... so it was more or less like "Barry Karp and his cousins" who is about to entertain every other month and try to keep them amused and tell funny stories and just keep the family together. It sort of petered out as far as both my wife and I were concerned. I imagine that in June we'll just gracefully drop out. . . . If they don't have someone like me to bind them together, to amuse them, to occupy their time suggesting things to do, they're not particularly interested in getting together with one another. They don't have any great love for each other.

When a married couple is inactive, there is greater concern than if only one of the couple is inactive. As long as the family is regularly represented, there is little fuss. Two of my women informants usually attended family club meetings without their husbands and were driven to the meetings by other relatives. Neither of their husbands liked to attend the meetings. In both instances they were the in-marrying spouse and did not derive as much enjoyment from the gatherings as their wives. One of the women spoke of her husband's perception of the family club in the following way:

His criticisms were that he just didn't want to be obliged to go, I think. He thought there was an obligation, I think, because he knew he *had* to go. Well, this is the kind of person he is. He doesn't want to be obligated to do anything, you know. Like this coming Saturday he knows he'd have to go there!

Particularly in family circles there is a tendency for the inactives to be the younger members. A young single adult may never attend meetings, but he or she is expected to bring a prospective wife or husband to meet the relatives. One young woman informant who was considered a "Bohemian" by her older relatives had not been to a family circle meeting for several years, but she was planning to take her fiance to a meeting. Her reasoning was that it was easier to meet all the relatives on her mother's side at one time instead of having to make a number of separate visits. And an inactive member who acts as an interested member of the family when he does attend a gathering will certainly be forgiven for his absences. But if he is seen as "very cold" he will gain little prestige in his relatives' eyes regardless of his presence.

Some of my informants were aware of the reluctance of young single adults to participate in the family club. But there is always the hope that when the young marry and have their own children, they will take more interest in the family club.

In talking about the future of a particular family circle, the WPA study (Rontch 1939:58) notes that

. . . the active people of the circle feel more correctly that time itself will be the best attraction of the young people. Let them get married. Let children begin to come, and with them will also come settling down. That is when one begins to think about cemetery plots and concerning benefits. Then one becomes lonesome for friends or relatives and for one's own. All this can be found within the family circle.

It isn't just among the young, however, that inactive members are found although I have stressed their inactive role because they are perceived as the greatest threat to the continuance of the family club. The data show that there are young marrieds, middle-aged, and old people among the inactives.

The reasons given for inactive status vary greatly. These include: (1) lack of dependable transportation, (2) illness, (3) lack of interest of spouse, (4) social values disparate to the group, (5) hostility to some members, (6) financial inability to sponsor a meeting, (7) baby-sitter problems, and (8) pressing business or professional activities. And as one informant explained to me, it is often difficult in a particular case to know whether the reason is valid or just an excuse. I do know, however, that where several reasons are involved, the less critical ones such as (1), (2), (3), (7), and (8), are given to relatives when the more behaviorally significant reason may be hostility to some members. Some of these reasons, expressed by inactive members for infrequent attendance to the family club's affairs, may eventually result in an inactive member finally dropping out altogether. But many members are satisfied to limp along in an inactive status for many years. They faithfully remit their dues but rarely or never attend a meeting or special affair. I believe that this form of token membership is related to the hesitancy of Jews to apostatize. The Torah speaks severely about the Jew who turns apostate. However, as long as a Jew does not deny that he is a Jew — and this may be totally unrelated to Jewish religious observances — he remains a member of "God's Chosen People". Even if he is an atheist but calls himself a Jew, he still belongs. But if he becomes a Christian, he may be ridiculed and despised and his family will denounce him. Among very Orthodox Jews the family may announce the apostate's "death" and carry out the necessary rituals related to his "dying". Socially speaking, he is truly dead.[5]

Traditionally, then, the negative sanctions among Jews for leaving one's group were tremendously strong. And if one leaves one's people one is leaving his kin as well so the idea of being a Jew and the social recognition of kin ties are intimately bound together. To belong to a family circle or cousins' club publicly acknowledges to one's relatives that one belongs to them. But to segregate oneself from a club may be interpreted as an active move away from kin and from a strong Jewish identification.

Today some members of family clubs seem less concerned about the "Jewish" — or more exactly, "Yiddish" — content of the club, and this is frequently lamented by the older members at meetings. And even if the Yiddish content is irritating to a member, he may still maintain membership to prevent unpleasant gossip about himself and a negative reflection on his parents to whom he is expected to bring a certain amount of glory and praise because of his accomplishments. So the dues are paid, and membership is retained, and Jewish and family identification is not jeopardized. After all, even a highly assimilated individual can't be all *goy* if he belongs to a Jewish family circle or cousins' club.

DROPOUTS

Within the context of family circles and cousins' clubs, the dropout is one who no longer comes to meetings or pays his dues. His status is very different from the inactive member who pays his dues but seldom attends meetings. Just as each group I studied had a number of inactives, each also had a few dropouts as well. None of my data suggest there is a particular personality type that tends to drop out but that the factors that account for the extrusion of members are primarily social, viz., intra-group conflict, geographic moves, marriage to a Gentile, and social differences. The dropout situation that most threatens the existence of the group is the intra-group conflict. Conflicts are of two types — those arising directly out of the affairs of the family club and those where the argument is external to the club's affairs. Nevertheless, both types of conflicts may result in several members withdrawing from the group. These are discussed in Chapter Six.

The most acceptable reason for dropping out is a move so far away that it is impossible to attend even an occasional meeting. The geographic dropout leaves on good terms with the family and may continue his contact with the group by correspondence although he is no longer a member. This member left New York to move to California with her family.

> *Dear Cousins,*
>
> *Thank you for your very thoughtful gift — Frank and I appreciate it very much. We thought about you Saturday night while at Aunt Sadie's. You must have had a good meeting as we always did have good times together! . . . Everyone here is very friendly. We all miss Chinatown, The Chinks out here are terrible! Hollywood is some place — you brush up against every movie star! Think nothing of it!*

What's new with the Cousins' Club? How is it progressing? . . .
Hoping you all make a trip to Sunny California. You are
always welcome to our restaurant! Regards from California's
Sons and Daughters. I'm a real native now.

Love from all always,
Lois and Frank

In some clubs marriage to a Gentile means exclusion from
membership either because of a formal ruling or informal pre-
judices against such intermarriages. One of the strongest rules on
intermarriage is in the constitution of a family circle studied by
the WPA Writers' Group. It stated that to be eligible for membership the individual must be of Jewish faith and if married or
wishing to marry, it must be according to the Orthodox law. I
have indicated earlier that these exclusionist principles based on
religion are more characteristic of the family circles organized
earlier in the century. At the present time there appear to be few
dropouts if a member marries a Gentile. Either the member has
already dropped out of the club if it is religiously oriented, or
among the more secular oriented family circles and cousins' clubs,
the marriage will be accepted as unfortunate but inevitable "in this
day and age", and the new spouse will be welcomed as a member.
From my data the only contemporary case of a major rift in a
family club because of an intermarriage was a case where the
marriage was interracial, and the member and his family attempted
unsuccessfully to secure membership for the spouse.

The last, but very important, reason for dropping out is because
of social differences. The upward-mobile person may find that he
no longer has time for the club, especially if he has moved far out
on Long Island to a fashionable suburb. I was told by one informant who was in the process of dropping out that while he
enjoyed his relatives, he really didn't have that much in common
with them. There was very little in the club for him, and he pre-
ferred to spend what leisure time he had with friends instead of a
lot of "distant relatives".

Similarly the downward-mobile individual may find that his life
style is negatively sanctioned, and after increasingly irregular
attendance, he stops attending meetings. This was true of the

following informant whose relatives thought she had made a poor match.

> [My husband didn't like the club] at all. Half the time he was dead tired and very tired and sleepy, and he was bored. He doesn't mingle much. There's only one cousin that he liked, and that was a cab driver like him, and when they'd get together, they'd talk. And then my cousin's wife would come in and say, "You two are always talking", and she'd pull him away. I'm telling you, it's so funny! And one cousin remarked about me that I had an inferiority complex. . . . She told my mother recently, "Pearl has an inferiority complex, and that's why she doesn't come to the meetings", and my mother told me about it, and, of course, I was hurt. I was hurt about it because I don't think I do. I think I did have a very inferior [sic] complex, but I think I've overcome that, and I think I'm much happier a person than my cousin is. . . . I, so, so I'm glad I don't go. The heck with it! It cost a lot of money, and there's no reward for us. We didn't care for it.

But the family club can play a very important part in the social life of a couple, and the gatherings and activities may be missed. My informant continued:

> So I told him the other night, I said, "You know we stopped going to the cousin club, and we've got to have some place to go. We just can't lie around watching television day-in and day-out, week-in and week-out. We've got to dress up with a purpose, with a destination!"

And then there are those social differences that relate more to religious differences than to occupational mobility. If a very secular-oriented member finds that his values are too diverse from his religiously-oriented relatives, he may drop out of the club. In the same way, religiously-oriented persons may drop out if their ritual values are blatantly violated. One of my informants explained why his parents were planning to drop out of their cousins' club:

> . . . my parents are Kosher, and the rest of the members are not . . . and one meeting the hostess served ham. She kept it in the kitchen, though. One of the members brought out a big fat [ham] sandwich and sat right in front of my parents [laughs] and started eating it. This was Freddie. They didn't particularly enjoy the experience. Not so much that they are intolerant of others who don't observe their Kosher, it's — they don't care

about that so much — but he just placed himself in such a position where it was so observable. It was the intent behind the act rather than the act itself.

Regardless of the reason, if a member drops out but remains in the metropolitan area, the group feels the loss as a threat to its goals of family solidarity and attempts are occasionally but repeatedly made to encourage the individual to return. These are usually made within the context of other family contacts, but a committee may be appointed to effect their return. This is especially true if the members were active ones but leave the club after an argument.

They were looking for help from the family circle, and it caused a big rift at that time. Gussie didn't come to a meeting for about three years. Max [Gussie's son] dropped out. . . . Trudy, that's Gussie's daughter, also didn't come to the meetings for quite a while. It took us a long time to get Gussie back to come to the meetings. She just didn't have the nerve to come back, but she finally made it. Debbie [another daughter] came back. We have Max on the books. We didn't want to drop him. But we do [suspend members if for] six months, or a year, they didn't pay dues. . . . [It's done by] sending a special delivery letter, waiting for an answer, sending another letter, talking, having a meeting. As a matter of fact, I was appointed and two cousins of ours were appointed a committee to go to Gussie and plead with her to come back to the family circle. We wrote to Gussie. We wrote to Sam [her husband]. We didn't go to them, I don't think, but we wrote nice letters. We tried to be nice, actually pleading with them to come back. But Gussie [only] comes to the meetings to her brother's house when he has them and at her mother's house if her mother has one.

NON-MEMBERS

A non-member is one who does not join a kinship club which he is eligible to join. A close study of the genealogies reveals some patterning regarding the non-members and appears related to the husband's social position. If in relation to the other men eligible for club membership a man is: (1) too intellectual, (2) too successful, (3) too Orthodox, or (4) in show business or the arts, he is less likely to be a member than the individual who seems more on a par with the others. But I am talking only about a tendency, for in the family clubs I studied there are, for example, university professors, rich businessmen, doctors, and meticulous observers of Orthodox ritual. Although in my sample none of the men with theatrical careers, e.g., orchestra leader, ballet dancer, and vocalist joined family clubs, I do know of one famous theatrical personality who is a member of a family circle. This is the folksy stand-up comic, Sam Levinson, who appeared on national television while this study was under way with his entire family circle. It seems more likely, however, that the style of life and the values inherent in a theatrical career are inconsistent with maintaining ties with an extensive range of kin, and membership in a family club by persons in the entertainment industry is unusual.

The other reason for potential members, genealogically speaking, not to be members is because they belong to "detached lines" from the apical ancestor. If a male or female cognate of an ascending generation terminates active relations with his kin for whatever reason, his descendants tend to follow the pattern. It is the knowledge of just such a possibility that helps motivate the formation and sustains the functioning of family circles and cousins' clubs.

MEMBERSHIP SIZE

The size of cognatic stocks from which members in family clubs are recruited varies greatly according to the members and size of the constituent nuclear families. Large families were in vogue among early Jewish immigrants, and nine, even 12 children, were not uncommon. It is these large sibling groups that provide the ramified network that, as descendants appear, are sometimes organized into family clubs. The patterns, often vagarious, of differential immigration, marriage, birth, and decedence shape each cognatic stock just as the more patent social factors of residential proximity and conflict patterns further shape the membership of the family club.

As family circles include all of the descendants of the apical ancestor as potential members, they are usually larger than the age-graded cousins' club. The largest family circle I have data on is international in its membership with approximately 2,000 members.[6] The smallest has 25, including 12 adults and 13 children. Most of the family circles fall within the range of 35 to 100 members while none of the cousins' clubs exceeds 40 members. Appendix D presents examples of family club membership within the genealogical context of their encompassing cognatic stocks.

FAMILY CLUBS AS REFERENCE GROUPS

There are numerous approaches to "reference group theory", and it is not my intention to survey these differences but to use the basic concept of a "reference group" to illuminate the variability in the meaning of the club membership to individual members. "Reference group theory" is one of the approaches that social scientists, especially social psychologists and sociologists, take towards the study of the functional relationship between the individual and his social environment. A "reference group" is one to which an individual "refers" as a model when he is assuming new values and behavioral traits or when he evaluates his own or others' values and behavior. Merton (1957:283–284) identifies the former type of reference group as ". . . the 'normative type' which sets and maintains standards for the individual, and the second is the 'comparison type' which provides a frame of comparison relative to which the individual evaluates himself and others." In either instance the individual's response to a reference group is neither dispassionate nor neutral but represents a high degree of personal involvement.

An individual's attitude towards a reference group may be polarized about negative or positive values or perhaps his attitude is one of troubled ambivalence. But if his attitude towards a group is one of complete lack of interest or "not caring," then for him, at least, it is not a reference group. Consequently, different individuals may have very diverse attitudes towards the same group. For one it will be a positive reference group, to another a negative reference group, while the attitudes of others will be ambivalent or uncaring.

From my data it is doubtful whether members of a family club, regardless of the degree of participation, ever relate to the club as a non-reference group, i.e., with complete lack of interest and unconcern. It is difficult not to care about a group when, as a member, you have assumed a set of rights and obligations within that group and close kin expect you to participate to the degree they think you are capable of or suffer the imposition of their informal negative sanctions. It is also my impression that those individuals who participate the most in family clubs perceive the club as a positive reference group, and those who participate the least – if distance is not a factor – perceive the club either in ambivalent or negative terms.

A complicating factor in the analysis of the individual's perception of the club as a reference group is that his relationship to the group sometimes changes markedly through time. Numerous illustrations of such temporal changes appear throughout these pages. The type of perceptual changes I have the most data on are those from positive to ambivalent or negative. If too many members become disenchanted with the club and with the life style of other members, the club is headed for collapse or at least a loss of membership. Many of the members in what I call "inactive" status fit this situation. However, a popular new president, an interesting new meeting format, or the resolution of a club conflict may act as the catalyst to change members' perceptions of the club as a negative or ambivalent reference group to a more positive one. Obviously, there is nothing preordained and necessarily constant about an individual's evaluation of his reference groups, and a detailed historical study of any single family club shows how great these changes may be as well as documenting changes in the group's structure and operations through time.

All of my informants who were nonmembers of a family club that they were eligible to join perceived the club as a negative reference group, i.e., a group whose values and behavior they denigrated. But there is bias in my sample for my genealogies show other individuals who are eligible to join, but because of circumstances prior to their birth or in childhood, their lineal line became disassociated from the others. As I have indicated, for these individuals the long-lapsed social ties to the club are unimportant. From informants' remarks about some of the living eligible individuals in these "detached lines", the club is perceived as unrelated and irrelevant to their social life and definitely not as a reference group.

As family clubs are primarily composed of nuclear families or marital pairs, it is also possible to analyze these constituent family units as individual reference groups with various positive, negative, and ambivalent implications for any particular member. From a member's point of view, this may be the most significant way to examine his relationships towards the multiple families that make up a family club. The data conclusively show that a member does not react to each family in the same way. While he is somewhat indifferent to some, there are others he may intensely dislike and still others he admires and attempts to emulate. Part of the complexity that affects the operations of any group is just this great variety in perceptions of the units that compose a group.

IMPLICATIONS OF FAMILY CLUBS FOR MEMBERS

In the following discussion I do not imply that a family club will perform all of the functions noted for a particular member. My purpose is only to show programmatically some of the behavioral implications that affiliation with a family club may have for members as revealed in the data.

Membership in a club means for most members that they are actively relating to a larger network of kin than they otherwise would. Whereas a member's "close" kin, depending on how "close" is defined, will probably perform many of the functions described below, he is also able to utilize his augmented network of kin in similar ways although perhaps not so frequently. Even inactive club members may sometimes need the help of fellow members and because of the club tie do not hesitate to call on a distant relative for assistance. Even those members who are "inactive" may ask for the help of club members. The help may be given by the group as a whole or by individual members, but in either case the petitioner as a member feels he has the *right* to expect help from his relatives. As these rights are not spelled out in detail, the perception of members' rights and obligations may vary and become the source of interpersonal conflict among members.

One of the most important functions that a family club may perform for its members is to provide a large network of kin for *emotional support* in times of crisis. In times of illness or at the *rites de passage* of birth, death, marriage, and "coming of age", the membership of the club rallies around the particular family to offer comfort and support. This was dramatized in the life of one woman informant with a severely handicapped child whose family club helped with the hospital bills, found her husband a better job while members also visited her occasionally or entertained her to help cheer her. Because of her tremendous economic, marital, and illness problems, she became inactive in her family club, but this did not preclude the club from offering her continued support.

Clubs may also provide personal services and favors for a member. Because of common membership in the club a member, for example, may call on a professor relative to get her son into college or call a doctor relative for an immediate consultation. One informant told me about moving into a new neighborhood where it was no longer convenient to continue using a particular doctor relative. But when one of his children became seriously ill on a Sunday evening and he couldn't find a nearby doctor, he called his relative. The relative, although annoyed, drove across town in "his big black Cadillac" to tend the child. My informant and the doctor are "distant cousins" and never see each other except at the meetings of the family circle. According to my informant, it is only because of this common club tie that they are "friends". Each invites the other to his daughters' weddings, and my informant was expecting a five-hundred dollar check as a wedding present to his youngest daughter. Other types of personal services and favors include running errands, helping with child care, getting consumer goods wholesale, passing on children's outgrown clothes, and helping in job and house hunting.

A related function is *economic aid*. Members may also perform a personal service to members *selling* services by "throwing business" their way whether it is to a member who is a watch repairman, a young doctor, or an owner of a dry cleaning business. Members who need business may become very active in the club with the hope of finding new customers as well as fun at club meetings. One young man, I was told, had succeeded in selling many of his relatives investments in Mutual Funds by assiduous work during the social part of the meeting. Sometimes members joke about a member advancing his business interests at club activities, but no one would suggest that he should desist. "Getting ahead" is recognized as important and proper, but borrowing money from members for risky business ventures may get a member and the club into difficulties. A member of one club had borrowed about four thousand dollars from several club members to open a "Bar and Grill" business. It promptly failed. Unable to repay the loan, he left the city with his wife and children and moved to Nevada. One married son remained in New York City, but "since the rift" no longer attends meetings. Another form of economic aid is the loans offered to members by some clubs, discussed in Chapter Four.

Another function of family clubs is assistance in *decision making*. Members often bring their problems, both large and small, to meetings where they are sympathetically discussed by other members during the informal part of the evening. It may be as insignificant as deciding on a color for the living room drapes or as major as what kind of car to buy or where to buy a house. This seeking and giving of advice is a very important conversational part of club gatherings.

Family clubs may also facilitate the *social mobility* of some members. Membership gives access to a variety of life and occupational styles and role models. Some may be higher status relatives otherwise unavailable for interaction, thus providing others status "by deference" (cf. Litwak 1960a). In addition, the club provides an opportunity to sustain kin relationships in a way that may facilitate requests for assistance in occupational advancement. For example, in one club two brothers helped their formerly unsuccessful cousin by setting him up in business. This active assistance was facilitated by joint membership in the family club. Since these cousins lived in different neighborhoods and moved in very different social circles, they would have had little basis for social contact without the regular meetings of the club.

Potential conflict between the interests of club membership and geographic mobility is limited, however, by the fact that these groups exist in a large metropolis where extensive job opportunities that do not require making a geographical move are more likely than in a small community or rural area. When members have independent businesses or professional practices where success depends on remaining in a given location and building up a clientele rather than being able to accept an opening wherever it may occur, geographic mobility may also not be required for success. Although there are many constraints against making geographic moves, when they do occur in the interest of occupational achievement, they are generally accepted by the club's members. An effort is then often made to maintain contact with the club by continuing correspondence and continuing to pay dues or through a formal club newsletter. As husbands and wives belong to the same groups, their loyalties are not split at times when moves must be considered.

Since family circles and cousins' clubs exist in a group of immigrant background, they have *acculturative functions* for some of their members. Here the differences between family circles and cousins' clubs are of great importance. The bonds of a family circle which transcends generations are very different from the sometimes single-generation ties of a cousins' club in this respect. Most of the cousins' clubs studied were founded by a group of first cousins who were usually the children of those who had emigrated from Europe. The cousins for the most part were those born in the United States. This "one-generation" structure of the cousins' club is a rare form of kinship organization. Undoubtedly, it has a special significance in relation to value differences that separate the immigrant generation from their more Americanized offspring. The cousins' club is apparently one way to maintain the traditionally Jewish value of family solidarity by organizing generationally while at the same time excluding an older generation whose viewpoint and life style are very different. One man explained that he joined a cousins' club rather than a *landsmanshaft fareyn* (an organization of those from the same area in the country of origin) because "I was looking for younger people; I wasn't looking for older people. . . . Their ideas are different, and they have different ways of doing things." Thus cousins' clubs and family circles differ greatly in their probable implication for acculturation of their members.

Family circles may be subject to cleavage along generational lines because of differences between generations in cultural values and styles of life. This implies that in the family circles that survive there is a certain degree of continuity of the values of the older generation, at least for a while. Although both family circles and cousins' clubs undoubtedly recognize the achievement of their members in moving toward Americanized ways of life, their impact in this respect is undoubtedly very different.

Cousins' clubs serve as a way of uniting the younger generation and maintaining their kinship solidarity. At the same time they may actually serve to strengthen the bonds of the younger generation against the older generation. This organized bond of solidarity among the younger generation may help it as a group to break away from the ways of life of the older generation who are not allowed to be full members of the cousins' clubs.

Individuals, too, may be assisted in making a transition to a new set of values. Family clubs may also offer collective opportunities for trying out new types of social activity, often things that the nuclear family would not do alone. Elaborate preparations and much energy may be devoted to collective efforts to ensure that the new type of activity will be carried out in proper style. For example, as shown in Chapter Five, much time may be spent investigating restaurants to determine the best one for a club party. Families sometimes stated explicitly that they participated in activities that they would not engage in alone. Thus, membership in a cousins' club may give support for a family's attempt to alter or augment its style of life.

Since these kinship clubs clearly function as an arena for social participation and status presentation of the constituent families, for example in competition over the refreshments served, they afford an opportunity for recognition of achievement in style of life as well as in occupation. At exceptional meetings the group may even give explicit recognition to the style in which a family entertains the club by a special vote of thanks. The clubs, therefore, undoubtedly play an important part in enhancing the family's ability to move into a new way of life. The functions of the organization in this respect will, of course, vary greatly from one individual to another and among clubs as well. But the major structural differences between family circles and cousins' clubs in their emphasis on bonds between and in their generations mean that their general functions in the process of acculturation are not the same.

I have phrased these implications of membership as if they were felt by members to be *positive* functions, but the picture is considerably more complicated than that. Not all members feel positively about the club's social functions of providing emotional support and personal services as well as assistance in decision making. Some members reported that they found this kind of help *intrusive* from certain relatives. And there is also the double-edged aspect of services rendered, welcome or not, of the expectation of reciprocity. In other words, involvement in a family club means that members will be to some extent personally involved in your life and you in theirs. If you have special knowledge or access to a wanted service, you will be expected by some members to assist them. The point is that regardless of your personal feelings about certain member relatives, by your membership in the club you have signaled others that you wish to be thought of as a relative. Members that otherwise might not feel close to you genealogically or personally are now free to call on you. It is this increased expectation of kinship rights and obligations binding the members closer together than would otherwise be the case that some of the members find irksome. They like the idea of family solidarity but at the same time prefer to keep the relationship with more distant kin more purely social. This, of course, is not always possible and make membership in the club to some members, especially those who are in a position to perform services for others, a burden and one they may willingly or grudgingly bear.

LEADERSHIP STATUSES AND ROLES

In family circles and cousins' clubs, leadership statuses may be considered as either formal or informal. The formal leaders are the elected and appointed officers responsible for conducting the affairs of the club for a specified time of usually one or two years. The informal leaders are those individuals who, although not holding office, are influential in club affairs. In the clubs that appear to be the most successful, the informal leaders supplement the skills of the formal leaders. Both types of leader are most often found among the active members, but occasionally an inactive member is voted into office in the hope that this will force him to participate more fully.

There are two types of roles related to these leadership statuses, "managerial" and "inspirational".[7] The managerial role refers to the administrative behavior of leaders directed toward the organization's goals. The inspirational role refers to the expressive behavior of leaders that excites and inspires affection among the members for the organization. Managerial roles are usually taken by the elected leaders while inspirational roles are taken by both the formal and informal leaders.

INSPIRATIONAL ROLES

In most of the groups there is a certain amount of sentiment expressed periodically during the meetings by different members about the importance and joy of having a family club. These sentimental self-congratulatory declamations are one expression of the expressive behavior that helps to bind the group together with affectionate kinship ties. However, among those groups that I know best, there may be one or two persons who because of their own personal charisma and dedication to the solidarity goals of the club are the most effective. My data on these individuals are very limited, partly because I did not realize their integrating significance until late in the study.

The individuals who assume these inspirational roles *vis-à-vis* the other members may be termed "affective pivotal kin", since so much of the group's integrating affectionate behavior is related to their behavior.[8] The few that I learned about were all individuals for whom most of the members felt deep affection, and they were all middle-aged or older. Such an individual might be described in the following way:

Well, he is our oldest member. He is a lawyer. His knowledge is full of every single thing that is needed, and he is sort of our guiding post, guiding light for the organization. He was more or less our guiding post until now, but at present he is an ill man, and he's just biding his time.

The most obvious examples of these pivotal kin are from family circles. I know of none who are members of cousins' clubs, although an "honorary member" or an aunt, uncle, or grandparent may play an inspirational role towards the members to a certain extent. But with the single exception of an honorary member of a cousins' club, I do not feel that their integrating influence is as great as those pivotal kin who are members of family circles. Here they may also take considerable managerial responsibility, so becoming of great functional importance to the club. In both a figurative and literal sense, the club revolves about them. The death of a significant individual may put the group into an organizational crisis, especially if it is a very large one and needs a strong central personality to keep the socially diverse family units together.

When compared to the annual "family reunion" kinship

organization of Old Americans (Ayoub 1966), the Jewish family clubs have a stronger social structure to support them through such a period of organizational crisis. From my knowledge of family reunions in Kansas and Vermont, as these groups become older and larger or when the pivotal kin member dies, they tend to dissolve. If they miss meeting one year, it is even more difficult to locate and bring the members together for the following year. But the family clubs have more opportunities to reconstitute because they meet regularly throughout the year, not annually. Although I do know of clubs that gradually dissolved owing to lack of attendance because there was no effective leader to rally the members around the principle of family solidarity, there is an intensity of feeling about "keeping the family together" in most family clubs that in my experience does not exist among the members of Old American family reunions. In Chapter Seven, I examine some of the historical factors contributing to the intensity of familial solidarity among Jewish family clubs.

MANAGERIAL ROLES

From my interview sample of kinship clubs only two groups — one a family circle and the other a cousins' club do not have officers. As a minimum the others have a president, secretary, and treasurer.[9] In the more informally managed clubs, the roles of the respective officers are not recorded but are known by tradition. For example, the president conducts the meetings and appoints standing and *ad hoc* committees; the secretary records the minutes of the meetings and sends out cards announcing the meetings; the treasurer collects dues, allocates the money as determined by the group, keeps a record of income and expenses, and deposits money in the group's bank account.

Some of the larger and more formally organized groups may separate the secretarial role into a recording secretary and a corresponding secretary. A very few may also have a social secretary. Occasionally a club will have a sergeant-at-arms to maintain order at the meetings. A single group has a "trustee" who is ". . . the custodian of all valuable papers, documents, deeds, and bonds of the family circle". Two of the largest and oldest family circles in the sample have a board of directors who meet independently of the family circle membership to plan and oversee the group's activities.

From one family circle constitution under the heading "duties of officers" the formally stated managerial role of officers are:

1. *President*: The President shall be the Chief Executive Officer of the family circle. He shall preside at meetings and shall appoint all committees. He shall be ex-officio a member of all committees.
2. *Vice-President*: The Vice-President shall assist the President in the discharge of his duties and shall help to maintain order and decorum at meetings. He shall as such officer also preside and assume the duties of President during the absence of the President.
3. *Recording Secretary*: The Recording Society shall keep an accurate record of all meetings of the family circle.
4. *Corresponding Secretary*: The Corresponding Secretary shall send out all notices.
5. *Social Secretary*: The Social Secretary shall send out greeting cards and shall perform such other duties as shall be required of her by the President.
6. *Treasurer*: The Treasurer shall be the Fiscal Officer of the Family Circle, shall be the custodian of all monies and securities of the Family Circle and shall keep full and accurate accounts of all receipts and disbursements. He shall deposit all monies and securities in the name of the Family Circle in such depositories as may be designated for that purpose by the Family Circle. He shall report on the condition of the finances at each regular meeting.

In some of the clubs without a social secretary, the chairman of the "Sunshine Committee" or the "Good and Welfare Committee" is responsible for sending out greeting cards for members' birthdays, anniversaries, and illness and for carrying out other expressive behaviors of good will. The family circle whose officers' roles are stated above also has several standing committees:

1. *Entertainment Committee:* The Entertainment Committee shall have charge of all affairs, social events, and similar occasions, and shall have authority to formulate plans therefore subject to the approval of the Family Circle.
2. *Membership Committee:* The Membership Committee shall investigate all new applicants for membership and interview said

applicants, shall maintain the membership of the Family Circle, and shall have such other duties as the President shall impose.

3. *Cemetery Committee:* The Cemetery Committee shall have charge of the Family Circle Burial Grounds, shall attend funerals and unveiling of monuments, and shall visit the families of the bereaved during the period of mourning.

A membership committee and a cemetery committee are not nearly as representative of the groups as the entertainment committee. All of the groups with officers have an entertainment committee that is either a permanent committee or an ad hoc committee appointed by the president to supervise a particular affair or outing of the club.

A common problem, but seldom considered a serious one, confronting the officers who conduct the meetings is that they are not provided with effective sanctions for maintaining order. As I will show in the chapter on club gatherings, the meetings are generally very free-wheeling affairs, and it is sometimes impossible to maintain order and decorum. That is why the role of the vice president quoted previously is to help ". . . maintain order and decorum at the meetings". Order is maintained or secured by the officers trying to out-shout (often accompanied by table pounding) the assemblage.

We just try to keep decorum. My brother-in-law's the president, and we try to . . . keep things in order, more or less. And I'm the secretary, and if they get out of hand, I shout louder than they do.

Or some groups have an elected or appointed sergeant-at-arms whose express function is to maintain order.

If they get too noisy — which they usually do — [the sergeant-at-arms] is the one that gets up . . . . We have a woman that has a voice like a foghorn when she yells, "Quiet!" and that quiets them down.

In another club it is the vice president who tries to maintain order while the office of sergeant-at-arms is treated as a joke.

Well, there's a lot of voice raising, a lot of voice raising. "Shut up down in front!" someone pipes up [and it is] usually the vice president, whoever he is at the time. And, of course, they'll always appoint someone figuratively as a sergeant-at-arms, and [someone will say], "Sergeant-at-arms, take care of that guy!"

And he'll say, "What?" You know, it's almost like a joke; the weakest one gets the sergeant-at-arms, or it seems that way to me. . . . Not in the sense of weak other than the fact that they're the quiet type and would never harm a soul or ask anyone to be quiet because, "Well, he's not bothering me, not really, just having a good time," you know.

A few groups give the officers the authority to levy nominal fines, e.g., 25 cents, to those who are too vocal, but it is more in the form of joking than a serious negative sanction. My notes on one cousins' club read:

The president can impose fines on the members if they don't behave correctly at the meetings; this can be from one cent to a quarter. There is much joking about this. Some of the people as they come in say, "brought a quarter with me tonight!" Fines are usually for talking when they should be listening to someone else.

SELECTION OF OFFICERS

I mentioned earlier that there are no regulations in any of the clubs as to limitations to holding office once you are a member. For example, both men and women may and do hold any office. However, there appear to be some correlations between sex and particular offices. Although both men and women are elected to be president and vice president, my examination of club documents and informant interviews indicate that men are elected much more frequently than women. Here is a typical kind of succession:

There's Marvin Glass who was the first president, his brother Joe Glass the second president, [and his] first cousin, I believe, Tom Glass being another president. Tom's sister Kitty is a former president, and the current president is Al Schacter. That is the order of the presidents.

In another interview I asked a woman about the sex of officers:

WM: Have any women held the office of president?

INF: No, but vice president. My sister Martha is vice president now.

WM: Do you think women will ever hold the presidency?

INF: Oh, yes, yes. We don't have any discrimination against women. [Both laugh.] It is just that women are more capable as far as the Good and Welfare Fund is concerned and so on than men are so we choose them for the jobs.

In one of the small family circles, however, all three of the original officers were women although since then the sexual division of officers has been varied. Women are usually club secretaries and the chairmen of "welfare" committees, but treasurers are almost as likely to be women as men.

I could find no patterning in relation to age and particular officers nor in kinship position. Speaking overall, however, neither the very young nor the very old are frequent office holders in the family circles. But since cousins' clubs are more closely age-graded than family circles, the association between age and office holding is unremarkable in the former.

I was very interested in the extent to which in-marrying affines hold office. I assumed there would be a bias towards cognates, but my data do not support this. Even in the office of president, affines seem to appear as frequently as cognates. I was present at the election of officers of a family circle that elected as president a young and vivacious female affine, although there were several male cognates present who had not held the office.

The most important factor in becoming the president is acknowledged acceptance of the goals of the club validated by regular attendance. The president is also always a person who is on good terms with the members. These factors are expressed by a male informant on the family circle and the cousins' club to which he belongs:

WM: What do you think are the criteria by which a person gets elected to be president?

INF: Number one is interest. Number two is attendance. Number three is sociability of the individual.

WM: What do you mean by that?

INF: Well, to be liked by the group that are habitual attenders. There's always a nucleus, let's say, of the eligibility group — according to the way we worked it out on the kinship chart, a couple of hundred members I guess — there's a nucleus of about 20, and I think that those 20 will eventually be president because they're liked in the nucleus, and they represent the core of the family circle. Other than — I don't think the finances enter into it at all. It's just sociability and attendance, and that's just about it as far as why they are elected president.

Or as the past president of a cousins' club said:

More or less they elected the cousin who they more or less knew would be favorable to all of them . . . because they felt that the president had to be somebody that everybody would like, and they would come to a meeting. . . . It is just that some are a little more favored than the others. In every family you don't get everyone that is just perfect.

The election of officers is held every one, two, or three years and is usually in the spring or the fall. There are usually stipulations as to how many terms an officer may be elected to the same office. In both the formal and informal club, the presidency tends to rotate regularly, whereas the subsidiary officers may stay in office a much longer time. If, for example, the secretary or treasurer likes the job and does it well, he may serve for as long as he likes. If it is a formal club but there are no restricting clauses on tenure, again there is no problem of serving multiple terms if the incumbent likes the job, and no one else wants it. Even if there is a limitations clause, this need not be a hindrance.

We have a problem of the secretary, the recording secretary. As I told you, she writes the meeting notice cards very well, and we're all afraid to compete with her, and the constitution states that officers can't hold a position more than two terms. But it was suggested . . . that somebody can be elected, resign after the first meeting, and then reinstate the former officer. This is what they're going to do with the recording secretary and the treasurer.

I then asked my informant why the treasurer was continuing in his office, and she replied, "Well, he happens to be such a charming fellow, and he is so nice, and we're sort of lackadaisical."

In none of the groups did I see a tendency to create oligarchies, a problem of some voluntary organizations (Sills 1968:369). In fact, persuading some active members to assume leadership roles is an annual crisis in many, if not all, of the groups. And those members who try to decline nominations decline not so much from modesty but because they do not wish the monthly responsibility of attending meetings and carrying out a leadership role. From what I know about some of the older family circles, this was not so great a problem in the past as it is now. The lack of competition for leadership within a group is one of the family clubs' weakest structural features.

Someone said, "We'll make you president", and I said, "I decline." They said, "You can't decline." I think that was almost like negative psychology. The moment I said, "I decline", they wanted me very strongly. But there was no nominee against me in a formal sense. They said, "You're it". I said, "Amen, well it's only for a year."

One of the cousins' clubs in an attempt to impose leadership roles on recalcitrant members amended their by-laws to read that "Two candidates, at least, must be nominated for each office" and that "A nominee for office when nominated by two people cannot refuse the nomination". In some of the smaller clubs, notably the cousins' clubs, the election of a member to the presidency may not be so much an honor as a prank played on someone who is not doing his share. Still, at the end of the president's term, appreciation for his services may be expressed either through a motion of thanks by the members or perhaps by a small gift.

According to the degree of formal structure in the club, there are two ways officers are selected, viz., by ballot or verbal consensus. In the formal groups the officers are elected by ballot. The names are selected by a nominating committee appointed by the outgoing president or they are nominated from the floor. But in the informal groups the procedure is more varied. The president may be elected either by ballot or by an informal verbal consensus among the members. The other officers are selected by the verbal consensus method or appointed on the spot by the new president.

4. Resources and records

The economic systems of family clubs are of considerable functional importance because they provide the significant behavioral arena for involving members in a *common* activity of planning and decision. In other words, although it is the ideal of family solidarity that brings the relatives together, it is the economic system they evolve that keeps them together. One informant was very clear:

> The dues were set up as $2 a meeting for no other reason than just to sort of have a reason to keep the people coming — that they have an investment of $2, and the money would probably be spent at the end of one complete year, which would be perhaps again from September through June. Then there would be an outing, or we'd all go out [and spend it].

Another informant told me:

> ... one meeting they got into an argument about the money. Somebody said, "Well, let's not pay any dues. Let's just get together." And a cousin said, "If there is no money involved, if the money is not there, we will not be tied together." And I said, "If you tie together without the money, it's the feelings people have towards each other, not the few dollars in the bank [that counts].

But her argument was ineffective, and the requirement for dues was not suspended. Even the two clubs I studied with no officers or formal decision-making procedures evolved simple economic systems that obliged individual members to contribute specific amounts of cash into a common pool for redistribution in the name of the group. One, a family circle, gives a gift of cash to members on their wedding anniversaries, and the other, a cousins' club, collects $3 from each couple per meeting to help pay for the food served by the hostess.

CLUB RESOURCES

The principal resource of family clubs is the money they hold in common. This is banked in the name of the club and then redistributed primarily to the members themselves according to the group's agreement. Another resource, but one held by relatively few groups, is the joint ownership of unused burial plots. Although a family circle may sometimes sell or trade a few plots at a profit, the club's graveyard is basically a non-negotiable investment. The occupied graves can't be sold, and the others are awaiting occupation by the members. So there is little opportunity to increase the resources of the group from these property holdings. In fact, the cemetery puts a heavy drain on the cash resources of a club. Some groups erect elaborate fences around the graveyard, purchase name tablets and markers, and must pay for maintaining the area. The following family circle luckily made a profit on its original burial plot but immediately put it into a monument.

> A few years ago there was another family circle that had a plot near ours that had used one part of their ground already, and they wanted to buy ours from us so they can have the two of them together. And we, I think they offered us $700 more than we paid for it, and so we exchanged with them. And to that we added some money, and we bought a monument that cost us, I think it was $1,200 or $1,500. I don't remember exactly.

Unless a group owns burial plots, its members are likely to have very few corporate possessions beyond their pool of cash. Some own stationery and postcards, the minutes and financial records, and perhaps a gavel. Few own anything more unless they have published a book about the club, an unusual occurrence. One group I know about published an anniversary volume with many photographs of the members, entitled, "The Tenzer Family Circle, 1927-1937", and another published a genealogy (Margareten et al. 1955) with photographs of ancestors and contemporaries. Thus, it is obvious that the negotiable property of kinship clubs is meager, indeed, with the exception of banked cash, and this rarely exceeds a few hundred dollars.

Nevertheless, the club's energies revolve around this common fund, and a great deal of club time is spent discussing and arguing about its allocation. The behavioral dramas of the club are played out around these resources, and to an outsider the involvement seems disproportionate to the sum involved. But the club's treasury to which all have contributed provides a topical stimulus for kin interaction among relatives who, in may instances, have little in common but a reciprocal kinship status. Thus, the group's economic problems and plans become a *raison d'être* for collaboration and interaction.

Also, because there is no rigorously sanctioned external expectation for Jewish families to join together in family clubs, there is always an honorific and, it seems to me, slightly "make-believe" quality about these role relationships that exist primarily because of club membership. Still, the relationships are real enough and have important consequences for the individual involved. If a club member who is a second cousin once removed calls you about a job in your trucking firm, you can't very well act as if you don't know him.

SOURCES OF INCOME

For a married couple belonging to a family club, dues vary from about $2 to $15 a year depending upon the organization, with $10 or $12 the more usual amount. In family circles there may be a further assessment of, say, $1 or $1.50 for each child. Some groups set dues at a yearly rate, others set them per meeting to make payment more convenient for the members. One group that collects money at each meeting to help pay for the food charges only if the member is present. If he does not attend the meetings, he does not pay. But this is unusual. The majority of the groups expect members to pay dues because they belong to the club and the expectation is unrelated to attendance. "Inactive" members may seldom attend meetings but remit their dues annually. A familiar sight at meetings of family clubs is the treasurer making his rounds among the members collecting dues.

The dues for single members are usually half of what married couples pay. Some groups, however, add two or three dollars to the single person's dues as a kind of penalty for being unmarried. Almost all groups make special arrangements for members, especially widows and the indigent, for whom it would be a hardship to pay dues. The dues may be waived or close kin may pay for them. One widow explained to me:

This year my boy is working so I was able to give, but I have noticed that up until now they didn't ask me because they knew I couldn't afford it. And this year they asked me if I could afford it, and I said, "Yes, I can," and I was very proud. When I didn't give . . . my brothers would cover my share so it was never very obvious, you see.

There was strong sentiment among all the groups that personal finances should never be a factor preventing an eligible relative from participating in the club. In this way, as in others, the groups are extremely egalitarian in ideal as well as in practice.

Although dues are by far the most important source of the club income, money may also be derived from raffles, fines, interest on loans, and the "anonymous" gift. Thus, wealthy members of the club may contribute to the treasury to help support its activities or it may be customary to make a special contribution in honor of, for example, a son's Bar Mitzvah or a relative's wedding anniversary. One large family circle receives donations in honor of recently deceased members.

When someone passes away, as you probably know, the Jewish people they have a period of *shive* which is, you know, a week after in which [the immediate family] remain at home and everybody calls on them. So it's customary when you go to someone's home to bring something. It started years ago when these people [in mourning] were not allowed to cook their own food, so for hundred and hundreds of years people would come in and bring something. And now we're at the point where it's a box of candy or it's flowers or a donation to the family circle in memory of the person. So we have a card that we send out, a printed card if someone would like to donate some money in honor of so-and-so. And we send a card to the family saying, not how much, but just a donation was made and in honor of so-and-so. It could be anything from a dollar up.

If members are jokingly fined for "disorderly conduct" during a meeting, or if loans are made at a low interest to members, this money too goes into the treasury. But a number of groups also have raffles, an income strategy that serves the double purpose of adding money to the treasury and fun to the meetings.

Every once in a while my sister will buy something so she can raffle that off . . . in the family. And we get, say, two raffles for a quarter or one for 15 cents, and it's a small thing. And we have fun with that too!

But a large family circle working diligently at selling raffle tickets to friends and neighbors as well as members may make a large sum of money:

> At the beginning when we first started this organization, we used to have a Sunshine Fund; we used to have raffles. The business members would supply a raffle gift, and we would raise money that way. . . . As a matter of fact, it was in — I think it was in three years we had raised over $1,000 in order to buy the family plot.

Not all raffles, however, serve the function of obtaining money for the club. This one is purely for entertainment:

> We have one other thing that's a little different maybe than usual. We have what we call a door prize. Now in this case we don't charge anything for the door prize. I mean it's just something that you, if you've won a gift, you bring in the next gift, see? And it's just something that keeps rotating like this. The children make up the numbers, and each one picks a number, and they pick one out of the hat. And whoever has the number gets the gift, and the next month they bring in another gift. . . and it works out nice. It's a little something different.

These three examples illustrate how a simple activity like a raffle may vary in its functional emphasis among the clubs.

ALLOCATION OF INCOME

The income of family clubs is allocated to four principal types of expenditures, viz., death benefits, welfare, gifts, and entertainment. Only some of the older family circles allocate funds to all four economic spheres. The younger family circles and cousins' clubs allocate money primarily to entertainment and perhaps a small amount to gifts.

DEATH ALLOCATIONS

Death benefits may include a burial plot, and the payment of part of the funeral expenses. In my interview sample, only three family circles provided members with death benefits, and in no case was I given access to their cemetery records. None of the other clubs I studied was interested in adding death benefits as a service to members, and some expressed the belief that it was a morbid subject and would actually hinder participation. Members of cousins' clubs in particular felt that burial of family members was the concern only of the immediate family. But in those family circles with death benefits, considerable attention is given to the management of cemetery affairs.

> ... up to last September we used to talk about cemetery quite a bit. Buying more ground, finishing up the plot with hedges, and whatever was necessary. But we lost two members, and now it's come down to the situation of fulfilling our promise to them of keeping the grounds in order.

And it is the older members of family circles who usually are most interested in the problems of the cemetery.

> We have a family — a centralized family plot — that, well, mostly the older people seem to be interested in that regardless of where they're going to be buried. That's very important to them. ... I think it is a little ludicrous, but it's some sort of formality there. At least you know that, well, should the husband pass away, well, there's a place for the wife or vice versa. And I don't know if it's so in other religions, but in our religion it's a pretty important factor.

Some of my younger college-educated informants who did not belong to their family circles were extremely critical about what they considered to be a preoccupation with the cemetery and perceived the club to be for the old and dying but certainly not for the young.

There are not too many topics a group can discuss in relation to its cemetery, but these few, for example decisions about a boundary fence or a family monument, the procedures for allocating the graves, and plans to buy or sell graves, are certain to stimulate an active, often angry, discussion. Josephy (1967:46) in her study of a single family circle observes that the:

> ... position of graves and the whole subject of cemetery affairs is a singularly sensitive topic. Recently, a whole branch of brothers, sisters, and their children stopped speaking with one another due to dissatisfaction over a particular burial site chosen for the husband of one of them. The end result was that the body was disinterred and moved to another site. ...

She also notes that the problem of burying non-Jews who are members has been brought up although presently there are no Gentile members. This issue was resolved in one of my family circles in this way:

[There] also came up the question of intermarriage. And we had the thought if there was an intermarriage, we would give $50 towards a plot that the party would need. Because all the Circle gives is the burial ground. We do the rest ourselves.

Some informants told me that the family circles earlier in the century had death benefits more extensive than providing a burial plot. The funeral itself might be paid for by the club, but among my family circles with cemeteries — with one exception where the family circle paid for the funeral of an indigent member — only the burial plot is supplied. The casket, funeral, individual monument, and, in two of my three groups, perpetual care of the grave, is the expense of the deceased's immediate family, not the club. But as long as a member pays his dues regularly, regardless of whether he ever attends meetings, he is entitled to his burial plot:

Last year one of our members died. We have never seen this man at our meeting. His wife . . . is a working woman. This man was the type that — I don't think I ever really met him. I don't think he was there although we did have a meeting one night at his home. It was a forced issue with his wife, and she had to take it. The president had forced the issue on her.

The problem then is where in the cemetery is a member to be buried who is so unconcerned about the family into which he married. His wife may want him near the central family monument, but the cemetery committee may think he should be in a more peripheral position. It is in the club's cemetery, as Josephy observes (1967:46), that the egalitarian ethic of the family club ceases to operate. Although informants jokingly say that burial is "first come, first served", social factors are frequently crucial in determining a member's final resting place. Once a member is buried, if he is married, an adjoining plot is reserved for his spouse. One group reserves plots for the surviving spouse and their children as well.

WELFARE ALLOCATIONS

Among the clubs that have them, welfare allocations are more varied than death benefits. Six of the family circles offered some type of formal help to members in need. Two of the groups offered small loans with a ceiling of $25. One informant explained that the amount was "... small so that they shouldn't think that the family would back them for whatever they want because we're not there to be bankers or anything." The statement is, I believe, fairly representative of the contemporary membership of these family circles. In the past one of the principal functions of these groups was loans and financial aid to needy members. But the position of Jews in the economy of New York is very different from what it was 50 years ago. A family circle is a primary group to which a member can now demonstrate his financial success in an affluent society; it is not a group to which one goes for money and certainly not for the sum of $25. One's prestige within the club is more valuable than that. It is, then, this mutual aid function of the early family circles that has fallen into disuse. Josephy (1967:58) in examining the changing function of the loan fund in her family circle comments:

> By the early 1940's there was a change in the type of aid requested. People no longer required aid to meet the requirements of daily existence, but for business expansion and improvements. However, there has been a diminishing number of requests for such loans in recent years. This is due to the comparative ease in obtaining loans from the commercial banks and loan associations and the preference for dealing with an impartial unknown. The extended family is not so frequently looked upon as the source area for aid and sustenance, but rather one prefers to exhibit at least a facade of success before one's lineage .... During World War II Family Circle funds were used to send gifts to those members or children of the members in the Armed Forces. ... After World War II the relief fund was reactivated. Supplemented by private contributions, the family cared for Displaced Persons and refugee relatives. ... However, bestowal was selective. When an indigent member requested that the Circle purchase a taxi for him, his request was denied, and he was referred to the State Rehabilitation Board.

Another family circle no longer solicits loans but simply gives a check to the few disadvantaged members:

> If any member is in need, every Jewish holiday such as Passover and our New Year, they get a check. I have an aunt who was

deaf, dumb, and blind — I have two aunts like that . . . and they get [$25] checks every holiday.

Or sometimes if a working-class member of a club has an extremely costly illness in his family, a special donation will be made.

When I came home from the hospital with my husband, they sent me a check of $100 to help pay some of the bills. I felt very badly about accepting it because I felt — I just didn't like it. I am a very independent person, and I didn't want to accept anything, but, of course, they wouldn't hear of it.

But specific examples of financial aid are difficult to obtain apparently because of the present disuse of the aid fund. More typical is the following example of an informant who couldn't think of any actual donations from her family circle's $1,500 welfare fund.

Perhaps we would help if a boy had to be confirmed, and the family wanted to make a little celebration, and they couldn't afford it. I don't think anybody is that much in the — maybe more or less it's somebody who had to settle in the country; perhaps someone who had an extended illness or somebody who's pretty old and not — but thinking more broadly speaking, I — most of the family is pretty well set financially.

One family circle, a small one and only five years old when I studied it, organized its mutual aid function on the format of a credit union. Individual members deposited money into the fund as their circumstances permitted, and this was then loaned to members at a six per cent rate of interest. Here are some sections from their original statement of purpose that was kept among the secretary's papers:

Membership

The members are to be paid interest proportionate to the amount of money each has in the group and upon the length of time it is there.

Interest to be divided at the end of the group's fiscal year. . . . Should a member decide to drop out of the group, he is not entitled to any interest if he leaves in the middle or any time during the year. If he leaves his money in until the end of the fiscal year he will receive any interest due him.

Meetings

Meetings are to be held in the members' houses. They are to be held on the first Sunday of each month.

Entertainment Fund

Each member will pay $.25 per week into the fund. The money will be held aside by the treasurer for the purpose of parties, shows, etc.; to be decided later on by the members, when enough money has accumulated in each individual's account to be able to use for some purpose.

Loans

The Loan Committee will pass on all loans given to the members. The Committee will consist of three (3) members selected by the group. All three are necessary to pass on all loans. If a regular member is not available, an alternate may pass on a loan. . . . The treasurer is always a regular member of the Loan Committee and must pass on all loans.

All money up to $25.00 of the Treasury can be loaned out. The loans are to be made on a first come, first served basis. Applications will be held on file, if the treasury is depleted until funds are again available.

The member making the application for a loan must sign a note with terms of repayment. Payments are to be made as agreed, with all of the money to be paid back within one year of the date that the loan was issued. (Payments, and rate of payments, and amount of time given to pay the loan is all contingent upon the amount of money loaned out and the Loan Committee). Interest on all loans is 6% payable in advance. In other words interest is deducted from the amount of the loan at the time the money is borrowed.

Officers

The officers of the group will be elected by the membership. Term of office to be one year. The officers are as follows: [President, treasurer, secretary].

The document further shows that the treasurer made the first loan for $110 and signed a note ". . . to return the money in one year with weekly payment of $2.00." Nine months after its founding, the following report from the treasurer is recorded in the minutes:

Cash in Bank	$ 423.65	
Loans Receivable	984.00	
Entertainment Fund		$ 144.15
Bank Charges. Int.		2.24
Interest on Loans		95.16
Members Shares		1,166.10
	$ 1,407.65	$1,407.65

At the end of the club's second year of operation, the treasurer submitted this report:

Assets		*Liabilities*	
Cash in Bank	$ 878.79	Interest from Loans	$ 138.00
Loans Receivable	1,481.00	Bank Interest	5.31
		Entertainment Fund	145.25
		Membership Shares	2,010.22
		Surplus	61.01
Total Assets	$2,359.79	*Total Liabilities*	$2,359.79

Shortly before I became acquainted with the club, members were slowing down on their borrowing, and a motion was passed making it compulsory for each member to have at least a hundred dollars out on loan. The mutual aid aspect of the group is central to its functioning, and because the mode of mutual aid is non-stigmatizing, it is quite different from the older "welfare" model of some family circles. Using the newer model of the credit union that encourages individual members to deposit money into the loan fund also permits a member to *make* money on his relative's loan. The family circle does not own the loan fund itself but acts only in an administrative capacity.

Another form of welfare practiced by some family clubs is financial support of community charities. This is a feature of a few of the older family circles, and an occasional cousins' club will make a nominal donation to a charity, e.g., to the *New York Times* "Neediest" that are publicized at Christmas time. Family circles, however, tend to give exclusively to Jewish service organizations, and the choice of the organization and the exact amount may take several meetings to resolve. One family circle was considering eliminating its philanthropic contributions because of the factionalism such giving creates among members. But most family clubs do not give to charity at all. In the clubs defined by members primarily as "social" — and most of the clubs I studied happened to be of this type — contributions to community charities are not thought to be an appropriate club activity but should be handled by the individual members themselves.

Another indication of the changing function of Jewish family clubs is the "welfare" findings of the WPA study in 1938. Among their sample of 112 kinship clubs, 65 per cent dispensed economic aid. This was further broken down in the following way: 37 per cent gave money both locally and to the "old home," 16 per cent gave only locally, and 12 per cent gave only to the "old home". In my sample of family clubs only 2 per cent dispensed formal economic aid.

GIFT ALLOCATIONS

In a strict sense, the welfare donations of family clubs to members and charitable institutions are "gifts", but in this section I am using the concept of gift in a more limited way to fit the ethnographic facts. Among my informants, the term "gift" is used only in socially positive situations and never in a situation where a recipient's dignity or self-esteem is compromised. The gifts given by the clubs are of modest cost ranging from about one to ten dollars. The presentation of a gift is always directly related to: (1) a member's status change, e.g., marriage or hospitalization, and (2) a holiday like Hanukah when gifts are traditionally exchanged.

The inclusion of a gift-giving function in the organization of some of the family clubs is an expression of the importance of gift giving in Jewish culture. The presentation of gifts among my informants was a carefully observed custom and reciprocity a definite expectation. Money is the most appropriate gift for a significant life-cycle ceremony, such as a Bar Mitzvah or a wedding. Money is also given to the couple when they announce their engagement at a party. The daughter of one of my informants had received about $400 in engagement gifts:

WM: If she got that much when she was engaged, then about how much will she get when she gets married?

INF: Well, the families, the close families, will give about $50 a piece. I mean that's what we've been giving.

WM: That's a lot. That's very different from my family at home in Kansas.

INF: Well, you are not Jewish, or no?

WM: No.

INF: No, then that's the difference. The style is entirely different. I know in your case they usually bring gifts in their display.

WM: That's right.

INF: And everyone brings a piece of junk, and by the time you get through, half that stuff is thrown out. You don't even use it. Am I right?

My informant thought her daughter would average about $20 from each of the 60 couples invited to the wedding and dinner party. This, she correctly calculated, would give the young couple around $1,200 with which to begin furnishing their apartment. By comparison, the gifts presented by the family clubs are interpreted by members more as gestures or tokens of goodwill.

Depending upon the custom of the club, gifts may be given to members at the following life-cycle points, the birth of a baby, a Bar Mitzvah, a graduation, a wedding, a special wedding anniversary, and a death. There is no established pattern among the clubs on the gift itself; some purchase presents, others give a cash gift. This is the gift-giving custom of a family circle:

Well, it's ten dollars for a wedding gift, which is usually cash. And I think a Bar Mitzvah is five dollars, which is cash. And a baby gift is usually three dollars, which is given to them in a gift. I mean, the social secretary buys it. On Hanukah there is a Hanukah party with gifts for the children under eighteen, which usually does not exceed a dollar or two.

Members are usually expected to thank the club in writing, and these notes of gratitude are then read aloud at the meetings.

Dear Cousins,

When I asked my Mommy who was the Cousins' Club I was quite surprised and happy to learn that I had so many. I hope that soon I can be a member of your club and that you won't charge me too much dues! It was very nice of all of you to send *me the $5 bill, but it is already invested in a bond for me, so I won't be able to spend it on my inititiation[sic] fees — ha ha!*

I hope that by the time you read this "thank you note" I will have met you all. If you don't come to see me, then I guess I will just have to come to you! Right now I weight 8 lbs. 12 oz. and mommy says I'm too heavy to hold while Daddy drives the car. So she has promised to take me out more as soon as I have my car bed — then watch me go visiting!

Thank you all again,
Love and Kisses
Your Brand new Cousin
Steven Andrew

Dear Family,
We wish to thank you for the wonderful party in celebration of our 25th Anniversary. May we be together for many years and spend such pleasant evenings.

Thanks again,
Marsha and Babe

In one of the clubs a member serving in the Navy was sent gift packages from the group, but these were not always acknowledged by him. At one meeting it was suggested that he be asked to send the club a thank you card. His answering letter, in part, follows:

I just received your package and I had to write to thank you very much for those gifts. I feel very bad about not having written more often to you. I haven't written in such a long time. I have wanted to write but one thing happens after another and I never seem to get around to it. It isn't an excuse because there really isn't any excuse for not writing. I must apologise and hope you will forgive my procrastination and fatuousness. I shall honestly try and write to the club. You are all swell and I am very lucky to have you all for my cousins. I'm very lucky. There are so few families that are lucky to be as intimate and happy as ours is. We may have occasional disagreements but they aren't anything since we all love each other. I do love you all and hope you all are always happy and feeling fine. . . . Once again let me thank you for the package.

The letter also illustrates the kind of emotional impact a kinship club may have on a sincere but erring member. For many members approval from the club is important.

Some clubs, in addition or in lieu of gifts to mark a special occasion or the illness of a member send a greeting card. In a way a greeting card itself is a miniature gift as it is publicly displayed in the recipient's home whereas most correspondence is not. The sending of greeting cards is usually the responsibility of the corresponding secretary and the events eliciting cards are similar to those for gifts.

A few of the groups have a reverse gift-giving custom. Instead of the club's presenting a gift to a celebrating member, the member contributes to the club. It may be a small amount as in the example below or considerably more.

> There is a sunshine fund. This sunshine fund being when a wedding or a birthday or an anniversary is announced, and we have — they have a record of all the birthdays and all the anniversaries and so on, usually the birthdays of the children . . . eighteen and below, you know, and when this is announced at the meeting, then what usually happens is that you donate to the sunshine fund a quarter [or] fifty cents. . . .

There are those groups — and they appear to be increasing in numbers — where no gifts are given in the name of the club. An informant from a "strictly social" cousins' club said that the topic of gifts and greeting cards came up at a recent meeting but ". . . was rejected by everyone. They said, 'If you have anything, send it individually.'" One of the family circles that has always given gifts recently partly abandoned the custom. The initial reason given to me was, "It cost so much money we just don't do that any more." The custom was to give five dollars to members at weddings, births, and deaths. For hospitalized members a gift for approximately five dollars was bought and delivered to the sick person by a committee from the club. But it was impossible to keep the purchased gifts exactly at five dollars. Because of this my informant later explained:

> There is a little prejudice. One gift is a little high, one is a little low; one is more noticeable, one isn't, and so it isn't done directly through the family circle that way any more. Now members give their own gifts to the ill. This way we find it's much better for ourselves. The Family Circle doesn't get invol-

ved and there is no question of giving to this one equal to giving to that one.

ENTERTAINMENT ALLOCATIONS

With the possible exception of some family circles with death benefits, the greatest annual allocation for most of the clubs is, undoubtedly, for entertainment. All of the groups with any resources at all have a fund for entertaining the members. In most of the cousins' clubs I studied, especially the newest ones, this was the only area of expense with the exception of perhaps a few greeting cards or token gifts. In these clubs it is the entertainment function that is of principal importance to the members.

Expense for entertainment may be classified into two broad and sometimes overlapping categories; parties, food and drink. The party category includes such group activities as attending movies, plays, and nightclubs, or a boat ride up the Hudson. Popular food expenditures are catered banquets, restaurant dining, picnics, and meeting refreshments. It is the involvement of saving together and then planning together a suitable entertainment on which to spend the savings that provides the content for much of the interaction among members during meetings.

In summary, while all of the clubs have some form of economic structure, they do not all allocate their funds with equal emphasis. The death and welfare benefits that are so central to many of the older family circles are being eliminated in response to the sweeping changes occurring in America's political and economic structure during the past 25 years. While entertainment was always an important function of kinship clubs, it is of increasing importance in family circles and of primary importance in the cousins' clubs. And as the direction of change in our society is for citizens, not kin, to pool their resources for providing mutual health and welfare benefits, the eventual demise of the traditional type of family circle seems certain. Its social structure and ethos is too closely related to a society that no longer exists. Programmed by immigrants in a strange and often inhospitable city, its values and concerns appear "old-fashioned" to the culturally assimilated potential members of today. But the principle of "keeping the family together" still has great appeal, and the cousins' club format is a singularly appropriate organizational innovation.

CLUB RECORDS

My main interest in family club documents is what they depict of members' values and behavior. I have, where appropriate, used selections to illustrate certain ethnological points of analysis. By now it must be clear that there are many types of family clubs in terms of the degree of formal organization and that there is considerable variation for any particular formalized feature. I can think of no single feature of family clubs where this diversity is more demonstrable than in the keeping of records and members' attitudes towards them.[1] All of the clubs with officers and dues tried with various degrees of success to maintain as a minimum some sort of record of meetings and who had paid his dues. There are family clubs with beautifully complete and soberly ordered records (usually older family circles) and others (usually cousins' clubs) where the keeping of records is joyfully cavalier and the content is clearly intended to add to the general merriment and fun. Sometimes they become precious and cute, and the humor is of the "family joke" variety. Such material is intended only for the consumption of members and is an interesting mode for creating a feeling of intimacy among them. After studying the meeting minutes of several groups, it is more understandable why most hesitated or refused me access to their documents. With a single exception, the minutes I examined were written quickly, stylistically odd, and grammatically uncorrected. They were written to be read aloud and then stuffed or filed away in the secretary's book. They certainly were never intended to be viewed by an outsider. My field notes reveal my incredulity:

Eli, I believe, was the old secretary and Renée the new secretary showed me some of his notes. She thought that they were hilarious, the way he recorded the details of the meeting in a semi-professional and so serious way. The minute book itself is a loose-leaf book and a #1 mess. Never have I seen records kept in a more alarmingly slipshod manner. This was the source of great amusement to the group. Mr. P. is a bit more serious about it and feels that Renée should really try to do a better job. . . . There is no constitution or charter, and all rules are in the record as minutes. Mr. P. may someday try to pull them all out and write a charter, but that is a big job.

Although informants may laugh about their disordered records, some members complain, but only mildly, about them:

Recording secretary Pauline was asked to read the minutes. . . . so she started reading it, the old business things that were on the previous meeting. It seems that Pauline wasn't very efficient at reading the minutes. There were several items she had omitted to mention. So it was asked if there were any comments on the old business. And so we offered to have new business, and throughout the proceedings of the new business my Uncle Morris kept tabs on Pauline, whether she was keeping the right notes. Of course, this wasn't very serious. This was all as a joke, asking her to read what had just happened, just to check up on her.

But the condition of the records seems never to be a major source of contention among members. Someone can usually remember a past decision if it isn't recorded and, after all, it is "more fun" to have things more informal. One very informal family circle didn't even bother to keep its minutes:

WM: I'd be extremely interested in having or being able to look through and study some of the minutes or records of your family circle.

INF: I have them available. I have a few of them. I don't have all of them. I'm just the secretary now for a couple of months, a few months, so I wouldn't have all the other data.

WM: Who keeps that?

INF: Well, my other sister was secretary, but I didn't find need for the other minutes so I just got rid of them. There was nothing in there that was important.

WM: You mean you threw them away?

INF: Yes.

WM: That makes an anthropologist gasp.

INF: Well, to me it was just excess. You know, I have a penchant for throwing things out. I hate to keep unnecessary things around. . . . The sooner I can get rid of it, the better I like it.

This particular interview was towards the beginning of my

research, and I was still under the impression that all family circles were formally structured organizations. Our discussion continues:

WM: What kind of records do you have of the organization? How many types of written records do you have?

INF: We don't have any charter, if you mean that. We are not chartered.

WM: Oh, don't you have rules or procedures?

INF: Well, we have rules and procedures.

WM: That's what I mean. Do you have anything like that written down?

INF: I don't have it written down. I know what they are. I don't have to have it written down.

WM: How come you know?

INF: Because we do it every time when we meet the same way.

WM: Oh, I see. Does anyone have it written down?

INF: My sister may have written it down at the first meeting or so, but after that it became just a matter of course.

WM: And that first has been thrown away anyway, hasn't it?

INF: Yes. You see when we get together the president calls the meeting to order. That's the first thing. . . .

Gradually I learned that family clubs do not necessarily keep records about their procedures and decisions in a methodologically precise manner. But then custom, as any anthropologist knows, need not be written down to make it behaviorally effective. So there is no single way of establishing and recording family club records. Procedures and group decisions may be rigorously set down in constitutions and by-laws by one group while another must hunt through the minutes, if they still have them, to find an old policy decision or rely on members' memories. But even having a constitution is no guarantee that it will settle arguments as hoped.

WM: Do you have a constitution?

INF: Yes, by-laws . . . a constitution which we were very exact in, otherwise there would be a lot of arguments (laughs).

WM: Now who drew those up for you?

INF: Well, I think there are one or two who had the different organizations that they used to belong to, Jewish lodges, and they still do, and they knew a lot about by-laws and all this, and they decided to do it very constitutionally, and everything is according to Hoyle.

WM: I see.

INF: And if anything comes up, it's always, "Look in the book! See what the book says!" And so you know with the con- stitution, we look it up and see. Of course, sometimes we have some people who disagree on it, you know, but this is the usual procedure.

All of the records in my sample are written in English, but in the WPA 1938 sample 62 per cent are in English, 35 per cent in Yiddish, and three per cent in a mixture of the two languages. Again this is an indication of the gradual easing out of the Yiddish content from the family circles and replacing it with American behavior patterns. The few members who lament this passing away of old traditions make their lamentations quietly because they also realize that the old ways alienate the young. The continuance of family solidarity is of greater importance than the continuance of fond traditions.

There are examples of family club records other than those per- taining to their social and economic organization, but they are scarce among my clubs. These records may be a printed or mimeo- graphed family history, a family genealogy, a club anniversary book, and a bulletin or newspaper. I have found these to exist only among family circles although a few cousins' clubs talk about making a family genealogy.[2] None seemed interested in a family history and they are too intimate a group to warrant a club bulletin. These "secondary" documents seem to be almost ex- clusively institutional components of the older and larger family circles. Only two family circles in my interview sample have a written family history; one has a printed genealogy; three have a family bulletin, but none has club anniversary books.

Of the three clubs with bulletins, one sends the monthly minutes to members living outside of the metropolitan area; the other two send a mimeographed bulletin to all members. I was told that the bulletins are very much appreciated even by members who never attend meetings as information on all the relatives is in it. Such events as marriages, births, illnesses, address changes, graduations, deaths, important trips and vacations, and significant business and professional achievements are recorded. According to one infor- mant:

The bulletin tells all the news that goes on in the family; who's ill, and who's in Florida; who's on vacation, and who's graduated, and who's married, and who's here, there, and the other place. It also congratulates people on their birthdays, anniversaries, and, of course, one of the members has to collect all this information.

Occasional bits of family history may be included as well as sentimental eulogies to the recently deceased. Announcements also abound. A few excerpts from one of the bulletins of a very large family circle follow:

Helen Jacobson writes: "That was a fine memo which you enclosed with the bill. I'm with you 100%. I consider membership of $2 a year a bargain. The Bulletin is great. Keep up the good work. You should read the Amboy paper at 10¢ per day and full of super market ads."

Julie Segal writes: "We must receive the Family Bulletin even if it is only one page in July and August. It's our only means of contact and the family tie that binds even if I have to rush to the genealogy to find out who's who. Keep up the good work. Love to all the family."

Dr. Abraham Zimmerman writes: "Healthy, Happy Chanykah greetings to all the family circle. It is a pleasure once again to pay our dues; we find it not only a privilege to be a part of the family, but we are proud to be known as such.

I thought at the same time I would write this bit of pleasant news — our granddaughter Bonnie Brody who is 12 years of age, performed with the New York City Opera Co. in two operas — *La Bohème* and *Don Rodrigo* — ... here in Los Angeles. Her sister Brenda who will be 9 in a week appeared with the San Francisco Ballet in the *"Nutcracker"* at the Shrine Auditorium. Both show good promises in the respective arts, Bonnie as an actress and Brenda as a ballet dancer. We wish for all the family a healthy and happy New Year.

These club bulletins present an interesting method for achieving family solidarity as face-to-face interaction is not involved. In a sense, members may feel a close identity with a very large network of kin without ever seeing them. This mode of vicarious and effortless "interaction" with relatives must, in part, account for the bulletins' popularity.

5. Social gatherings

The gatherings sponsored by a family club bring together not only those relatives with whom a member is socially intimate but, more importantly, those relatives with whom he ordinarily would interact only at infrequent kin ceremonial occasions or perhaps not at all. Membership in a family club, however, gives a person an opportunity to interact regularly with those relatives he would like to see or feels he should see, but with whom an intimate relationship is precluded because of social differences, geographic distances, and/or temperament differences. For most families it would also be temporally impossible and socially undesirable to maintain intimate interaction via reciprocal home visits with all of the nuclear families in the family group. The functional appeal of the family club is that it allows the individual to discharge his felt obligations for kin interaction without necessitating the degree of personal intimacy and social reciprocity that exists among intimate kin.

Since the main goal of a family club is to bring kin together regularly, the success of a club is measured by its ability to sponsor kin assemblages. Most of the structural features discussed in the three previous chapters are consciously designed to facilitate the formation of these gatherings. It is the club gatherings, i.e., the regular meetings and special parties of the family circle and cousins' club that I now examine.

MEETINGS

When and where
The kin assemblages of family circles and cousins' clubs center around two principal types of gatherings: meetings and parties. The

term "meetings" refers to gatherings of kinship clubs where the officers preside over the affairs of the group and "parties" refers to club gatherings planned expressly for fun and entertainment.

Family clubs usually meet monthly or bi-monthly although a meeting is always subject to change if unusual circumstances occur. As the goal of the club is to bring the family together, if a large wedding or other ceremonial kin occasion occurs among the members, the regular meeting is canceled as the kin will all see each other at the ceremonial gathering. Similarly, if the club has arranged a theater or restaurant party, no meeting is held that month, or if many of the members are in retail businesses, the meeting may be canceled in December because of the members' evening working hours.

Almost all groups give up meetings during the summer months of June, July, and August because vacation plans drastically cut down on attendance. An occasional group does not meet during January and February, months when a number of older affluent members winter in Florida. So within any one family club the actual frequency of meetings varies although the principle is usually one of monthly or bi-monthly gatherings. The exception are clubs which are having difficulty assembling relatives for meetings, and then in every case I know about the meetings gradually become spaced further apart. One family circle now meets only three times a year but is considering reorganizing as a cousins' club as a revitalization technique.

Family circles, because of the inclusion of children, tend to schedule their meetings on Sunday afternoon or early evening to maximize the number who can attend. Cousins' clubs, primarily a gathering of adult age mates, prefer Saturday night, although some clubs schedule meetings for Friday or Sunday night. All predetermine the day by establishing a regular meeting time such as the first Sunday or the third Saturday of the month so that members may reserve it for the club's meeting.

The hours of the meetings also vary with the afternoon meetings scheduled at around three or four o'clock and evening meetings at around eight or nine o'clock. But few of the groups actually get the meeting under way until an hour or more after the scheduled time. As one informant told me, her club's meeting was scheduled at "the Jewish eight o'clock", meaning that many members did not actually arrive until about nine o'clock, while an informant on another group said that the meeting was scheduled at 7:30 but that ". . . most of the people come late. Actually, I don't know who ever comes at 7:30". But those who habitually come to meetings *very* late are likely to be criticized by the somewhat more punctual.

> It's supposed to start anywhere from 8:30 to 9:00, but a good number of the couples have a way of walking in like Hollywood starlets at 11:00. . . . This seems to be habitual, and there's no reason for it. They're not any more remote [in distance] than some of the people who get there on time.

A meeting seldom lasts for less than three hours and sometimes may continue for up to five or even six hours if the conversation, entertainment, and food are unusually appealing. Most of the groups, even the smaller ones, send out a postcard announcing the time and place a week or two before each meeting.

The larger groups and especially family circles may meet in a hired meeting hall or the public rooms of a centrally located hotel if the membership is too large to be comfortably contained in the homes and apartments of members.

> Our family circle would try to get a place that was centrally located, which was very difficult because you have to take into consideration that people come from different parts of the borough or different parts of the city. . . . I remember they had it in downtown Brooklyn, and then they had it in Manhattan. . . .

Cousins' clubs, because they are smaller, usually meet in the members' residences and this is considered to be eminently more satisfactory. Many of the family circles have a history of meeting at different times in both public and home settings.

> We had taken a meeting room at one of those places on 14th Street. I don't remember the name of the place — at 14th and Broadway. But it was very cold. It wasn't the feeling of being together, a family feeling. We went back to the homes. . . . Then again the same thing happened. It was the winter time — that was really the main problem with the snow and the rain — and we started again taking a room at a hotel. Again, it wasn't what we really wanted.

> I've been married for 18 years, and I knew of the existence of my husband's family circle for about 20 years and . . . the question of procedure has changed a bit. First, I remember there were times when they would have the function or the meeting at

someone's home, but then, of course, that became too complicated so they would have it at a hotel or meeting hall where
you'd gather in a room.

But the greater expense of the public meeting room and its lack of
homelike warmth are in some instances more of a liability than the
central location an asset.

When the family circle was first started, the meetings were
held in the Hotel Diplomat in New York City in the evening . . .
and they would start at about eight and last till about 10:30.
But then it got kind of expensive because they had to pay for
the room, and it usually became quite an elaborate spread that
somebody brought rather than catered. And it was a lot of work,
and it was much easier to have it in someone's home. And finally
they succumbed to the idea that having it in someone's home
might be more convenient than travelling downtown to a hotel.

These dues were for, as I said, paying for a hall, paying for
food, for beverages at the meeting. But they found that it
wasn't enough money because they didn't collect enough money
— the treasury wasn't big enough to do this. So, therefore, they
tried meeting in each other's homes, which they found to their
liking because it was a warmer atmosphere.

The home meetings of cousins' clubs and the smaller family
circles are rotated so that in some groups a couple sponsors a
meeting in their home about every three years. The frequency of
giving a meeting, however, depends upon the number of member
couples and the number with apartments or homes of adequate
size. In other clubs the members must sponsor a meeting almost
every year. The principal responsibility of the host and hostess
giving the meeting is to provide and/or serve the refreshments. The
meeting list of sponsors is usually drawn up among the members
far in advance, but it is frequently changed for the members' convenience.

Well, originally we always left it up to the members to decide,
"Well, I'm ready for one," you know. And at one time we used
to bring it up at every meeting. "Well, where will be the next
meeting?," you know. But then we decided it would be best to
plan out a year, so at the beginning of the year we plan them out.
And each one says, "Well, I'll take then," and, "I'll take that."
And sometimes you take a month, and you decide, "Well, this
isn't convenient for me," so you speak to the one that — let's

say you decide this year I have February. Now let's suppose I find it inconvenient in February, and I decide . . . I'd like to get it, let's say May. Well, I go to the one who's going to have the May meeting, and I say, "Look, I'm having it in February; you're having it in May. It's very inconvenient for me to have it in February; would you please take February, and I'll take May?" Usually the other person will be obliging. . . . There's always someone that you can rotate with, and it's worked out fairly well. Of course, there are times, as I say, we all have our discussions, our difficulties.

Procedures and styles
The meetings held in public rooms appear to be somewhat more formal than those held in members' homes, and the absence or presence of children also helps to determine the meeting style. While none of the meetings is truly decorous in procedure, some are more undisciplined and joyous than others. If young children are present, the meeting will be "hectic" because the children ". . . will be screeching and running around you know". If the group is exclusively adult, the noise level may not vary much, but the moral level will drop slightly as members "let their hair down" to tell off-color jokes and indulge in lively horse play.

Well, as I said before, my husband's family [circle], they play cards, they enjoy that and . . . telling jokes, you know, the off-color sort. That's with my husband's family. [Laughs]. But with my family [circle], while they do that on occasion, it's not primary. I mean we have fun otherwise, that is, with the dancing. We love to dance. We love to sing, and that's what we do most of the time.

Regardless of the club, the meeting procedure is similar. On arrival the members visit with each other, but the sexes are mostly segregated; the men visiting together (usually in the kitchen) and the women visiting among themselves in the living room. Then begins the onerous task of quieting the members to begin the business meeting. Finally the meeting is called to order, and amid much over-talking and general noise, the officers give their reports and the issues of old business and new business are debated with vigor and occasional rancor. The meeting, seldom lasting more than one hour or two at the most, is adjourned and the members are then served the refreshments or supper and continue to gossip and visit. Some groups have "entertainment", usually children performing or they play cards or other games. Eventually members begin to leave, but it is a gradual procedure similar to the way the groups build up gradually at the beginning. This is how one young male informant described a meeting of his cousins' club.

All right, I'll describe it from the time we arrived. We arrived quite early. My father likes to get to places early. We're usually the first ones, and we met the host. The meeting is held at private houses. When we came they were watching television. They had their daughter there and her husband. . . . The host was my father's brother – my uncle and aunt. And when we got there, we just talked to each other. We had brought my other uncle Arthur, who is noted for his jokes – most of them dirty – supplied us with several of them on the side . . . and we just waited until the other members of the cousins' club had arrived, and we were watching television and talking. . . . The ladies were sitting in what actually was a dining room – the television was in the dining room – and they were sitting down, and the dining room television was on. Then they turned it off and put on some records with music. . . . These were records like Mantovani orchestrations or various medleys. They were just talking, and we were roaming around, and this continued until all the guests came, and we greeted them and talked to them. And the women would break up into a group and the men in another group. There wasn't much order to the whole thing. It was very informal at first. Then we assembled in the living room and tried to get some order. . . . It was about 10:00 and we were there for about three-quarters of an hour before the meeting started, and I would say half of the fun was getting the people in order. There wasn't very much of an attempt made, but there were several personalities trying to get things going; my uncle Arthur who with some antics and some jokes and some other things but nothing very serious. . . . The officers try by very earnest means, very earnest looking faces, "Come on, let's get into order," plus no one is very interested at the beginning anyway. The talking and the jokes and comments go on. It's very hard. It took about 35 minutes or so before order was gotten, and when the meeting was called to order, they followed some semblance of procedure.

Not all clubs have the refreshments after the meeting, however.

Several serve when all member guests have arrived and then have the business meeting afterwards. At one of the family circle meetings I attended, my notes outline the evening's events:

1. We [my wife and I] arrive at nine, the first ones present. The hostess Mrs. L. greets us ... and makes us feel at home.... She was a most charming, considerate hostess, emptying ashtrays, offering food and drink, etc.
2. Mr. L. offers us "schnapps", and we drink and joke in the kitchen. Other guests arrive, and we are usually introduced.
3. Much drinking but no one stoned. Buffet in dining room. We wait for Lennie's wife to arrive with some more relatives. They lose their way and don't arrive until almost 11:30. Gang gets louder and louder — tell dirty jokes. Women mostly in dining room.
4. Meeting finally gets under way. New officers are "appointed". New president tries to make plans for the future. Succeeds fairly well.
5. Jim gives his watch to Lennie as outgoing president. Jim's wife Harriet is the new president. But not first woman president as Lennie originally thought.
6. About a quarter of one people begin to leave. At about 1:30 we leave with Uncle Ira's son and wife. They take us down to the Eighth Avenue subway in upper Manhattan, but we take cab home. Exhausted!

Later in my notes, I observe that the interaction style is:

... noisy and warm. Lennie had told me that "the women are all screamers," and he was right. Older generation women were the noisy ones although not exclusively.... At least three of the women were in their forties or younger and they made a lot of noise.... I sat by Harriet for some time, and she kept commenting on the noise. "It's not fun, just noise!" Also said that they usually always played poker — that was all they did — no conversation really, i.e., "interesting" conversation from her point of view. She said the group was primarily enjoyed by the older members. A short while later she was appointed the new president.... After being appointed president by the group, she got their attention by talking quietly, i.e., she would not raise her voice to their level. Then like a bunch of school children, the members shushed each other. At that she had plenty of difficulty in maintaining order what with the kibitzers, etc.

These notes are on a family circle that was in the habit of meeting in hotels. The group was going downhill quite fast and the younger members seldom attended. My principal informant conceded the group was poorly organized. The minutes were lost and the treasurer usually forgot to bring her records to meetings. The president thought the dues were $6 per year, but the treasurer told me they had been raised to $8. It was only because this particular meeting was being held in the home of a prosperous older member that so many attended. But what was interesting was how Harriet, after being elected president, proceeded to institute measures that would modernize the family circle along some of the lines of the cousin' club to which she belonged. Since the issues discussed are frequently crucial ones in all family clubs, my notes continue.

Some of the things Harriet wanted and offered for discussion — such a noisy discussion! — are as follows:

1. Meetings should be held only in members' homes. This was quickly accepted. Harriet volunteered to take the next meeting. Then they will go in alphabetical order of members' last names. Those with small apartments will be bypassed. The idea is that a family will have the meeting only once about every three years. None of this was voted on but there was no one with a contrary opinion.

2. Meetings will be held in the summer too, i.e. throughout the year. They will occur every other month. Old style was every other month but with no meetings in the summer months.

3. A newsletter will be sent to all members about a week or so before the meeting. A member was appointed to be responsible for getting it out. She was chosen because she had a duplicating machine in her home. Members will send her changes of addresses, family news, etc. for the paper. Detailed directions on how to get to the meeting home will also be included. In fact, in the discussion this was to be the main function of the card, but in the talk they enlarged it into a news sheet. At present a card is sent to each member giving the date and hotel where the meeting will be held.

4. Only coffee and cake can be served by the host and hostess plus schnapps and, of course, fruit and tidbits can be around

the room. On this point Harriet was most adamant and there was a furor of discussion and controversy. It got mixed up with another issue of whether ten dollars should be given to the host and hostess by the club to defray the coffee and cake expense. The men were particularly argumentative (negatively) on this issue, but it wasn't until Harriet got the two issues separated that any headway was made. She then limited discussion to the "coffee and cake" deal, explaining that if they didn't have this limitation, competition would develop. This, she said, had happened in the cousins' club until they passed the "coffee and cake" ruling. Sue and other ladies said they didn't want to have to compete on the food and finally got the thing pushed through. One of the younger girls, Lena's daughter, protested earlier that she should be allowed to serve lox and bagels if she wanted to, but they said absolutely no. Just coffee and cake — no more, no less. Bennie protested that if they had a feed in his house the night before, he should be allowed to serve the family the food that was left over. But again he was told that that was forbidden — he should throw it in the garbage — no exceptions were to be made! Then the ten dollar thing was discussed vociferously and finally was voted down. As Lennie said, any of the family members should be able to afford to offer his relatives some coffee and cake!

5. The time of the meeting was discussed. Someone wanted to alternate Saturday and Sunday evenings because so many of the men were merchants and couldn't get away on Saturday nights. Believe they left the meeting time open depending on the host and hostess and other activities.

6. Also discussion on whether to have the meeting if there had been a family occasion during the month. No definite decision on this point either.

7. Harriet said that she would work on a plan for the activities at the meeting so that some could play games if they wanted to.

8. The organization will now try to interest more of the younger members and get them to come to the meetings. In fact, the whole new format is designed to get the young people in; why else, as Mr L. said, should you have a family circle? It should keep the family together!

My wife's notes on this particular meeting are even more candid: We were the first guests to arrive, and the refreshments of candy, chips, fruit, and nuts were arranged all around the living room. A buffet of bagels with an assortment of fillings, cakes, pastries, and coffee was in the dining room, the bar was set up in the kitchen. The house was decorated rather brightly in color; the furniture gave a comfortable appearance. . . . Mrs. L. was very pleased that we came, and she was a warm and friendly hostess. She stayed right with us until we had a drink, made by Mr. L., something to eat, and had shown WM her family picture album. People arrived slowly until about eleven. They had mixed drinks and the buffet as they arrived; the socializing was all before the meeting. The L. brothers greeted us as "cousins" as this was the third meeting we had had with them. Minnie's was the outstanding voice in the crowd. Her husband had died recently and she said, "It could have been worse. He could have been here, and I could have been there!" Quite the joke of the family. She wanted to tell us all of the family doings for years, "but don't print it".

The meeting was called to order by Lennie. It was the night for installation of officers. Lennie had been president for the past three terms and, unfortunately, there was no nomination committee before the meeting; therefore, all was to be accomplished in the one evening. Now the turmoil commenced.

Lennie's wife wanted to run the show, and in terms of being heard and direction of voice, she did so. She nominated Harriet, who was not a regular attendant of the club, for the president. Then Lennie's wife was nominated, and one man. Mr. L., who was over eighty, did control the group by standing every once in a while to quiet everyone down. He was a grand gentleman, host, and the outstanding male influence in the group. He had everyone's respect and used it to the fullest extent which resulted in just a little less than chaos. All at once Harriet was president, sat in the president's chair; Lennie's wife was vice president and sat nearby, and the battle of president versus club began.

Because Harriet's tactics were so different, it did give her a little edge. She spoke in a very quiet voice assuming that others would have to stop talking in order to hear. Consequently, she was heard more than any other one individual although this was about one-fourth of her speaking time. She made many references to her cousins' club to reorganize this club. Surprisingly enough, this was taken quite well, and the comparison of clubs didn't offend anyone. It appeared that the family circle was so near to failure that they were willing to try any new ideas to keep going. A new office was appointed, that of an investment committee. They were to report on tips for investing and let members of the club in on it in order for all the family to benefit. The particular stock being discussed informally was a new medication . . . and many were going to invest in this stock right away. At 1:00 a strong need for adjournment was felt by all. Not all of the meetings we attended were as boisterous and exciting as this one, but it is closer to the expressive style of meetings reported by informants. When discussing meetings with me, informants invariably stressed the gaiety and craziness of the group's behavior. Only one of the groups we attended failed to live up to this self-image. This was a small meeting of a cousins' club, and for reasons that are not completely clear to me, the members' behavior was quite restrained, perfunctory, and lacking in sparkle and fun. We left the meeting soon after refreshments were served as our presence seemed to be casting a pall on the activities, and we did not really feel included. Although the interaction style was restrained, the procedures are very typical for a small home meeting. There were 14 members present and six guests, including the parents of an affinal member, a neighbor couple from down the hall, and my wife and myself. The following are excerpts from my notes:

When my wife and I with our informant couple, Alan and Irene, arrived at the apartment, we were met at the door by the hostess, Kitty. She welcomed us, and then we walked past the living room where the women who were already sitting said, "hello" to us. We went on to the bedroom where we left our coats. Alan and I then walked towards the kitchen since all of the men were in there except Joel, a young affine at his first meeting, who was sitting in the living room rather to one side from the women. . . . Sammy was making hors d'oeuvres in the kitchen, and Bill and Jerry were talking about automobiles at the breakfast table. Sammy asked me if I would like a drink, and I said, "yes". Then I noticed I was the only person having a drink although there were about four different whiskey and scotch bottles on the drainboard. . . . Alan, on his own initiative, explained to me who all the women were in the living room since I had caught a good glimpse of them and knew where they were sitting and something of what they looked like. JM had at first come into the kitchen where she exchanged pleasantries with Bill and Jerry but then evidently noticing that this was a man's world, went into the living room where she joined Irene. We arrived at the apartment a little after nine, and we had an hour to go, in fact, a little over an hour, before the meeting actually began. . . . I had gotten the impression from Irene that this was a very warm and demonstrative family that kissed each other a lot. However, I observed that as the different people arrived, the pleasantries that were exchanged were of a rather formal, stilted type, and there was none of the immediacy in the type of greetings rendered that I had expected. Although a rather talkative group, they were not noisy in the same way that the Siegel Family Circle [this is another family circle and not the one just described] members were nor did they have the same degree of spontaneous warmth. Alan and I moved into the living room and stood by the chest where we continued to talk for a considerable time. Nancy joined us for a while as did Joyce [my wife] and Irene.

Then David, the president, said that it was about time that we get together; the meeting got under way, and we all found seats in the living room. . . . The meeting was very informal as I had expected, and there was considerable joking on various points, such as this was David's last session to be president, and he was warning everyone not to cross-talk or interrupt because he felt like giving fines that night as it was his last chance. Alan then jokingly suggested several times that he was going to impeach David and, therefore, he would not be completing his term and, therefore, would be eligible for re-election at the next meeting for another term. Jane, the secretary, and David both joked about how they were glad this was the last time they had to hold office. . . . At first no one had to be recognized by the president to speak even though there was some kind of an attempt for parliamentary procedure with the president demanding at intervals that there be order or else, rising up in his chair and snapping his fingers at the group, for them to be quiet. However, his manner was warm and he did not seem to offend the group.

After the meeting was called to order Jane read the minutes of the last meeting although she said she didn't want to because they were so long. However, someone told her that she had to read them as that was a part of the procedure. After reading the notes and having them approved and seconded David asked if there was any old business to be brought up. His wife brought up the problem she had mentioned at the last meeting of whether the cousins' club should give money to one of the *New York Times* "neediest" charity cases. . . . There was considerable difficulty in getting the motion into the proper words because Jane had not quite understood the original phrasing of the motion. There was much advice all around on how the motion should be stated and much advice to the president on whether the motion should be voted on immediately or discussed further.

In some ways the president's role here was an interesting one in that at times — but not all the time — he seemed to be formalizing what was a group consensus, that is, he would formalize what he felt the group appeared to be clamoring for. Also, it seemed that it need not be the majority that wanted something, but it was rather who was the loudest and the most persistent in getting his views across that the president listened to. . . . If someone would give the president as bad a time as the person before, then he might listen to the other person next. In other words, it was rather a travesty on parliamentary procedure. There was a lot of discussion by many of the people . . . with Sammy bringing in a sobering and sane point of view occasionally when things began getting too complex. . . . Bonnie then made a final motion that included the donation of the dues of the club for one month to help a needy family listed in the *New York Times*. This was voted on by a show of hands and was apparently passed although there was no formal counting. . . . There was no asking for all those who opposed the vote, nor were there any complaints when it wasn't asked.

The next problem was to pick a committee to choose the needy family. This was kicked around for a few minutes among the members, and finally Bonnie, Irene, and David said that they would do this task. . . . At one point the treasurer was asked for her report, but she laughingly said that she had left it at home and that, in truth, she couldn't even find the thing but that she hoped that she would have located it by next meeting. . . . Incidentally, there was quite a lot of joking about money. For example, at one point the new members, Joel and Cheryl, were brought into the group, and Bill made some joke about that now they would get some money out of them, and everyone laughed. . . . Finally when no one brought up any new business, David said that he guessed that that was it. Some of the people started getting up, especially the host and hostess, to prepare the "spread" . . . and a table had been put up at the end of the room in front of the chest and covered with a tablecloth. Soda and ginger ale were placed on it, and bagels and lox and cream cheese had been arranged on the table in the nearby kitchen. . . . The meeting had lasted from about 10:14 to 11:15 . . . and at around 11:30 we began to make going-away motions. . . . I then got the coats, and we left saying goodbye to the group as a whole. Most of them looked up and said good-bye to us. Alan then drove us to the subway station.

Although the meetings of the four kinship clubs I attended were each different in details from the others, the general outline of events was quite similar. One of the cousins' clubs is of special interest, however, as its members are primarily suburbanites with the New York City residents in a minority. The meeting procedures were very similar to the other groups, but what was strikingly different was the relative importance of men and women in the proceedings. In the city-based groups the women seemed to dominate the activities, but in the suburban-based group, it was the men who played the more active role. This is a single case, and I do not know if the difference holds for other suburban-based clubs. Still, the diversity is of interest, and the behavior of the suburban club might relate to a more complete assimilation to American male-female roles. My notes describe some of these differences.

I could not have been more struck by the difference in the behavior of the MNO Club (they don't say "cousins' club" when talking about the organization). The style of interaction is completely different from the two previously visited groups. Whereas in these two groups benevolent harrassment is the order of behavior as well as for any and everyone to speak at the same time, the behavior style of the MNO members as a whole is very different. They were much more orderly, and when there was dominance in the discussion, it was by men, not women. This is one group that the women do not dominate and run. . . . In this sense they are almost a reversal of the Siegel Family Circle where the women dominate the meeting and the conversation, and the men have a very secondary and passive role. But with the MNO Club, it was the men who were joking with each other, making most of the suggestions, and women usually spoke only when they were called on or asked to speak to a particular point. They did not, as a rule, volunteer suggestions, and decisions definitely seemed to be made by the men. There was no feeling that the women were squashed as there was with the men in the Siegel organization but simply that the women just weren't as interested in this part of the activities of the organization. . . . In many ways, I would say that these people are quite well assimilated into American culture. For the most part, they would fit into almost any Old American group. One could not say this for the members of the first two groups studied. . . . There was nothing distinctive about the dress of this group except that they were dressed in comfortable sport clothes. . . . Also, in regard to speech patterns, this group was not following the "Brooklynese" type of speech. It is interesting that the five members with more of a "Brooklyn-Bronx" accent and who spoke with the more traditional "Jewish" inflections and word order were not core members of the club; they were definitely on the periphery.

By way of contrast here are my wife's notes on a meeting of the Siegel Family Circle.

Within five minutes there was no doubt that this was a woman's world. The men played at being officers of the club, offering opinions, being listened to, and all the other things men should do, but . . . the women decided, talked, cooked, talked, entertained, talked, persuaded, talked, and introduced most of the business and social issues. I hope the impression isn't one of women uniting to take action. The impression intended is that each lady participated for her own ideas and purposes. This may seem impossible as an audience is usually needed; however, it should be clear that a form of order was not uppermost in the minds of this happy, friendly, "united" group.

I have no reliable data on the relative dominance of men and women in the very large and more formally organized family circles that meet in public rooms. The findings of the WPA study would indicate that in at least some of the groups men dominate for there are several statements about the wealthy member merchants dominating the proceedings, but no examples are given.

The WPA study (Rontch 1939:55–56) does give an example of a meeting that for my purposes illustrates two points — that the liveliness of meetings has not changed much in the past 30 odd years and that great attention may be given to seemingly unimportant issues, a point that holds for my groups, too.

Now a tremendous debate develops concerning the question about a fifteenth anniversary banquet of the society. Everybody takes part in this discussion. Everyone wants to give his opinion. Only last year they celebrated the tenth anniversary, but they are only four years away from the fifteenth anniversary and believe in preparedness; therefore, they are ready to take up this matter now. There were three propositions that came out of the discussion. As a ticket for a couple would cost about $8 and none of them are too rich, let's make it a little bit easier in one of the following three ways. Pay 50 cents at every quarter, and in four years the ticket will be paid for. Second proposition, pay 25 cents every quarter, and at the end of the fourth year, two dollars at one time. The third proposition is to pay two dollars each year at one time. After a discussion of over an hour and a half, they take it to a vote, and the first proposition wins.

After this a member of the Cemetery Committee gives a report concerning the new stone wall, which they have put up at their cemetery. He praises the work and mentions correctly all of the names that are inscribed on both sides of the wall. The report is accepted, and it is decided to pay the bill to the workman who did it.

There were also certain questions taken up regarding the help of the Bialistocker Relief with 100 dollars. After a discussion this proposal to give the Bialistock Relief Society $100 is approved. The meeting closed in the same spirit of happiness and tumult as it opened. The women say goodbye to each other with kisses and the men with warm handshakes. They send regards to the absentees and wish each other to be inscribed in the Book of Life and not to forget to come, with G-d's help, to the next meeting two weeks later.

The style of dress at family clubs varies from business suits for men and cocktail dresses for women to sports shirts and slacks for men and more casual outfits for women. The time of year, the place, the meeting program, and the custom of the group all affect the sartorial style. Generally speaking, the women are dressed more formally than the men, and "When you come, one or two women will look you up and down to see what you're wearing, to see if you have got a new coat or something like that." Fashion and clothes are also discussed among the women at the meeting as well as pregnancies, babies, house furnishings, illnesses, food, marriages, and deaths. The talk of the women is much more kin and domestic oriented than that of the men who prefer to talk about business, investments, sports, automobiles, and to tell off-color jokes.

Still, any really important gossip is heard by all. Although gossiping about family, public events, and famous personalities are important sources of conversation, members also take the opportunity of being together to stress their status accomplishments.

... it's the time for bragging about your children. "My son got this degree", "My son got the other degree". . . . I have – my, this is interesting – my father's youngest brother married a woman who's very active in our organization. She's not the blood relative, but she's extremely active, and she had a son who received a scholarship to the University of Minnesota and now he won a fellowship to Columbia. And, of course, she's very proud of him. It's a chance to brag to your cousins and to your relatives. And he just gave his girlfriend a ring, and, of course, this was discussed, what kind of a ring, what they're going to do, and what their plans are. And they always discuss these things at the meetings and about vacations they went on . . . or how many people they had to dinner for this holiday or the other. It's all very amiable, very pleasant, and even the arguments, the heated discussions, are not really very bad.

There is also considerable banter among the members.

Jean – who pays $25 a throw for the psychiatrist – whenever she was insulted by her husband, which wasn't too frequently, she would say, "Better not do that; you are making me insecure, and I might cost you money besides." [Laughs] Referring to the psychiatrist's terminology, it was another way to get attention. You know, "You're making me feel insecure," or "You're not listening to me," such things like that. Actually, I don't see why they need psychiatry; they're so frank about their problems, and they discuss them so openly they *know* what the trouble is. I think the psychiatrist is just a paid listener.

The interaction style is generally open and animated, and the repartee can be exceedingly fast and bright with the more restrained members providing an audience for the adept performers.

Entertainment and games

While conversation among the members is certainly the most important social activity occurring at a family club meeting, some groups also plan entertainment to precede or follow the meeting. The most common form of entertainment is cards. None of the groups I know about play bridge, but poker is popular among the men and in one of the family circles both men and women play together. The more usual custom, however, is for the men to play poker and the women to play Mah Jongg, or, less frequently, gin rummy. The poker stakes are never very high, and the winnings may be kept by the winner, or returned to the players at the end of the evening or donated to the family club. If children are present, they may be asked to perform. At one family circle meeting I attended a grade school boy belted out "Mammy" in a bumptious imitation of Eddie Cantor and several little girls performed a group of dances with the Irish jig the most applauded. Or perhaps some of the members will put on a skit or mock wedding.

A few meetings ago they had a mock wedding, and it was just riotous. You know this doctor relative of mine is short and bald, and he must be in his late fifties, and he was a flower girl . . . dressed up with a wig and all. And my uncle, who is very tall, he's about six-two and a big man with a ruddy complexion, he was the bride . . . and it was a lot of fun. . . . The groom was my doctor's wife. [Laughs] The bride was like this [makes high motion], and the groom was like this [makes low motion]. And they had a flower girl, and it was really very nice.

One cousins' club has a member who frequently brings along his collection of pornographic films to show to the men. Some of the larger family circles plan entertainment to make the meetings more attractive to the younger adults to increase their attendance. This might be hiring a dance instructor to give lessons after the meeting or a director to stage an impromptu play by the members.

Food and drinks

In most cultures the ritual serving of food to guests is important; in traditional Jewish culture it is uniquely important. It is not enough for a hostess to offer a cup of coffee to a visitor, food must accompany it. And the more food that is offered, the more extravagantly the guest is welcomed. Reciprocally, the guest must eat the proffered food to show his appreciation of his hostess. At a family gathering or other festive occasion, a hostess feels willingly obligated to serve as fine a repast as her means allow. The last thing she wants is for her guests to think she is sparing or stingy. This bountiful attitude towards food and guests has interesting implications for the family clubs because refreshments are usually contributed by the members on an alternating basis. More often than not, the serving is somewhat elaborate.

. . . I know when I entertained them, I tended to do everything I could do, and it did run into a lot of money. . . . My husband is a butcher so . . . if I were serving meat I would have, perhaps, a tongue prepared and a roast beef prepared and sometimes a turkey. But then again, there's beverages, there's candy, there's fruit, there's cake, there's coffee, and liquor. And I felt, gee, it's a horrible feeling if you're entertaining; what if you get caught short? I think that's what it is mostly, you know. You go and buy more just to make sure you have enough, and this is what makes it so expensive. I think it's just human nature if people try and do so much, you know.

At this particular house that I last attended a meeting there was kosher delicatessen; all varieties of platters of meat and sort of a smorgasbord, you know. . . . They make sandwiches, and they had all the relishes and so forth. And he, the host, being a baker, or formerly a baker . . . there were an awful lot of cakes there and delicious varieties of foods.

If there's an engagement or anything like that, I've seen them really, you know, go all out and serve beautifully, you know like sort of to say, "Well, this is my way of celebrating with my family." You know you can't invite all the family to the wedding so they sort of bring in intoxicating beverages . . . bring in platters, cold-cut things and you know it makes it kind of a smorgasbord. . . . They've done it from time to time to celebrate an engagement or a wedding or a confirmation or perhaps the recovery, you know, of an extended illness.

The result is, even if the club begins with the idea of serving simply, each woman feels that she should serve as much as — or perhaps a bit more than — the preceding hostess. It is one of the most consistent regularities in the data.

Originally it started out that they were going to serve coffee and cake and then someone along the way decided that they were going to make a dip, just sort of pretzels, peanuts, and an onion dip. And that resulted that the next one decided, well, I'll make a small roast chicken and serve it cold, and by the time it got around, they were making feasts.

Well, we started out having, you know, just coffee and cake or sandwiches. Now they have gone into dinners. [Laughs] It's forced me into culinary arts so I have to live up to my reputation because — well, I'm international in my outlook — so I've gone in for Oriental cooking. And they all look forward to my Oriental cooking or East Indian, you see, or Mexican or anything like that.

Originally we had started out by saying, well, we'll make it very simple. But, of course, you know that there's always — well, this one says, "Well, this is an occasion so I've made a little more; I've just moved," or "I've had a party" or something.

When we started, it was originally coffee, cake, food, candy, various simple things. When we went to the hotel on Fourteenth Street, we used to order coffee and cake from the restaurant and have it sent up. And whoever was hostess would pay for it. When we went back to the homes, we started food. Sometimes it was a special occasion; then we started to try and outdo each other as we went along. It came to the point that we put a stop to it. . . . Now we are back again trying to outdo each other with the food. At the last meeting I wanted to bring this up again, but the meeting was closed. I asked if I can reopen the meeting, and they said no. So I'm going to stick to the routine that we're going through, but I'm going to try to say something about it.

The following club, like the others, has no limitation rule on food. No, there's no ruling at all. It's whatever you want. . . . For instance, we have a party, a Bar Mitzvah party, a little more is served. That I can understand. In a new home I can understand. But we don't all have new homes, but we all feel obligated to do a little more than we have been doing. And it puts a taxation on us financially. But physically there's so much work involved, and you're really exhausted. You really dread having the meeting because of all the work involved.

Another problem is that the very simple menu isn't always appreciated.

Sometimes someone will say, "Well, you know you're too elaborate. You're not supposed to have any more than bagels and lox and cream cheese." But you know, to be truthful, lox are kind of dry . . . I mean in the long run most people serve what they want.

When the women decide among themselves that they must return to less elaborate serving, from my knowledge, it is never successful. Only a club motion limiting the kind of food served can be effective — and then not always — in eliminating the culinary competition.

Whoever started it started with lavish refreshments and then the next one had to do a little better till it became ridiculous. And the people who couldn't afford it just couldn't invite them so nobody offered to entertain the cousins; you just couldn't. I mean spend $100 for a meeting, that's what it amounted to — turkey, cold cuts, liquor. So then they realized what it was, and we called a meeting and put in a ruling you're not allowed more than bagels and lox and maybe coffee cake . . . but nobody is allowed to show off. Like somebody wants to, she makes stuffed cabbage, but still it's not an expense.

But it is not always easy to get such a ruling passed. Earlier in this chapter I reported the difficulties the new president of a dying family circle had in instituting a "coffee and cake" ruling.

But there are other ways besides legislating the kind of food to be served to help eliminate or at least cut down the competitive serving of refreshments. Some of the family circles which gather in hotel meeting rooms have the refreshments catered by the hotel and paid for from the treasury. Or there may be a refreshment committee for each meeting with individual women bringing a part of the refreshments. Some of the clubs establish a policy that although the hostess prepares and serves the refreshments, she is reimbursed a set amount of, for example, $25 or $30. While this last method of handling refreshments does not necessarily cut down on the competition, the contribution makes it less of a financial burden on a housewife's budget to sponsor a meeting.

Whether the food served is kosher or not also varies, but it varies not so much with the club as with the individual hostess. The following interview with a male informant on his cousins' club illustrates how complex the situation may be. His wife keeps the only non-kosher home among the members of the cousins' club.

INF: All the cousins keep kosher homes. And if you'll check the kinship charts, you'll see that a few of them are butchers, kosher butchers, which makes them even more strongly akin to orthodoxy in that it would be hypocritical to sell kosher meat and keep a non-kosher home. It wouldn't be right . . .

WM: Does this make for any problems when they come into your house for a meeting?

INF: Not at all. Because for the simple reason that they all eat outside of the home. This is part of a little hypocrisy that I don't understand. But it's something that I've felt for a long time. Although I was brought up that way, Bill — to respect towards a parent — my mother will not eat any meat in my house. Only because she's a kosher woman, she won't eat meat in my house. She'll eat dairy products, but she will not eat meat. And the younger generation, again my . . . cousins, they eat un-kosher foods outside of the home. But in their own homes they will not eat anything or serve anything that is un-kosher.

WM: Now, at your meeting there wouldn't be any mixing of dairy and meat?

INF: No, never, never. . . . In other words, when we went to Estelle's house, and it was the last meeting . . . she was serving Chinese food. Now this is something that is wrong, but it turns out that she made it all herself. She bought the rice and the chicken — not pork — and the noodles and made some sort of delicious sauce and beef, and it was quite good. She followed some sort of kosher type recipe for making Chinese food, and, believe me, it was good. And it was sort of a novelty for her and for the rest of the group because they're welcome to eat it in the restaurant. They don't mind.

WM: Pork too?

INF: Well, no. Now we come to another ticklish area. Again a good number of these cousins still observe the dietary laws outside of their home. . . . Now by that I mean if I serve bacon and eggs, for argument's sake, I don't know that everyone would eat the bacon. They realize that they are eating meat in a non-kosher home because in a kosher home, as you probably know, you need two sets of silverware, and two sets of dishes. Two sets of everything: Pots, towels, if you keep it proper. And they know when they come to my house, even if they eat tuna fish salad, meat could have been served on that tuna fish salad dish just the day before. But they are willing to understand that they can't compel me to go out and buy separate dishes for them, but they will eat dairy. In other words, there are certain minimizing influences that they can sort of console themselves with or say, well, I understand . . . dairy is okay. But a good number of the cousins . . . probably don't eat non-kosher, for example, ham, bacon, pork, seafood, of a shell nature. You know Jewish people are not allowed to eat seafood of a shell nature. It must have scales. Whereas my wife and I, well, we swing: clams, oysters, anything! These cousins, I doubt if they'd touch that.

In other words, while my informant's cousins keep kosher households and rigidly maintain a distinction between dishes for serving kosher meat and dishes for serving dairy products, they are not so orthodox that they won't eat from dishes in someone else's house where dairy and meat products are served on the same set of dishes. Also, although they would only serve kosher meats in their own home, they do not hesitate to eat non-kosher meat in restaurants. Where they do draw the line, however — and from my experience with the clubs it is a very rigid one — most will not eat those foods that are categorically proscribed from consumption in any form, such as shell fish and pork.

Besides the cousins' club, this informant also belongs to a family circle with both rigidly kosher and non-kosher families. I asked him if there are ever any conflicts over the serving of refreshments among them:

INF: Not too much, no. Because the non-kosher would never

serve meat. See, they can serve dairy and get away with it to the people who are kosher because dairy, for some reason or other, doesn't have the connotation of being, ah, ah . . .

WM: *Treyf?* [i.e., ritually unfit for consumption.]

INF: I didn't want to say that. That's right exactly. In the sense that they will eat cheese and egg salad and anything of this variety as long as they don't eat an unkosher chicken served either roast or boiled or however they do it, or eat unkosher delicatessen foods — anything like dairy, what we think of as dairy like cheese, milk, butter, as long as no meat is served.

But even if a non-kosher hostess doesn't mix dairy and meat, there are rigidly orthodox members in some groups who will eat no food unless it has come from a kosher kitchen. Another person told me,

Oh, it's ridiculous. Sometimes they have a meeting at someone's house, and it's a big to-do; should they drink from the cup because they're not kosher, or something like that. Usually they have just a cup of coffee or "Who baked the cake?" you know, "Whose house did it come from?"

Or if a club banquet is to be held in a hotel or restaurant, there may be a heated discussion as to whether or not it should be kosher.

We usually have the annual banquet at the Henry Hudson Hotel . . . as they make a nice affair. Oh, and then we had a big argument this year over whether the dinner was going to be kosher or not. Mostly all of us are not Orthodox. I'm not Orthodox. We each observe our faith in different degrees, and each one thinks that they're so right. When we started we could get a very nice dinner for less money and at a nice place if it were not kosher.

In some of the smaller organizations there is less diversity in degrees of being kosher, and one of the family circles I studied was completely non-kosher. My wife's field notes show that the dietary law against mixing dairy and meat products were not observed at the meeting we attended.

Several tables were set up in the dining room. The children waited on the table, the hostesses served from the kitchen. A "Texas Round-up" meal of steak sandwiches, salad and French fries was served with quart bottles of a variety of sweet carbonated warm soda placed in the center of the table. Shots of scotch were offered the men (and me!) during the meal. I took the shot . . . then found myself in a dilemma because none of the women were drinking, and the men drank it in one gulp . . . so without a woman's model to follow I decided not to drink the scotch at all. . . . The dinner was brought to a close with cheese cake, coffee, and cream, and the knowledge that no one was kosher in the group.

The Jews long have been known for their sobriety, and drinking liquor to the point of exhilaration is traditionally restricted to festive occasions, such as weddings. Consequently, the consumption of liquor is not an important part of the family clubs, although it is frequently available.

Nobody that I know of is a big drinker in the family circle. . . . Drinking is a minor part. In fact, I don't remember the last time I saw someone ask for a drink at one of these meetings. There's always whiskey on the table. It's always put out but rarely touched.

This is especially true of the older style family circles that meet in the daytime with both children and adults present. Women generally do not drink at these affairs, and if a man takes a drink, it is consumed in a shot glass. There rarely is ice or the mixing of high-balls.

This may be different for the family circles and cousins' clubs that meet in the evening and in the members' homes. Here the serving and drinking of alcohol may be a more important part of the evening's activities. The men drink "shots" or "highballs", perhaps scotch or rye mixed with ginger ale or soda. The women, however, if they drink at all, may prefer " . . . something easy to take like orange juice and a little bit of vodka". Only one of the clubs I studied actually served cocktails. This was a very small family circle with several inter-faith marriages that gave late dinner parties lasting until 2:00 or 3:00 a.m. But the most typical attitude towards the serving and drinking of alcohol seems to be, "Oh, there's plenty of liquor there, but . . . it's not a drinking crowd; let's put it that way." From all of my informants I heard of only one incident where a male member drank too much. He quietly left the gathering, was sick outside, then waited the rest of the evening in the car for his wife and the couple who had brought them. The fact that he drank more than he could handle was considered to be inappropriate and imprudent behavior.

A drink served with food and favored by men and women, regardless of whether or not alcohol is served, is fruit-flavored soda water served without ice from quart bottles. Coffee is also popular and usually is served with the dessert. I have already indicated that the hors d'oeuvres may be elaborate and varied, but there was one so standard that it made us feel immediately at home when we saw it. My wife writes, "The first familiar sight in the house was a pineapple split in sections with a cherry on top of each bit. This particular hors d'oeuvre was exactly the same served at the other clubs attended, and I have never seen it anywhere else."

PARTIES

Whereas a meeting is the most frequent form of assemblage initiated by family clubs, much of the meeting time and club resources are expended on parties. By parties I refer to the gala occasions when the club gathers together *without* a meeting. This distinction between "meeting" and "party" or "outing" is made by the members. Clubs usually do not have a meeting and a party the same month, and if a party is scheduled, the meeting, as mentioned earlier, is not held.

Without the parties there would be no dramatic climax structure to the club's activities. It takes several months of regular meetings to discuss and plan for one party and at least that long to accumulate the necessary funds, because in most instances, a party is paid for from the club's treasury. The extensive planning and the cost means that at the most only three or four parties can be given during the year and in some groups even fewer. The parties then are the activities that give meaning to the regular meetings and a tangible and rewarding purpose for contributing to the treasury. The party represents the "payoff" or "reward" in material terms for belonging to a family club. Even members who seldom or never attend regular meetings often appear at a party not only to enjoy the festivities but to get a tangible return on their dues. However, there is considerable variation on the financial arrangements for parties. All parties are not paid for from the treasury, while for some the members must pay a supplement to the club's contribution. Differences in arrangements are primarily dependent on the treasury balance and the elaborateness of the scheduled party.

The monthly reports of the Entertainment Committee recorded in the minutes of one small and well-organized family circle give some indication of the range of entertainments considered. Here are the reports for four different months:

An affair at Club Sabra costs $175.00 for ten people excluding hat check and parking. Question arose if member does not attend function can they withdraw entertainment funds? According to the minutes, they cannot. The following resort hotels are to be checked by the group: Este Manor — Monticello, Goldman's — Pleasantville, New Jersey, Concord — Kiamesha, Windsor—South Fallsburg, Zeiger—Fallsburg, Neville—Ellenville, Evans—Kiamesha.

Picnic tabled due to a lack of transportation. Going away to the country: Minnie made a motion that the club finance a weekend in the country with each member's account taxed later on or each member to return the advance paid for the weekend later on. Bea seconded the motion. Motion carried unanimously.

The committee received a suggestion from Lola about Albert's Restaurant in the Village . . . Leah, who has become the unofficial "committee" volunteered to investigate. For New Year's, the group decided to attend a Broadway show and then dinner in Chinatown . . . $70.00 was issued to Leah for the tickets.

Albert's Restaurant gives a meal (choice of steak or ham-steak) a ride on a float and choice of three plays. You must be at the restaurant at 6 p.m. Belle reported on the meal she had there and found it good. The group decided to attend together but privately on an individual basis.

These outings or parties given by family clubs may be conveniently classified into four types: entertainment parties, dinner parties, outings, and children's parties. The reasons given for having parties vary. The parties for children are to bring the younger generation together to further their mutual acquaintance. But the other parties may be to celebrate an anniversary of the club, the anniversary or accomplishment of a member, or, as is most frequently the case, "just for fun".

The entertainment parties appear to be the most popular type among the newer family clubs. These are parties where the members go in a group to enjoy one of the city's public entertainments. Broadway plays, particularly musicals and comedies, first-run entravaganza-type movies at Broadway theatres, and nightclubs are the three types of entertainment frequently chosen. Although the Manhattan nightclubs chosen tend to be of the "tourist" variety, most of the nightclub parties I learned about were in neighborhood establishments with shows catering specifically to a Jewish clientele.

Banquets or restaurant dinner parties are given less frequently than entertainment parties by most clubs because of their expense. Some clubs, however, do not give any entertainment parties but save all of their money during the year for a single elaborate affair. My wife and I attended one such annual affair as the guests of a cousins' club. It was held in a suburban country club and billed among the members as an inaugural dinner dance. The club was taken over completely by the cousins and their guests. The bar served rye and scotch, and a variety of fancy hors d'oeuvres also were served. The men were dressed in business suits and the women in cocktail dresses and as it was early spring many arrived in mink stoles. My notes observe that, "It was a rather dignified but warm occasion." A band played throughout the evening, and the dinner was roast beef. We arrived at around 8:00 p.m., and dinner was served at about 9:30 at tables with white tablecloths and place cards. At 10:30 a large decorated anniversary cake was wheeled into the center of the dance floor and then was cut and served with an ice-cream sundae. While we were having coffee, the mistress of ceremonies rapped for attention at the microphone and began the small program that apparently she had arranged. My notes continued:

> It was all in verse, and she read about the Cousins' Club, how old it was . . . and it was done in rather clever style. She then called up the old officers and each one was personally thanked in rhyme for the job he had done. The gift for the outgoing president . . . was not available because her husband had forgotten to bring it from the store. She promised him, however, that he would receive it. . . . After the outgoing members had been given a round of applause they returned to their seats and the new officers were called forward. Only the president and the vice president are new and they were elected by the steering committee. There is no open ballot of all the members. More

verse was read about them, and they each said a word about what they would do for the club this year, that is, that they would try to do their best and so forth. All this was done with much levity. The installation was anything but a solemn occasion. It was more a floor show.

After the new officers had been installed, someone got up and suggested that everyone give a round of applause to the mistress of ceremony. She came off as the belle of the ball and the most important person. No one else was given the same degree of applause, not even the popular outgoing president. Just after these ceremonies ended about 11:30, the president and his wife, with whom we were sitting, excused themselves. . . . We then left a few minutes before twelve.

It had been a very pleasant and entertaining evening, but in talking with different members of the club, I learned how difficult it is to give an elaborate party that satisfies everyone. Some of the more traditional cousins thought the band should have played many more Yiddish and Hebrew melodies to encourage more group dancing. They said the older generation had been disappointed. As at most big dinner parties of cousins' clubs, the parents of the cousins are invited. In this group they are also given the status of honorary members. One member also disapproved of the way the cake had been cut. In past years a piece of the cake was presented to each of the older generation as part of the cutting ceremony, but this evening it had been dispensed with. The style of the dinner party was American Country Club, and it was obvious that there was not enough traditional Jewish content to satisfy some of the members and honorary members.

Most of the clubs try to have some kind of outing for the adults and their children during the summer when there are no regular meetings. It may be a beach party, a park picnic, a "cookout" at the home of a member, or if the club wants a more expensive and prestigous outing, they will spend a day or weekend at a resort hotel in the Catskills.

In June, instead of having a formal meeting, the family circle has a vacation outing. Originally we started off with trips to Bear Mountain; then we started going one day to a place up in Spring Valley. We used to go for one day, and now we have started to go on weekends. . . . The family circle, I think, pays a quarter of the total bill. We pay the rest. We try to have members save during the year so that when the time comes, well, the money is there. There are times not all the members go. If they feel they can't go, there is no imposition. The first year that we had gone, this was our fifth anniversary, and whatever member did not attend was given a silver tray as a reimbursement of the fact that they didn't spend the money for them, couldn't enjoy themselves with us, and just a reminder of the anniversary.

Some of the resorts advertise directly for the business of family clubs. This ad appeared in the *New York Times:*

FAMILY REUNIONS
Cousins Clubs, Family Circles, Club benefits, anniversaries. We have the most mod. facilities and pleasant surroundings to make your affair a success within a mod. budget. Day camp. Pool. Tennis. Dancing. Ranch and golf nearby. Write Deerpark Farms, Cuddebackville, N.Y. or call LO 80700.

One of the largest family circles I studied has an "Annual National Convention" each year at a resort hotel near New York, but it is held during the winter rather than in the summer. Expenses are paid for by the members themselves although the reservations are handled by the officers of the club and secured at a special rate. The expense per person for room and meals varies from $30 to $42 depending upon the type of accommodations desired. The club's news bulletin following the family convention was filled with glowing reports of the weekend. Here are three:

The weekend at the Brunswick gave us great pleasure. This was due to the club president and the staff. The entertainment was excellent, out of this world. We really and truly were pleasantly surprised and appreciate all that took place this weekend. We also had an added surprise by a few hours of our brother's and sister-in-law's visit for dinner Saturday night. . . . Even the weather cooperated. The sun shone as warm and beautiful as in Tel Aviv, Israel, when we left in November. I must add the religious services were appreciated by our men and all enjoyed the table service and what can we say about the food, — it was great. We enjoyed the weekend so much we hope we will induce our two daughters and their families to join us

G-d willing next year. We make our reservations right now . . .
G-d bless and keep all the members of the mishpokhe. Max and
Sally Green.

To the family circle weekend, greeting I want to send. What a
cultured and refined group you are; for that I give you a
personal star.

That the lovely Lehmans in your midst you count; for that
your value in height does mount. New in your group I join you
tonight; together with you in lots of joy and delight.

Long life, good health and pleasure without end; may your
existence forever attend. Yiddishkeit, and Torah culture in you
I admire, may these ends forever be your desire. That the New
Brunswick for the weekend you chose, is because thoroughness
and beauty are to you close.

Mingling of young and old is a delight to see, may these
characteristics with you always be. My joy to be among you is
quite unbounded; and my thankfulness for the discovery well
founded.

With grace and tranquility make merry tonight; may all your
dear hearts find endless delight.

Next year with G-d's help may this fete be repeated, and not
an iota of joy be deleted. By Miriam Davis.

John Lobel — age 7 — I liked the show and the ice-skating and
the puppets.

The most frequent type of outing and the least pretentious is a
picnic.

One year I think we had a picnic in somebody's back yard . . .
and once we had another one at a member's country place, and
her daughter was, I think, 12 or something, and she wanted to
have a little more of a celebration so she invited us all there.

They'll have this family grouping at Van Courtland or another
large park where they can all find facilities for barbecues and
so on.

An outing also provides an opportunity for the wealthy suburban
or country residents of the club to invite the members to their
homes and a chance for the apartment dwellers to escape the city.

We have one of the relatives, I think his name is [pauses but
can't remember], well, anyhow, they have an estate . . . which

is a fabulous place. . . . It was during the summer, and they invited all the family circle members to come, and they had a barbecue. And they supplied the cold drinks and the watermelon, and they had a beautiful pool and the most gorgeous grounds you've ever seen. And you were invited to come and spend the day with them, and they had various barbecues set up, which is very nice. I didn't even know them! The only communication I had with them was, well, in the arrangements for the day and instructions on how to get out there and what to bring along. We did bring our food along, but the other things were provided, and it was really a very lovely day. And it was all natural, you know like a Utopia, beautiful place! And it seems that they got all this area — well, he's a doctor, it seems that he performed some kind of a miraculous operation for a resident, a man of that town who was a gangster, and he owned all this territory, all this land. And he was so grateful to him that he gave it to him outright practically. I suppose all he has to pay is the taxes. But it is a fabulous place with fishing, everything that you can ask for . . ."

The most popular type of party for clubs members' children is a Hanukah Party. Hanukah is the Hebrew holiday commemorating the victory of the Maccabees and always falls near Christmas. It is sometimes called the "Festival of Lights" because on each of eight successive nights a candle is lighted until all eight are lit.

Gifts are exchanged, or given on each night of Hanukah so that Jewish children in the Diaspora will not be inclined to observe the Christian holiday of Christmas with its veneration of the Evergreen Tree and the elaborate gift system now prevailing. There are special foods for Hanukah, including Latkes or potato pancakes; special games (with the *Dreidel* or spinning top), and many other activities attractive to children and young people (Newman 1965:176).

Thus the Hanukah party serves two functions: (1) to bring the young, unacquainted relatives together and (2) to celebrate a Jewish holiday to counter the pageantry and glitter of the Christian Christmas.

The Hanukah party may be held in a home, a restaurant, a hotel, or in the recreational rooms of a Jewish synagogue or temple. It is always a rather large and lively affair. The party is planned by a committee from the club. Refreshments are served and games may be played, but the most important activity is usually the presentation of a Hanukah present to each child. In one family circle a major concession is made to Christian custom as the gifts are presented by a male club member dressed as a jovial Santa Claus. Although some of the children of members have Christmas trees in their own homes, none of the clubs uses a Christmas tree for decoration at the Hanukah party. It would be unthinkable.[1] However, it is not unlikely that in time the Hanukah party may even become an actual Christmas party among some clubs. One now has a Hanukah party for the children, but the separate adult holiday party is called a Christmas party.

Here is an adult's account of a Hanukah party that appeared in one of the family circle bulletins. It was attended by both children and adults.

What happened at the Chanukah Party? All I remember is that I was stormed with Chanukah greetings before I even had a chance to take off my coat. The aroma of delicious fresh brewed coffee by Ethel Klein and Betsy Greenfeld and others drifted out into the foyer. I followed my nose. The table inside was laden with all sorts of cakes, cookies, pretzels, potato chips. Sidney Tobias' usual variety of candies, and nuts, fruit and other goodies.

With a little effort the happy guests were quieted down and a wonderful show began. It was planned especially for the children. The performer had them laughing, crying and under his spell all afternoon. Cynthia Brody and Hannah Moskowitz distributed the gifts. The children were delighted. Florence Greenfeld lit the Chanukah candles and everyone joined in the singing with true Chanukah spirit. We all said good-bye with a promise to meet again and soon at the next meeting.

The presents distributed are inexpensive, but in some groups great care is taken to see that the gift is appropriate for the individual child. Each child may be expected to ". . . stand up and recite a poem or something; sing a little song or something", or as in the previous example, a professional performer entertains them.

6. Feuds and fissions

THE CULTURAL BACKGROUND OF CONFLICT

One of the principal sources of excitement within a group is conflict among its members. While often disavowed and regretted, intra-group conflict does animate and intensify the group experience. Just so, a family club without conflict would be an unthinkable institution. But while conflict is enlivening, it is also divisive and may prevent an organization from achieving its goals. The success of an organization is usually dependent upon its ability to prevent and/or resolve serious interpersonal conflicts among its members.

Different cultural groups vary extremely in the extent to which they permit or discourage conflict between members. The family clubs have a high toleration for interpersonal conflict that is related to the characteristic frank and expressive interaction style. It is a style that is bold, often audacious and challenging, and demands an emphatic response. When I first began my work with Jewish informants of Eastern European cultural background, I often felt threatened by the abrupt frankness. But as I learned not to withdraw, my interviews became both more valuable and entertaining. When I could argue back at an informant this stimulated him, in turn, to be even more thorough and convincing. It also seemed to make the interview more interesting and worthwhile to the informant because he had someone to "push" against. I learned that I could never truly "win" my point, but neither was there any animosity because I did not come around to my informant's point of view. It was the disputation or "status jockeying" that was exciting and important. It makes one think quickly in an effort to marshall convincing evidence. More important, it gives one a feeling of exaltation to carry off one's own part of the disputation with aplomb. What at first felt uncomfortably like an inappropriate argument, I later came to feel as a stimulating discussion about a disagreement. Later, when I asked one of my informants whether her family circle had any conflicts or problems at the meetings, I know exactly what she meant when she replied, "Oh, we don't have arguments! We have disagreements!"

The general interaction style, then, is one that includes disputation as a legitimate and non-threatening medium of discourse. This is an important consideration when one attempts to isolate and analyze intra-group conflict in Jewish family clubs. What would sound like a conflict resulting in a serious disengagement of the participants to a person from a subculture with a more tranquil interaction style, can be an exciting disagreement with no consequences for social disengagement among members of a Jewish family club.

Zborowski and Herzog (1952) provide some data on the cultural behavior of Eastern European Jews that helps to explain this interaction style by relating it historically to the *shtetl* culture. In the *shtetl* community the criteria for determining status are "fluid" and must continually be validated. Consequently, one must constantly exhibit his claims to status in interactions with others. And since one's status position must be constantly validated through interpersonal encounters, the position of authority figures is both vulnerable and tentative. For in the *shtetl*,

> The authority of any leader is not absolute but relative – the shtetl recognizes no absolutes. Almost any category is subject to invasion from another category. Almost any agent is subject to replacement under exceptional circumstances. Any generalization has its exceptions. Any statement has its qualifications. Any authority, even that of God, is subject to check, question and criticism (Zborowski and Herzog 1952:420–421).

In spirit and practice it is truly an egalitarian culture. Zborowski and Herzog emphasize that because authority is accepted only with qualifications, it remains authoritative only as long as it expresses one's own point of view. Without agreement, there is an open challenge.

Related to the precariousness of one's status because of the behavioral expectation that one must continually defend one's own status while contesting another's, is the *shtetl's* highly active and expressive style of verbal interaction. So it is the winning and the incessant validation of status, Zborowski and Herzog (1952: 420) tell us, that primarily accounts for the exuberant, animated life of the *shtetl* community.

While this challenging and disputatious interaction style is as indigenous to the contemporary New York Jewish family club as it was to the Eastern European Jewish *shtetl*, its intensity and floridness appears to differ in degree. The interaction style I learned about in my research on family clubs is a paler replication of the *shtetl* interaction style that enlivens the pages of the Zborowski and Herzog study. But although the outlines of the pattern have been softened in the process of immigration and acculturation, the pattern itself persists and is vividly recognizable.

An interaction style as highly emotive and disputatious as I have described may easily move into genuine quarrelling if a participant "pushes" too hard, is too intractable, or ignores his associates. Within the social context of a family club this may result in an overt conflict, that is, an open verbal clash among relatives, or else a covert conflict, that is, expressions of veiled or indirect hostility among relatives. Examples of both types of conflict are frequent in my data although not complete enough to assess their relative importance. However, the interview and participant observation data indicate that interpersonal conflict is an integral part of club organization. Members are expected to be frank in expressing their feelings about issues. One member of a family circle with a good-natured and realistic appraisal of his club suggested the name "Friendly Scrappers" in a contest for a new family circle name. His suggestion lost but again points to the toleration of disputation within friendship. These are not mutually exclusive behaviors and interpersonal clashes are expected at meetings. As one informant explained:

> They sort of start off with a meeting. You know, old news, new news, you know, anything that you've got to report, anything important. And then there's always the side remarks, suggestions. Then there's a couple that clash, yeah, the clashing factors. . . . Once in a while I've seen one or two of them get a little bit mad at each other.

Although "clashing factors" are a regular part of club assemblages, they are not supposed to develop to the point of membership withdrawals or dividing the club into conflicting enemy camps. Nevertheless, this does sometimes happen.

EXAMPLES OF OVERT AND COVERT CONFLICT

This section examines conflicts that disrupt the functioning of the group and threaten its goal of family solidarity. Illustrations of various forms of conflict are given. In the last section of the chapter some of the social consequences of conflict are considered as they relate to the social organization of family clubs.

Intra-group overt and covert conflict may be further broken down into *intrinsic* and *extrinsic* conflict. Intrinsic conflict refers to conflict occurring within the family club itself and extrinsic conflict refers to conflict among members that occurs external to club affairs but negatively affects the functioning of the group. These two sets of polar concepts, overt-covert and intrinsic-extrinsic, are used to conceptually organize types of family club conflict.

Overt conflicts

Most of the conflict data are about *overt intrinsic conflicts* and involve an open quarrel or argument among members at the club meeting. I have no examples of conflict at club parties although behavior at a party may be the subject of an argument at a meeting. A frequent source of conflict involves the allocation of the club's resources. The following argument over false teeth finally collapsed a cousins' club that from its inception was continually weakened by conflict.

The cousins' club met once a month for two or three years, then they broke up. There was an argument that one of the cousins was in need, and someone suggested that — they didn't have much money — but they should take all the money and help this cousin. She had very poor teeth. She had to have dentures made. This was the argument of the dentures! Someone said, "Well, she is a young girl, and she should have them; it is necessary!" The other cousins felt there were other people in the family who were also needy who didn't complain, and nobody knew what was going on in their home. And they felt that the immediate sisters and brothers of this girl should be the ones to pay for the dental work if she needed it.

One family circle had a conflict over the proposed purchase of a television set for an invalid member that resulted in the withdrawal of several members.

At one of the meetings a topic of a television arose for my husband's aunt. So if they want to buy a television, let them buy a television! It didn't bother me. They wanted all the children to get a television. But Rachel, another member, was such an obnoxious thing that she caused more damage than anything else.... This is the only really sore point that really we've had. This family circle was supposed to be a social thing. But as one member has said, you have to have something basic to keep it together; otherwise it won't work. And so we decided on the family plot. And it happens to be true because the family circle has lasted such a long time. But the family circle did decide if anyone needed anything or in an emergency, we would give up to $25.... Anyway my husband's aunt became an invalid and refused to go to live in a nursing home. She wanted to die in her own bed, which she later did.... But the family couldn't get together on the television. What happened at one meeting, one member got up and started ridiculing another member ... and he started hitting below the belt at the meeting saying "Tom doesn't want to give," and this one doesn't want to give, and that one doesn't want to give ... and it hurt; it hurt very much. It hurt me also because at that time and place it wasn't for the family circle a problem. They felt that if they would throw it open in the air to the whole family, they can do something. They were looking for help from the family circle, and it caused a big rift at that time.... No one likes me in my husband's family. I'm too outspoken [laughs]. I don't think that it was a problem for the family, for the com - plete family of Levins. Just the immediate legal Levin family, not everybody else's Levins! Well, they didn't give it to her. I said, "In the first place, what is your mother going to do with a television?" Not that I resented her having it, but the woman can't get off the bed. She's always falling, she can't see what she's doing. What does she really need a television for? They wanted to get the television really for Rachel who lives with her mother so it would make her a little happy.... But they didn't get her the television because she really became sick after that. But allocation of funds is only one of many causes of conflict. I know of one family circle that disbanded before World War II because of the virulent arguments between opposing members of Socialist and Communist persuasion and another that failed because of the verbal clashes between Zionist and Marxist members. One informants' family circle was rocked by a dispute between a widowed member and a majority of the membership who would not rescind an exclusionist article in the constitution limiting membership to Jews. The widow's son was married to a Korean girl, but membership in the club was denied her on racial grounds.

INF: It's a very serious problem we have now. One of our cousins' child married a Korean girl. Now according to our by-laws, you must be Jewish to be in our organization. . . . Well, this is the mother of the boy. She cried so bitterly. She's very — she was deathly sick after this wedding, she did not approve of it. And she said, "I have to plead now for my daughter-in-law. I want her so to be one of us." And I don't know what about the outcome but, you know, everyone's afraid to give an opinion.

WM: At the meetings?

INF: Yes. Everything was out in the open, but our by-laws say no. He can be a member, but the wife can never be.

WM: But what about the children?

INF: That's just the thing. We've never had anyone of a different race. We've had a different religion, but we've never had a different race.

WM: Have there been intermarriages before with Christians?

INF: Yes. . . . They cannot be members. The one that is not of our faith cannot be a member. . . . It's strange, though, when I can talk to somebody and say, "Well, I wouldn't care for my children to marry into a different faith." But what am I going to do? I try to be broadminded that way, but when that hits home, it's another story. All, all that you talk doesn't mean anything. When it hits you, it's a feeling. Oh, I've heard that this cousin was just crying about it at the last meeting saying "How could you vote no?" You see your cousin, and you know her all her life, and she's so heartbroken. How could you face her face-full? "I don't want your daughter-in-law in our group!" You know, it's a terrible thing. . . . This has really taken an awful lot because they don't want to hurt them. . . . It's been very rough.

WM: How long have they been married?

INF: I imagine about four or five years. But at first when they were married, his mother was deathly ill. She was away for a while. It was such a shock to her. She just couldn't take it so she was away for a while. But now that things are quieting down, she would like her children to be members.

WM: Did she bring this up?

INF: Yes, and the girl is definitely interested because she does come. In fact, I heard at the last banquet that she wore the most gorgeous dress . . . and she was absolutely beautiful. And, of course, everybody — you can't help it.

WM: Well, now, what if she would, you know, convert to some part of the Jewish faith?

INF: I don't know. It's the different race. . . . The race is a very different matter. I mean a *very* different matter. You know, when emotions are involved, it's very difficult, very difficult. And she's such a nice person, this cousin, you know. Standing up crying in front of all these people. It just tears your heart out.

WM: What did she say?

INF: I guess each mother feels, you know, "What if it were my child?" I guess that has a lot to do with it. She said, "I'm heartbroken enough. Do I have to plead to my own family? Even this has to be made so hard?"

Another type of conflict is *overt extrinsic conflicts*. These refer to quarrels among members about matters quite extrinsic to the kinship club. In these examples the quarrelling spreads, feuding coalitions are established, and the club collapses. Especially vulnerable to this kind of conflict are clubs with several members in business together whose business arguments divide the families and if not resolved, the club as well.[1] The following conflict reported by an informant originated in a matter quite external to the affairs of the family circle. But even planning a Caribbean cruise may become a central conflict in a family club.

INF: At my sister's home at one of the meetings there was an undercurrent of heated discussion with three groups — three couples of cousins. It seemed that these three couples had decided . . . that they were going on a cruise, and one of the couples wanted her mother to go along because she was alone, and she wanted to take a trip. And, of course, she's a woman in her seventies, and she's very attractive and very — a good-looking woman and quite capable of being on her own. But she just felt that if she became ill or if something happend on the way, she would be with someone but not spending any time at all with the younger couples. And they had a rip-roaring argument because one of the couples . . . did not think that it was appropriate. And this was a *heated* argument!

WM: Now who brought this up at the meeting?

INF: Well, it started as an undercurrent, and then everybody chimed in.

WM: So this was part of the regular meeting?

INF: It was just one of those things that come up, and these things are *always* coming up.

This particular argument did not result in anyone's leaving the club, but relationships were strained between two of the couples for some time.

Covert conflicts

In covert conflicts the issues are never verbally stated. An individual who, for example, perceives a status insult does not directly challenge his protagonist but responds in an indirect fashion. Frequently he withdraws from interaction or in symmetrical fashion, "returns the insult". Covert conflict is insidious in the sense that when it occurs within a group, interpersonal communications may become increasingly distorted if the initial conflict is not perceived by all the group.

A good example of a *covert intrinsic conflict* was described in Chapter Three where a member of a club conspicuously ate a ham sandwich in the presence of Orthodox members. In this instance the status insult was one in a series where the Orthodox couple felt that the cousins' club was too divergent from their own values. They were planning to drop out of the club as soon as they could do it gracefully.

In another case the transgressed individual pointedly withdrew from the situation as a way of communicating his displeasure. In this instance two of the younger women cousins were talking about their experiences in psychoanalysis, a topic he felt to be inappropriate.

My cousins Judy and Charlotte talked about their experience with their personal psychiatrist. I mentioned that before, and my mother is very interested. She was sitting along beside them talking to them about their father and any other thing else that happened to come up. This was informal conversation after the formal assemblage. This my Uncle Mose didn't approve of so he took his wife Fay physically [laughs] out of the room and out into the driveway.

Covert extrinsic conflicts are sometimes played out around invitations to family celebrations, such as a wedding or a Bar Mitzvah. Because of the exacting reciprocal expectations pertaining to such affairs, a slight is readily recognized. In this example a member living in the suburbs first slighted relatives at his son's Bar Mitzvah. Later he attended the Bar Mitzvah of a relative's son but gave no gift. Finally he dropped out of the club, but the quarrel was never verbally overt.

And then there was something to do with a Bar Mitzvah that he had up at his place. They came up there. He invited everyone to stay overnight, and when they came, he just disregarded them, and they felt very hurt. . . . He didn't bother with them apparently. If it wasn't for my sister-in-law, my husband's sister, who was there at the time — they came expecting to find a place to change or something and freshen up after the trip, and the wife said, oh, she had no time; she had to go up and rest, and she just left them. And they were guests, and they didn't know where to turn. You know, they didn't know where to go, and they felt a little hurt, you know. So my sister-in-law came along, and she saw them, and she asked, you know, what happened. And she took them upstairs and got them changed and dressed. But they were feeling a little hurt. And since that time it's been cold. . . . And then afterwards there was a Bar Mitzvah here. He, they came down, and they didn't give a gift here. And I can see there was a lot of things going around, and they stopped coming. They're out of the club.

All of these examples of intra-group conflict are alike in having a negative outcome affecting the club's solidarity although some are obviously more severe than others. In the next section I examine some of the ways in which conflict can further group solidarity.

CONFLICT AND GROUP SOLIDARITY

Conflict is characteristic of all human groups, but interpretations of its functional importance may vary. Probably most important in the study of formal organizations is the function of conflict in relation to the group's own avowed organizational goals. To understand this it is necessary to look more closely at the *consequences* of conflict. Among family clubs the goals or purposes are universally described as promoting family solidarity. Thus, conflicts among kin that result in a clarification of controversial issues can actually promote continued family interaction. Participants, as they continue to learn about the value differences among members through conflicts, may also learn to avoid some of the most disruptive types of direct confrontations.

Also, many of the members enjoy the conflicts both as participants and observers. Informants often laughed when they told me about club conflicts and indicated even directly that the club conflicts were an important part of the fun. As long as the consequence of a conflict is not divisive, it may contribute to the solidarity of the group by providing an arena of excitment, even danger, for relationships among kin that otherwise might be pallid and ceremonial. For some of the relatives who have little in common except a common ancestor, a certain amount of conflict within the group provides lively topics for gossip directly related to the family club and a contact for tenuous relationships that exist primarily to fulfill an ideal of family togetherness. And, of course, the characteristic disputatious interaction style makes it possible for considerable immediacy and excitement to be generated at a meeting.

Although I can't adequately document this point, I feel it is this style of interaction more than any other single factor that makes these groups interesting and viable for the member. Even the most trivial decision of the club may become an exciting arena of disputation as the participants jockey for recognition and status within the group. And when an ethic of equality is maintained among the members, deference behaviors become unimportant for women's views are as important as men's; affines' views are as important as cognates'; youngsters' views are as important as oldsters', and views of the poor are heard as readily as those of the rich.

In an egalitarian organization where everybody can and probably will be heard from and where the interaction style promotes expressiveness and frankness, conflict becomes an integral part of the group's activities and, in organizational terms, an important structural component. When conflict is so integrated into the affairs of a group, it is not possible then for all confrontations to end amiably and without divisive feeling of enmity. By including conflict as a positively sanctioned activity, the clubs play with an exciting but dangerous behavioral system that may undermine the goal of family solidarity and destroy the club. Or it may provide the setting and material for playing out conflicts among members that result in the estrangement and separation of some of them. In one of his early papers on family psychiatry, Nathan Ackerman (1938:51—52) describes a conflict in a family circle that illustrates the kind of discontinuity that may occur between a club's goal of promoting family solidarity and some of the actual outcomes.

In my memory is engraved the record of an incident that bears a touch of absurd melodrama, but one which likewise points to a basic truth about family psychology. I shall relate the story to you since it illustrates so well the curious, para-doxical nature of family affairs. To get the point of the story I shall have to give you a little background.

The family I have in mind was a large one with many rami-fications and numerous members scattered near and far. The senior member, a man of 80 years and himself the father of nine children, made an urgent and eloquent plea for greater family unity. In deference to the "wise old man", a family lodge was established, and he was unanimously elected to the president's chair. The lodge included in its membership the entire family, even the most remote relatives who lived at a far distance. It was founded with several purposes in mind; to promote family sentiment, to foster mutual devotion, and to provide concrete aid for less fortunate members. Among other good and bad things, a treasury and loan fund was instituted. An achievement of uncertain value was the purchase and cultivation of a family cemetery. At a business meeting of the lodge the members were at one time trying to agree on matters relating to this cemetery; for instance, how much must each member pay for the privilege of being buried there, and what was to be the "seating arrangement" so to speak, etc. After considerable haggling they finally reached an agreement on these questions.

Soon they were again bickering with one another as to whether it would be most fitting for the cemetery to be bounded by a hedge, flowers or a fence. The two elder sons of the president of the lodge argued heatedly on this question. With exactly contraposed views, they grew vehement in their oratory, their anger waxed; things went from bad to worse, and they insulted one another freely. Their father, the honorary president and founder of the lodge, attempted to intercede, but his words fell on deaf ears. Finally, the younger brother shouted out bitterly to the older: "I wouldn't be buried next to you if this were God's cemetery." In the epilogue of this story, the brothers never again spoke to one another, but the existence of the family lodge and cemetery was perpetuated.

It is profitable to mull a little on such a story. Think of it — a family lodge, inspired by a father's desire to strengthen the love ties between family members results in lifelong animosity between his own two sons. The love of one brother for another changes to intense hate because they cannot agree on whether the family cemetery, in which they are both to be buried six feet under, should be bounded by a hedge or a fence. The irony of it is superb.

Although conflict is a structured expectation within the context of family clubs, there is a point at which the consequences of a conflict become divisive instead of integrating. No one can say beforehand where that point is exactly. But as in the previous example, there is no doubt at what point the disputation becomes implacable and its behavioral implications disjunctive.

But an egalitarian ethic and disputatious interaction style are not the only variables that structurally predispose family clubs to promote interpersonal skirmishes. First, these are voluntary groups. As membership in a club is voluntary, a member is free to join or to discontinue his tie at will. Furthermore, the club is dependent on the constant recruitment of new members with the hope of keeping them active if it wishes to remain a viable and vital organization. Also, many members feel that the club needs them more than they need the club, and they maintain membership almost as a kinship favor. These factors also help to make it impossible for the clubs to establish a strong authority structure within which an officer could intervene in members' disputes. The criterion for judging the success of a president is how many members he is able to get out to meetings and parties, not his ability to control the family. His power is interpreted in terms of the extensiveness of his positive personal ties to members. His job is to preside as best he can over the affairs of the club, but he and the other officers have no strong economic or social sanctions that they may impose on an errant or difficult member. Some clubs may empower the president to impose a fine for disorderly conduct during the meeting, but the fine is so small — 25 cents at the most — that it becomes part of a joking relationship with the officers and is willingly paid. There is not a hint of punishment or guilt or shame in the entire transaction. Only the club through its membership has the power to expel a member, and none of the clubs I studied had resorted to this extreme sanction.

Some do, as I indicated in an earlier section, drop individuals from membership, but only after the individual has clearly demonstrated that he no longer values his tie to the club. The only time a member is officially dropped is when over a period of years he has neglected to pay his dues or has not tried to repay a loan that he contracted. But for either reason financial default is an insufficient reason to drop a member; he must first absent himself from the club gatherings for a considerable period and refuse to acknowledge communications from the club. In other words, regardless of a member's behavior, as long as he maintains interaction with the club, he is tolerated and accepted as a member.

Another factor that contributes to conflict among members is the variability of their social backgrounds. Earlier I mentioned how cousins' clubs are an organizational innovation to maintain the ethic of family solidarity but structured to eliminate the old-fashioned "Yiddish"-oriented generation whose values and behavior are in discord with their children and grandchildren. Family circles have the difficult job of providing entertainment that is interesting to the old, the middle-aged, and the young. Besides generational differences, there are also political differences, life style differences, religious differences, educational differences, occupational differences, neighborhood differences, kinship differences, and sex differences, any of which can contribute to the development of animosities and problems in communication.

For the reasons described above, family clubs are weak structures in terms of gaining and establishing control over the behavior of members. The sanctions they can impose as a corporate group are ineffective and inconsequential. When compared to some of the strong descent groups in primitive and folk societies that control and determine a member's access to marriage, land, goods, occupations, and community leadership roles, family clubs are understandably weak. All that most clubs can offer to their members is a regulated access to relatives, an admittedly flimsy basis for establishing strong corporate groups. Some of the older clubs, especially family circles, have attempted to build in economic functions giving members access to graves and loans, but in an affluent society with a wide range of private and government service institutions, the economic help proffered is negligible. In fact, some of the data collected in the larger study on relationships between the nuclear family and its network of kin indicate that the family would prefer to utilize community, not kin sources for economic aid (Leichter and Mitchell 1967:76–77).

In summary it is amazing that family clubs, given their structural predisposition to promoting conflict among kin, are as effective as they are in containing and controlling conflicts. But the behavioral ramifications of: (1) the culturally determined kinship tie among members and (2) the strong ethic for continued and everlasting family solidarity, are a powerful countervailing force when intra-group conflicts pass into a disruptive phase. It is the tension between these contrasting centripetal and centrifugal forces — the desire to keep together and the desire to validate one's own status, often at the expense of others — that animates and colors the social life of family clubs.

7. Why family clubs?
An explanatory model

In the preceding chapters I have presented empirical data on the structure and organization of New York City's Jewish family clubs. But the anthropologist has a responsibility, as Arensberg (1957: 101) reminds us, not only to describe the social arrangements of the institution he is studying but to account for its presence as well. To account for a cultural institution or to answer Homans' and Schneider's (1955:15) question of how a particular institution or established norm of conduct becomes what it is, social scientists utilize a number of different explanatory models (cf. e.g., Buckley 1967:66–94, Brown 1963, Nagel 1961:503–546, Sutherland 1973). However, the choice of an explanatory model to some extent is dependent upon the specific questions asked about the data.

Throughout my work on the family clubs one of the problems that intrigued me was trying to identify the factors that contributed to the emergence of family clubs as social systems. The explanatory model presented in this chapter, consequently, is more concerned with causal relations of the "historical" and "efficient" type than, for example, a model concerned with teleological or final causes or with a synchronic equilibrium model. The reason for my primary interest in a causal explanatory model is the apparent uniqueness of the Jewish family club. I think it is of anthropological importance to isolate the determinants precipitating the emergence of these groups in American society. My explanatory model is, therefore, limited to taking the family club as the dependent event and identifying the multiple contributing determinants.

I am aware that this form of causal theory does some violence to what Buckley (1967:74) calls the "truly systemic process of emergence" by isolating some of the causal factors from one another. But any form of explanatory analysis — even that of general systems theory — is limited by the spatial patterns of the printed page to focus conceptually on parts or aspects of the flow of behavior that only theoretically — certainly not descriptively — may be immediately apprehended as a changing behavioral whole. However, in the spirit of modern science and general systems theory in particular, I have tried throughout the monograph to examine the fluid nature of the structure of the family club as a complex adaptive system. This precludes the attainment of a precise structural neatness, but it more closely approximates the dynamic quality of sociocultural systems as I understand them.

The following discussion of explanatory factors or determinants is organized into three areas, viz., historical factors, cultural factors, and socioeconomic factors.[1] Some factors are treated at greater length while those previously discussed in other contexts are simply mentioned. Admittedly, there is considerable substantive overlap.

CULTURAL DETERMINANTS

Family solidarity
It is popular knowledge in American society that Jewish families are "close". All of the information on the Eastern European Jewish family in the *shtetl* (e.g., Zborowski and Herzog 1952) and in America during: (1) the years of immigration (e.g., Bressler 1952), (2) the years preceding World War II (e.g., Brav 1940), and (3) post-World War II (e.g., Strodtbeck 1958; Leichter and Mitchell 1967) indicate that the popular conception is a valid one. But it is also surprising among a group in which family solidarity is allegedly so strong that little empirical research has been done on the topic. Balswick (1966), in an article entitled, "Are American-Jewish families closely knit?," reviewed the research literature to answer his question. Although he (1966:167) noted that there was a "shortage of both theoretical and empirical material" on the topic, he concluded that the findings indicate that the American-Jewish family is not only "closely knit", but

"is more closely knit than non-Jewish families with which it has been compared" (1966:167).[2]

But the factor of Jewish solidarity is insufficient to explain why a psychological desire to maintain close relations with kin would result in family clubs. There is evidence that other American immigrant groups also have close kin ties, but the family club has not emerged among them as a prevalent form of social organization. Jewish family solidarity is certainly an important determinant, but the family club as a social phenomenon demands a more adequate explanation that reflects the complexity of factors that affect the formation and organization of any social system.

The penchant to organize

Another characteristic of Jewish-American culture is the inclination to create numerous secular and religious voluntary associations. Undoubtedly, this is related to the independent attitude of many Jews who prefer to belong to organizations that exactly reflect their philosophical values and meet their specific instrumental and expressive needs. There is also the important fact that Jews in the Diaspora have always been a political and social minority excluded from many of the economic, educational, and social affairs and benefits of the dominant society that enveloped them. As a consequence Jews traditionally were forced into a form of social parochialism, and, turning in on themselves, developed an intensive community life reflected in the variety of their clubs and associations.

This Jewish penchant to create voluntary associations was already prominent both in Eastern Europe (Baron 1964) and in New York (Grinstein 1945) early in the nineteenth century, long before the great influx of Eastern European immigrants into America. Thus the tendency to organize associations was a separately established facet of Jewish-American life and Jewish-Eastern European life as well. If anything, Eastern European Jews in America found an even greater need to create associations than in their homeland. A turn-of-the-century observer (Paulding 1905: 197) of the New York Jewish ghetto writes that, "Anyone who knows the East Side knows that it swarms with clubs almost as much as it swarms with sweat-shops and peddlers' carts." And as this monograph and other recent studies demonstrate, e.g., Gans (1958), Goldberg and Sharp (1958), Sutker (1958), Wright and

Hyman (1958), and Kramer and Leventman (1961), there is no decrease today of American Jews creating and joining voluntary associations.

Membership in voluntary associations is also more characteristic of Jews than either Protestants or Catholics (Wright and Hyman 1958:294). No one, as far as I know, has attempted a multi-factorial explanation of the American Jew's propensity to create and affiliate with voluntary associations. There is simply the social fact that they do. But the finding does help to explain why some Jewish families, using descent as a primary restrictive criterion, organize "voluntary associations" in the form of family circles and cousins' clubs.

HISTORICAL DETERMINANTS[3]

Margaret Mead (1964:296) has observed that "In making a cultural innovation the first question one must ask is whether there is an existing form that can be used with some slight modification or whether some radical new invention must be made." When first encountered the Jewish family club appears to be a "radical invention". But when viewed within the historical context of Eastern European Jewish culture, both within the Pale and as transplanted in the lives and institutions of immigrants to New York, the family club represents the expression of familiar cultural forms within a new social institution. Because in Western industrialized society we do not expect to see the family formally organized along bureaucratic lines, the family circle and cousins' club is initially startling. Our image of the kinds of social ties among related families is that they are informal and structured only by the need and desire for kin relationships. To integrate a group of related families into an organization with its own economic and authority structure seems peculiar if not bizarre.

This section examines the historical antecedents of the Jewish family club in terms of: (1) traditional Eastern European organizations, (2) the indigenous American-Jewish organizations, and (3) the organizations developed in the process of the Eastern European immigrants' acculturation. In spite of the fact that these data are not always as full as one would wish, a case may be made for the family club as an innovation from *conventional* Jewish cultural forms. Although I cannot always point to empirical evidence documenting the direct serial influence of the cultural forms discussed one upon the other, the structural similarities among the organizations regardless of their purposes or goals are impressive.

The kahal and the synagogue
One of the oldest concepts of social organization among the Jews is the *kahal*, the inclusive community organization that controls all of its religious and secular institutions. Traditionally it was governed by a group of officials composed of a president and elders and was supported by taxation. As the size of the community varied, so did the number of institutions included in the *kahal*, but in larger communities it might include several synagogues, lower and higher courts, numerous schools, a bathhouse, and an inn for travelers. A large number of *kahal* employees was necessary to operate these institutions, including street cleaners, policemen, administrative personnel, sextons, judges, teachers, and rabbis. I have already noted that in America the Jewish community was never politically ghettoized as in much of Europe. In colonial New York, Shearith Israel called its synagogue organization a *kahal* in the sense that all of the problems and activities of the New York Jewish community came under its jurisdiction. In eighteenth century New York it was a simple and expedient matter as the synagogue and the Jewish community were coextensive. But in 1825 when the Congregation Bnai Jeshurun was organized, it also called itself a *kahal* as did the multitude of other new synagogues formed in the first part of the nineteenth century. In other words, each synagogue laid claim to representing the entire Jewish community. As this fashion violated the ancient concept of *kahal* that permits but one inclusive organization for a particular area, the term was eventually abandoned. Grinstein (1945:12) writes that in New York

... a superimposed *kahal* could not be created. The reason for the many synagogues and societies in New York was that each group wished to guide its own affairs without dictation from above. Each synagogue and each society jealously guarded its rights and privileges in true American fashion. No communal organization could have been reared in New York City which could have told Shearith Israel, Bnai Jeshurun, or even the

Russian Beth Hamidrash how it should act in any given matter. Freedom of action was cherished by groups as well as by individuals, and was upheld and defended in the name of the new cultural standard of democracy which gained ground so rapidly among the Jews.

The *kahal*, although a critical form of social structure in European Jewish communities, disappeared in New York City. It was the individual synagogues that became the foci of the Jewish community, and in the earliest period of New York's history all of the community's activities were centered there.

Since the time that, according to theological tradition, God gave Moses the Ten Commandments on Mt. Sinai, the Jews have been concerned with laws and regulations for proper conduct. Centuries before Jacob Barsimon became the first Jew to live in New York City, European Jewish communities compiled their local laws, called *takkanot*. But in New York it was the synagogues that were concerned with drawing up regulations, and they followed the pattern for American institutions by calling them "constitutions" and "by-laws". When Shearith Israel drew up regulations in 1805, they were divided for the first time into two groups called "constitutions" and "by-laws", and the multitude of synagogues established in the nineteenth century followed this example. Each synagogue was administered by elected boards of trustees with a president or *parnass* at its head.

One of the president's many earlier prerogatives was to levy fines on members for misconduct; important among these was failing to come to order. Thus the problem of disorderly meetings is an old one and not peculiar to family clubs — synagogues and other Jewish organizations also must deal with the problem of eliciting orderly behavior at communal gatherings. There is a paradox here that seems to be central to American-Eastern European Jewish culture. On the one hand there is the propensity to form and join associations while on the other hand there is the individual's insistence on maintaining his personal identity within the group. Consequently, those who must administer a group's affairs find themselves in conflict with the members who hinder the orderly conduct of business by their expressive spontaneity. Yet even in the smaller family clubs a form of parliamentary procedure is agreed upon by the membership because, as one informant told me, "Otherwise we would never get anything accomplished." Belonging to a group or association does not carry with it the obligation of submerging a part of oneself but as I interpret it, provides yet another social arena for self-expression. The balance between self-expression within the group and the maintenance of order to accomplish the group's business and realize its goals is a delicate one and, as we saw in the family clubs, difficult to achieve.

But the important point in a discussion of these early New York synagogues is that their authority structure with elected and appointed officers and constitutions and by-laws to guide the affairs of the group is, in structural terms basically the same as that of family clubs. Another type of Jewish institution that is of even greater importance and a direct organizational model for family clubs, especially the older family circles, is the mutual aid society.

Mutual aid societies
Mutual aid societies are, as the name implies, voluntary associations organized for the mutual help of their members. They apparently emerge when agrarian or rural populations are influenced by urbanization. There is a large literature describing these groups in the social context of so-called "underdeveloped" or "emergent" nations, e.g., Marris (1961), Little (1965), Freedman (1957), and Meillassoux (1968). Wherever they exist, they variously appear to be associated with conditions of rapid social change, economic deprivation, or when migrant populations must readily adapt to a strange milieu.

Mutual aid societies became of great importance in the lives of the Eastern European Jewish immigrants to New York, and Grinstein (1945: 103) has attempted to document their source.

Among the Jews of Europe mutual aid societies several centuries old continued to flourish. Those which were mainly burial societies, called *Hebrah Kaddisha*, could be found in every town and hamlet in Europe which housed a Jewish population. Out of these organizations grew the mutual aid societies which, particularly in the large cities, came into existence at the beginning of the modern era, if not earlier. Part of the tradition of the Jews who come to America was, therefore, the maintenance of burial and mutual aid societies. Furthermore, there existed in New York City, Christian societies, such as the General Society of Mechanics and Tradesmen, which provided sick benefits, aids in distress, assistance to widows and orphans, and other benefits, which undoubtedly influenced the Jews to found similar societies of their own. . . . Thus two factors — the burial and aid societies of European Jewish communities and the non-Jewish mutual aid societies in New York — may be considered as the sources for the rise of Jewish mutual aid societies in the city. All of the early societies were started within synagogues as a type of adjunctive service. The first of these was the Hebrew Mutual Benefit Society organized by members of Bnai Jeshurun in 1826, which served as the model for the numerous societies that grew up in New York. The Hebrew Mutual, still an active organization, initially combined burial and funeral arrangements for members with sick benefits and financial help to widows and orphans. Its main purpose was to aid its own members and their families and was little concerned with public philanthropy. Some synagogues had several societies; Anshe Chesed had four, viz., the Society of Brotherly Love, the New York Assistance Society for Widows and Orphans, the Society Gates of Hope, and the Montefiore Society. The authority structure of these mutual aid societies was very similar to the synagogue with elected offices, constitutions, and by-laws.

But the tie between the synagogue and the mutual aid society was eventually broken. Grinstein (1945: 108) attributes this to the factionalism prevailing in most synagogues that threatened to disrupt the continuity and unity of the affiliated but separate mutual aid societies. Before 1850, all of the New York Jewish cemeteries were owned by synagogues but around that date societies began to buy their own cemeteries and gradually became completely independent associations.

Fraternal orders
Closely related to the mutual aid societies are the Jewish fraternal orders that became popular in the latter half of the nineteenth century. The earliest order founded was the Independent Order of Bani Brith in 1843.[4] It began as an order of German Jews, but within a few years Jews of other national backgrounds were admitted.

The Jewish fraternal orders combined mutual aid with Masonic styled ritual trappings and were nationally organized with numerous separate lodges. As in most lodges, their authority structure was less democratic than the synagogues and mutual aid societies. Like the societies, the mutual aid aspects included burial and sick benefits and aid to widows and orphans. Neither the mutual aid societies nor the fraternal lodges were much concerned with charitable activities for nonmembers. The responsibility for the Jewish poor was still taken by the synagogues and philanthropies specifically organized for that purpose. These societies and lodges were immensely popular among the Jewish immigrants and provided a social as well as a helping tie to men in similar circumstances.

It was this [mutual aid] feature that made them fundamental necessities for the immigrant Jew, a stranger in a new land, struggling to make ends meet. Pride would not permit him to accept charity; he could, however, meet his problems while retaining his self-respect with the help of his lodge brethren or aid obtained from the society's treasury (Grinstein 1945: 113).

Benevolent societies

Philanthropy always has been an important part of Jewish communal life and largess a principal avenue to personal or organizational prestige. Consequently, the New York Jewish community historically has had a large number of societies, often with the word "benevolent" in the name, organized for various charitable purposes. The first of these groups was organized in 1822 by Ashkenazic members of Shearith Israel and called the Hebrew Benevolent Society.

The authority structure of benevolent societies was similar to the synagogues and mutual aid societies. An important function of some of the groups was free loans, a function incorporated into some of the family circles. But in terms of the benevolent societies' concern with charity or services for the larger community, they had little influence on the organization of family clubs. When family clubs do include service and economic functions, they are, as we have seen, like the mutual aid society and fraternal order, that is, primarily concerned with the welfare of club members and not the community at large.

The organizations of Eastern European Jews in New York

The synagogue, mutual aid society, fraternal order, and benevolent society were all established forms of New York Jewish organizational life when the great influx of Eastern European Jews began. At first dependent on seeking membership in the established American-Jewish organizations, the Eastern Europeans soon began to organize their own prayer groups, then synagogues, and eventually mutual aid societies. There was the added inducement that many of the earlier organizations were dominated by German Jews, and members resented the intrusion of the newcomers who knew no German and were considered rustic and provincial in manner. The mutual aid societies or *landsmanshaftn* of the immigrant Eastern European Jews were beginning to be organized independently of synagogue ties by 1880, and they soon gained the same social and economic importance as attained by the earlier-settled national Jewish groups. Eventually some of the mutual aid groups affiliated with fraternal orders, thus adding glamour of ceremonial and prestigious-sounding titles to what were still essentially mutual aid societies. The fraternal orders or lodges retained their high social status until the comparatively recent formation of Jewish country clubs, and the "lodgniks" are now superseded in status by the "clubniks", those financially successful Jews who belong to country clubs (Kramer and Leventman 1961: 62–74).

Just as the Eastern European Jewish immigrant's mutual aid society and fraternal order were modeled on indigenous New York Jewish organizations, so were their benevolent societies, that, as prosperity grew, began to flourish. The membership of many of these associations was determined by place of origin in the homeland. As immigrants to a city with a multitude of conflicting Christian and Jewish subcultures, they bound themselves to those whose ways and names were most familiar. And, just as some of the indigenous associations had organized women's auxiliary groups, so did the newcomers from the Pale. All of these organizations, both the new and the old, were interested in advancing sociability among their members, and while the business meetings were always the primary social activity, there were occasional balls, outings, and dinners to add drama and festivity to the affairs of the group.[5]

In summary, there is nothing novel about the organization of family clubs except that the membership is composed of cognates (and their spouses) descended from a common ancestral pair. And that is an unprecedented and unusual novelty. But the organizational outline of the family club is borrowed *in toto* from the Jewish associations that preceded it. Its strongest legacy is from the mutual aid society, and both the family club and the fraternal order may be viewed as two — clearly very different — adaptations of this basic associational type; the family club sought organizational solidarity around putative kinship ties while the fraternal order sought solidarity by stressing the ceremonial tie of fictive brotherhood. But the psychological and social implications of putative and fictive kin ties are as different as the cultural sanctions that enforce and maintain them. In the next section I examine some of the determinants based on the recognition of the role of putative kinship in society and its articulation with other behavioral systems.

SOCIOECONOMIC DETERMINANTS

Industrialization and geographic mobility
The geographic dispersal of an urban population is often functionally related to an advancing industrialization. As wealth is generated by the production and distribution of goods, the workers and entrepreneurs in a democratic capitalist society become increasingly upward mobile. With their increased wages and wealth they are able to move geographically through the community to the neighborhoods to which they aspire, thereby gaining a visual validation of their rising economic and social status.

I have shown in Chapter One that the Eastern European Jewish immigrants did not all stay in the area of first settlement on the lower East side. As industrialization advanced and the city prospered and grew, so did the Jews, and they spread throughout the city ever looking for a new and better neighborhood in which to raise their children, eventually spilling out by the hundreds of thousands into the suburban areas of Greater New York. Parents were separated from their married children and married siblings from one another although there was an attempt to reside near some genealogically close kin (Mitchell 1965b).

The ties to more distant kin, e.g., aunts, uncles, and cousins were even more seriously disrupted by the dispersal of relatives throughout the metropolitan area. This is certainly one of the most important of the efficient causes of family clubs as the geographic dispersal of kin threatened the principle of family solidarity. The remedy was to organize the family along familiar associational lines, guaranteeing regular interaction and reestablishing the primacy of family solidarity not only as a cherished value but, to some extent, as an actualized value as well.

Differential social mobility

An advancing industrialization and urbanization may be correlated with geographic and social mobility among a population. Both of these processes disrupt established patterns of kin interaction. But just as all members of a person's kindred do not move to new neighborhoods, not all advance equally in terms of social mobility. The reality of differential social mobility implies that there are different rates and forms of assimilation and adaptation among an individual's kin. This is certainly true for the New York Jewish population of Eastern European descent. As an immigrant population orginally characterized by poverty, Orthodoxy, and small trades, its patterns of action soon became differentiated in the contact situation in terms of income, religious orientation, and occupational choice. Acculturation, never a monolineal process, continued to separate kin as choices were influenced by American culture, a prosperous open society that encouraged experimentation and change. To be rich, to be a Reformed Jew, to be a Socialist or Anarchist, or to be a doctor, entertainer, or executive were all viable roles, but these differences in values and life styles separated the individual from those kin whose adaptation to American society was less successful or adventuresome or at least different from his own.

The twin processes of industrialization and urbanization here, as elsewhere, generated definite and frequently unanticipated consequences for the kinship system. For the Eastern European Jewish immigrants the related processes of geographic mobility and differential social mobility broke up the valued face-to-face action patterns among kin. This was an obvious, necessary condition that preceeded the invention of the family club as a method for restructuring the broken kin interaction patterns.

The occupational system and urban kinship

Talcott Parsons' classic discussion of the American urban middle-class kinship system and its structural relationship with the occupational system also helps to explain how the family clubs emerged in the form they did, not in a genetic sense but by indicating some of the limiting economic conditions that take precedence over kinship structure.

Observing first that the primary source of family income is from occupational earnings, Parsons sets forth the hypothesis that it is the modern occupational system and its mode of articulation with the family that accounts for the structural differences between the American kinship system and the kinship systems of pre-industrial societies (1955:11). Thus, "In the occupational world, status is achieved by the individual and is contingent on his continuing performance" (1955:11–12). In other words, in most instances "a person holds a 'job' as an individual, not by virtue of his status in a family" (1954:190).

This means that in our society there is a high premium on individual abilities, social mobility, and, if necessary, geographic mobility. Therefore, if the occupational system is to operate effectively, it must be segregated from kinship groups where status is more often ascribed than achieved. The nuclear family as a separate residential unit can meet all of these requirements and hence is the principal solidarity unit of kin in our society. Parsons then interprets the conjugal ties as the "main structural keystone of the kinship system" (1954:187). At marriage the individual is "drastically segregated" from his family of orientation by virtue of his membership in his family of procreation with its "common household, income and community status" (1954:186).

From the data presented on Jewish family clubs, we see that they do not interfere with any of these structural requirements. They are not residential kin groups and are never coterminous with an occupational unit. Furthermore, the jural authority of the officers is slight and pertains exclusively to the activities of the group and does not extend to the occupational sphere. These family clubs also emphasize the structural importance of the con-jugal tie by including a cognate and his spouse as members with equal rights.

In some circumstances membership in the group can even be a factor in facilitating mobility, and since the activities of the club are segregated from business and friendship contacts, association with kin of lower status does not jeopardize the status positions achieved by performance in other groups. Although clubs do not necessarily encourage geographic mobility, neither do they give the individual access to basic economic resources that would com-pel him to remain in close propinquity. In short, the Jewish family club is structurally compatible with the requirements of the occupational system in an urban-industrialized society. It is this that has helped to maintain its viability and continuity.

There is the final point that the occupational system of a metropolis like New York provides extensive job opportunities facilitating upward social mobility without leaving the metropolitan area. This means that a high proportion of Eastern European Jews have remained in the area so that some cognatic stocks are of sufficient size, given adequate motivation, to warrant organizing.[6]

Industrial technology and kinship relations

While an advanced form of industrialization may disrupt traditional patterns of kinship by scattering kin over an ever-widening area and by generating social status differences among them as well, the complex technology of industrialization has actually facilitated interaction among dispersed kin by providing a variety of new modes for rapid communication. This has made it possible for widely-separated kin to establish a high rate of interaction if they wish.

The most dramatic of these is the telephone that gives separated individuals instant contact, regardless of the distance. We have only begun to assess the importance of this form of communication for modifying our convential theories about the relationship between a society's ecology, technology, and kinship, theories that are based primarily on the study of primitive and peasant peoples. Residence pattern categories and ideas about the significance of geographic proximity to kin must be modified to include the data on kinship in urban-industrialized societies if a comparative anthropology is to be advanced.[7]

New York City is a city divided by bays and wide waterways, but the bridges and highways, the automobile, and the subway system facilitate face-to-face visits among kin. Those living in the city may visit suburban relatives and easily return home the same day. Although industrialization and urbanization disrupted the traditional kinship patterns of the Eastern European Jewish immigrants, the complex system of communications that accompanied these processes helped compensate for the dispersal of kin throughout a great metropolitan area and contributed to the feasibility of family clubs. It was still possible to see relatives if you really wanted to do so.

The foregoing discussion of cultural, historical, and socioeconomic determinants has examined some of the factors involved in the emergence of family clubs among Eastern European Jewish immigrants to New York City. The cultural patterns of family solidarity and a penchant to create associations were harmoniously combined in the creation of the family club when industrialization and urbanization attenuated the ties among kin. The organizational model of existing Jewish clubs and lodges was appropriated to structure the activities of the first family clubs, the family circles. These clubs incorporated the primacy of the marital bond and remained segregated in function from the occupational system. The increasingly complex communications systems of the city facilitated social contact so that regular meetings of relatives widely dispersed in the urban area were possible. As assimilation to American culture intensified conflict between the older tradition-directed generations and the younger American-born generation, cousins organized clubs that excluded their parents and grandparents from full participation in the group's activities. By the time the cousins' club emerged as an alternative to the family circle, just prior to World War II, sweeping social and economic changes had occurred in American society, and the mutual aid model of the family circle was no longer appropriate.

At this point in time, it is impossible to predict with any certainty the future of these family clubs. One consistent finding, however, is that as the old groups continue and new groups are founded, it is the social function — not the economic one — that is of utmost importance to the members. Whether the family club will eventually disappear as urban Jews continue to assimilate into the American population or whether it will become a persisting structural symbol of Jewish family identity, no one yet can say.

8. Family clubs and kinship theory

Since WWII the spread of industrialization has relentlessly accelerated, and urbanization, even in such outposts as Papua New
Guinea (cf. Rew 1974), is an increasingly important social phenomenon. For the first time in world history, as Goode (1963a:238)
observes, the focus of industrialization and urbanization affect
all human societies. An outgrowth of these often cataclysmic
changes in the world's cultures is a deepened interest and concern
by social scientists in the relationship between the combined
forces of urbanization and industrialization and the family. More
broadly stated (cf. Fried 1967), the problem is an evolutionary
one of examining the connections between economic systems and
kinship systems.

   The focus of this chapter, although germane to Fried's broad
problem, is more narrow in scope. Having in the previous pages
documented the ethnographic emergence and presence of Jewish
family circles and cousins' clubs in American society, I want to
reflect on the theoretical implications these family clubs have for
conceptualizing the nature of kinship in urban-industrial society.[1]

A PROBLEM OF CLASSIFICATION

Throughout this book I have steadfastly avoided referring to
family circles and cousins' clubs by a traditional social rubric.
Rather than get caught up in partisan arguments of whether one or
the other might be best classified as, e.g., a descent group, an age-
grade society, a voluntary association, a formal organization, etc.,
I thought the most prudent procedure was to coin the theoretically
innocent term "family club" as a generic term for both the family

circle and cousins' club and get on with the business of presenting my ethnographic data. And that has been the main purpose of this monograph — to describe the social organization of Jewish family clubs and indicate their historical and contemporary relationship to Jewish culture and American society.

The problem remains of how to classify family clubs in relation to other types of social groups. This cannot be done conveniently because existing typologies do not anticipate either the formation or the social scientist's discovery of family clubs. And, although it might be a tempting tactic to some, I do not think the cause of social anthropology as a generalizing science is furthered by simply designating the family club as a *sui generis* social form, thereby setting it within the pale of the uniquely unimportant.

My approach to established classifications is that they are mutable, and I agree with Leach (1961:26) that they are never more than temporary *ad hoc* expedients. As new data become available, it is the conceptual schemes and typologies, not the data, that must be adjusted.[2]

In preparing this monograph there were three important group concepts that seemed especially appropriate to a discussion of family clubs. These were (1) descent group, (2) voluntary association, and (3) formal organization. Each is an established social science concept with a referent and literature of its own. The first two, i.e., *descent group* and *voluntary association*, are contrasting concepts developed primarily by anthropologists in the study of primitive and pre-industrial societies. The concept of *formal organization* was developed by sociologists in the study of urban-industrialized societies. I shall look briefly at each of these concepts in turn to discover the degree of fit between the abstract concept and the Jewish family club. Perhaps some alterations must be made along the way.

The family club as descent group
No one has been more critical of the classifying interests of Radcliffe-Brown's followers than Leach (1961). He has accused them of being "anthropological butterfly collectors" preoccupied with universalizing hair-splitting classifications of social phenomena instead of seeking generalizations, preferably "speculative" ones. In spite of Leach's valid stricture that classification in social anthropology has serious logical and operational limitations and

should not become the primary goal of research, classification does provide a framework, albeit conceptually biased, for comparing societies and their social institutions. And comparison by classification is still a heuristically valuable analytical technique.

What, then is a family club? Is it a descent group? We may begin our butterfly-collecting by entering the thicket of descent group theory.

Simply stated, there are two competing referents for descent group: (1) a group that restricts membership exclusively by genealogical criteria and (2) a group that restricts membership by multiple criteria including genealogical ones. The first referent restricts a descent group to unilineally bounded groups while the second also includes descent groups discussed in the literature as "nonunilinear", "ambilineal", "cognatic", and "bilateral".[3] If we accept the first referent we having nothing to discuss, for according to this narrow definition the family club is definitely not a descent group.

Among others, Firth (1963), Scheffler (1966) and Schneider (1965) all argue convincingly for the second and more flexible approach to the descent group concept. Let us take a closer look at the more broadly tailored usage. According to Firth (1963:36):

. . . if the group under discussion is of a continuative, corporate type, comprising persons organized and united primarily on a consanguineal kin basis, with a collective name transmitted from one generation to another; if it is a significant structural unit of the society, performing multiple social tasks, then there seems no good reason to deny it the character of a descent group.

The family clubs certainly fit the first three criteria but how "significant" family clubs are as structural units in American society is another question. That they are significant in the New York City Jewish subculture, I believe can be argued on the basis of the materials presented in this book. Granting this, family clubs are indeed descent groups. To be more exact they are *cognatic* descent groups since they comprise "those descendants of a married pair reckoned through both male and female offspring and operationally defined, so that they share common aims and actions in a corporate manner" (Firth 1963:23).

In the study of cognatic descent groups, anthropologists are obviously interested in the range of criteria imposed to determine membership within the group. Firth (1963:23) cites seven general factors around which specific criteria are organized which indicate who is eligible to belong to the descent group in question. It should be highly instructive to see just how family clubs organize membership criteria around these seven points. I shall examine each one in turn.

1. *Name*
Family clubs are referred to by members either as a family circle or cousins' club with the surname of the male apical ancestor usually prefixed.[4]

2. *Situation*
According to Firth, restrictions on the specific situation in which a descent group is deemed operative are related to a *specific resource* and/or *specific occasion*. In reference to a specific resource, family clubs generally restrict membership to those who pay dues for financing the services and activities of the group. In reference to a specific occasion, the custom of regular meetings and occasional parties and outings also helps at times to restrict membership to those who are interested in participating in these events.

3. *Generation depth*
In the family circle there is no limiting criterion regarding generation depth; the entire cognatic stock of the apical ancestral pair are eligible to affiliate. But cousins' clubs limit membership to a group of first cousins and their adult descendants.

4. *Lineality*
Lineality refers to the genealogical continuity of the group in terms of transmission of membership rights. Both the family circle and cousins' club are *ambilineal* in the sense that continuity through the generations is provided by using male or female links without set order.

5. *Point of attachment (laterality)*
This refers to the principle designating persons through whom membership in the descent group may be claimed. Firth notes that a rule for attachment may be (1) unilateral, i.e., exclusively through the male parent or exclusively through the female parent, (2) ambilateral, i.e., through either the male or female parent, and

(3) bilateral, i.e., through both the male and female parent.

The major distinguishing feature of ambilaterality is that it denotes a principle of *variability* in the point of attachment — there is no consistent point through which all individuals affiliate with the descent group and this is certainly true for the family clubs. But as the rule for attachment for members of a family club is through either the male or female parent or spouse, I would extend the meaning of ambilateral affiliation to include attachment through the spouse as well.

In his discussion of laterality Firth also distinguishes between "definitive descent systems" and "optative descent systems". The first refers to those systems where the individual *must* belong to the descent group and the second to those systems where elements of choice or personal selectivity are involved. As affiliation with family clubs is voluntary, they are classified as optative descent systems. To implement a valid membership claim, it is only necessary to pay the required dues.

6. *Residence rule*

Residence with or near a cognatic descent group may be an important criterion in determining membership and continued absence may invalidate the rights to membership. Although a rule of residence may be significant in structuring the membership of descent groups in primitive societies where access to the basic economic resources is based on kinship, it is not applicable to family clubs in an urban-industrialized state. As a formal rule of limitation, residence is inoperative for family clubs. Individuals may live anywhere in the world, seldom if ever attend a meeting, and still be bona fide members.

7. *Marriage rule*

In many societies descent groups are important for defining who may or may not marry but this is not true for Jewish family clubs where marriage is regulated independently from the group.[5]

To summarize this formalistic discussion, the factors operative in structuring the membership of the family circle and cousins' club as cognatic descent groups are (1) name, (2) situation, (3) generation depth (cousins' club only), (4) lineality, and (5) point of attachment. Rules of residence and marriage are not operative.

But it should be added that in reference to cousins' clubs, *age*, a factor not included by Firth, is a very important criterion limiting membership.[6] Cousins' clubs are age-graded; children and adolescents are restricted from membership.

There is yet another ethnographic factor relevant to membership in descent groups not included in Firth's discussion. This is that in some societies there may be differential access to membership.[7] A *limited descent group system*, then, is one where affiliation to a descent group is available for some, but not all of the members of the society. An *absolute descent group system* is one where every member of the society (or every member of a sub-culture in a complex society) may affiliate with a descent group. Among New York City Jews of Eastern European ancestry the opportunity to affiliate with a family club is not universal and it therefore is of the limited type.

Another distinguishing characteristic of the Jewish family club as a form of cognatic descent group is the inclusion of specified affines, i.e., spouses of cognates, as members with *full* rights and obligations. In terms of kinship expectations related to group membership, consanguinity and affinity are indistinguishable and, I would add, irrelevant. This is because the social integers of family clubs are not, as in many unilineal descent groups, individuals, but *married couples* in the cousins' club and *nuclear families* in the family circle. In both, however, it is the marital pair — husband and wife — that is the primary structural unit.

In conclusion, on the basis of the accepted definitions and qualifying discussion just presented, family clubs may be classified as cognatic descent groups.

The family club as formal organization
Just as the marital pair is the basic structural unit of the family club, it is the "formal organization" that is the primary structural unit of American society (cf. Etzioni 1964:1) These are, e.g. the corporations, schools, prisons, political parties, garden clubs, and fraternal orders that interpenetrate American social life.

Sociologists have emphasized the importance of formal organizations in urban-industrial societies and the study of them is a central concern of their discipline.[8] When the sociologist talks about "organizations" he is not talking about a household or nuclear family as an organization in the anthropological sense. He is using "organization" as a technical term to conceptually isolate social units deliberately planned to attain specific goals. These social units are also referred to in the literature with the delimiting adjective "bureaucratic" or "complex" as well as "formal". Regardless of the specific term, there is considerable agreement on what they are. Here is one of the more succinct definitions.

Organizations are characterized by: (1) divisions of labor, power, and communications responsibilities, divisions which are not random or traditionally patterned, but deliberately planned to enhance the realization of specific goals; (2) the presence of one or more power centers which control the concerted efforts of the organization and direct them toward its goals . . . (3) substitution of personnel, i.e., unsatisfactory persons can be removed and others assigned their tasks. . . . Hence, organizations are much more in control of their nature and destiny than any other social grouping (Etzioni 1964:3).

These three criteria for defining a formal organization fall neatly around the family club: (1) its structure is deliberately planned to promote family solidarity, (2) its officers are given the responsibility for achieving these goals, and (3) regular elections make it possible to rotate officers to the club's advantage. The fit is perfect.

The family club as voluntary association
Both anthropologists and sociologists have maintained an active interest in the "voluntary" or "mutual benefit" association and contributed to the voluminous literature.

Sills' (1968:362–363) definition of an association is ". . . an organized groups of persons: (1) that is formed in order to further some common interest of its members, (2) in which membership is voluntary in the sense that it is neither mandatory nor acquired through birth, and (3) that exists independently of the state". A primary distinction between a descent group and an association is that membership in a descent group is determined partly or in whole by kinship ties that are irrelevant to membership in an association. It was Heinrich Schurtz' (1902) classic study of men's associations that first brought the voluntary association to the attention of social scientists and caused Lowie (1947:257) to exalt that Schurtz' was ". . . the glory of having saved ethnologists from absorption in the sib organization . . .". And since that time descent groups and voluntary associations have been viewed as mutually exclusive types of social groups.[9] Although the family club fits an important criterion of associations in that membership is voluntary, it falls irrevocably outside the classification because the right to membership, although activated voluntarily, is acquired "through birth" or, more broadly stated, through ties of kinship and marriage. Because kin ties as a basis of membership are rigorously excluded from all definitions of the association, the family club can not be classified as an association in the technical sense.

Catching the butterfly

In attempting to classify the Jewish family club we found that it fits the requirements of both the cognatic descent group and the formal organization but not those of the voluntary association. Still, it might be interesting to pursue this problem of classification a bit further. Perhaps we can create a typology that takes cognizance of some of the modalities we have mentioned but passed over. First, let us look again at the concept of voluntary association.

Because anthropoligists have concentrated their research on pre-industrial societies, many of the associations reported by them are loosely structured and based upon custom. Sociologists, on the other hand, have concentrated on the study of associations in industrialized societies where most associations have the formalized bureaucratic structure of a formal organization. As Sills (1968:368) observes, "formal organization-like associations" are ubiquitous throughout the world in urban-industrial societies and increasingly numerous in those societies now undergoing development. The formal association is now almost as familiar in Asia (cf. Freedman 1957, Norbeck 1962, T'ien 1953) and Africa (cf. Beidelman 1970, Little 1965, Meillassoux 1968) as in America and Europe.

Therefore it is useful to divide associations into two broad types: (1) *formal associations* whose social structure and continuity are greatly influenced by legalistic charters and by-laws setting forth their organization and purposes, and (2) *traditional associations* whose origins are usually unknown and whose social structure and continuity depend upon social custom without written instruction. This typology, while it does not express the nuances of an increasingly complex continuum, does acknowledge the two major forms of organization an association may take.

By using the same reasoning used in differentiating formal and traditional associations, we may differentiate formal and traditional descent groups as well. This results in a four cell classification of associations and descent groups as presented in Table 11. From our ethnographic knowledge about Jewish family clubs, it is obvious that the majority of family circles and cousins' clubs fit into the single cell, "formal descent group", indicating they are groups organized around a rule of descent and a set of codified expectations regarding their purpose and functions. Such a typology allows us not only to classify accurately Jewish family clubs, but an even wider variety of groups while honoring both the ethnographic data and the logic of the taxonomic scheme.

To summarize, on the basis of the foregoing discussion, the Jewish family circle and cousins' club are here classified as *formal descent groups*. As a sub-type of descent group, they are cognatic; as a sub-type of cognatic descent group, they are ambilineages.[10]

Table 11. *Ethnographic examples of associations and descent groups according to the organizational mode**

| Social unit | Organizational mode | |
	Traditional	Formal
Association	Black Mouth Society (Hidatsa)	Société d'Aide et de Coopération (Bamako, Mali)
Descent Group	Yapiaun patrilineage (Arapesh)	Weinstock Family Circle (New York City)

*For references to ethnographic examples, see Bowers (1965:184–194) on the Black Mouth Society, Mead (1947:182) on the Yapiaun patrilineage, and Meillassoux (1968:80–83) on the Société d'Aide et de Coopération.

DESCENT GROUPS AND INDUSTRIALIZATION

Work on defining the relations between industrialization and kinship is still more of a theoretical enterprise for social scientists than an empirical one. That the relationship exists is undisputed; it is the *nature* of the relationship that is at issue. Work on this problem is impeded by the complexity of determinants in industrialized societies, confusion in the conceptualization of kin units, the great variety of family systems that may exist prior to indus-trialization, and the lack of case studies based on field work.

Everyone seems to agree, however, that corporate descent groups and the extended family are structurally incompatible with the geographic and occupational requirements of the occupational system in idustrialized societies. This leaves the nuclear family as the most functionally adaptive kin unit although theorists no longer assume that the kin ties of the nuclear family necessarily atrophy to the point of social unimportance. On the contrary, studies, e.g., Goode (1963b), Hammel and Yarbrough (1973), Litwak (1960a, 1960b), Loudon (1961), Rosenberg and Anspach (1973), and Young and Geertz (1961), indicate that the nuclear family in industrial societies generally knows and interacts with a wide range of kin. Goode refers to this as the "conjugal family system", but at the end of a lengthy and searching book on the subject (1963b:369), he is still unclear about the theoretical re-lations between the family and industrialization.

On the basis of Goode's work and Zelditch's two scholarly reviews of the research literature on industrialization and kinship (1964a:723—728, 1964b:492—497), it cannot be assumed that there is a single factor, e.g. industrialization, breaking down the traditional corporate kin units of a society. The implementation of political changes rooted in an ethos of increased personal freedom (whether imposed from without or generated from within), a non-industrial expanding economy, and some forms of urbani-zation all may serve to undermine the economic and authority structure of corporate kin groups and render them ineffective, and Goode (1963b:370) and Greenfield (1961) suggest the hypothesis that changes towards a conjugal family system independent of industrialization may even facilitate the process of industriali-zation.

Another problem involves the functions of descent groups in an urban-industrial society. The principal functions of descent groups in primitive and folk societies are economic and political, e.g., they may provide access to the basic resources of the society, regulate marriage and alliances, and allocate decision-making statuses in the larger society. In an urban-industrial society these important societal functions are not the concern of the descent group system but are taken over by other institutions. Conse-quently kinship roles are generally segregated from occupational and political roles. It appears that the primary *societal* function of the descent group in fully industrialized societies is neither economic nor political but purely social, i.e. its function is integrative in its attempt to stimulate closer interaction among kin.

Much has been written about the loss of functions of the nuclear family in urban-industrial society as instrumental functions gradually are transferred to the formal organizations of, for example, education, health services, industrial production and distribution, and government. Ego's kin are no longer his principal source of help although a modicum of reciprocal rights and obligations in the form of services and exchanges remains important. In view of the overall social structure of an advanced urban-industrial society, the large-scale service and economic formal organization can usually offer the individual the greatest help with the most privacy — help that is not status-reducing as it may be when it is given by kin. Help from kin is more socially visible and, in an achievement-oriented society, may publicize a person's failure to cope successfully.

Consequently, in comparison with primitive and folk societies where kinship units are not rigorously differentiated from other societal systems, the interactional character of kin ties in Western urban-industrial societies is primarily affective. This has led Zelditch (1964a:726) to refer to these kin networks as "expressive kindreds" centered as they are on visiting and recreational activities and the provision of minor exchanges and/or services. The formation of descent groups like the family circle and cousins' club within such kin networks does not change the expressive emphasis. It simply creates a formal organization to facilitate the playing of affective kinship roles among members of a cognatic stock and in this sense might even be called an "expressive descent group".

It is impossible at this time to assess accurately the cross-cultural extensiveness of descent groups in urban industrial societies. However, if the interest in kinship in urban-industrial societies continues to increase and prevailing *a priori* theoretical formulations continue to be modified, it should not be surprising to find further reports in the literature on what I have called "family clubs". To demonstrate that the family circle and cousins' club are not peculiar hybrids standing in a class alone, I need mention only Ayoub's (1966) study of American "family reunions" and Marris' (1961:31—36) discussion of "family meetings" among residents of

Lagos, Nigeria. Although there are differences among "family circles", "cousins' clubs", "family reunions", and "family meetings" in terms of their organization and degree of corporateness, they appear similar enough to be loosely classed together for the time being.[11]

The family reunion may be informal or formally organized; participation and/or membership is voluntary and, like the family circle, recruitment is from a cognatic stock with spouses completely integrated. The principal activity is an annual reunion featuring a picnic. Ayoub (1966:417) has classified these groups as "occasional kin groups", but they also may be considered as weakly-structured cognatic descent groups.[12]

The city of Lagos has a population of around 400,000 with the majority of Yoruba ancestry. Like the Jewish family clubs, the "family meetings" vary in size and extensiveness of formal organization. Meetings are weekly or monthly, and 61 per cent of heads of households included in Marris' study attended such meetings regularly during the year. The groups have elected officers, dues, and some mutual aid functions. The Yoruba are traditionally patrilineal, but the data (Marris 1961:33—34) indicate that an individual may filiate with *both* his father's and mother's group. The groups are strictly cognatic and spouses are *not* incorporated.

In conclusion, I want to make a final theoretical point specifically relevant to the family circle and cousins' club that is central to the entire monograph. It is one I have touched upon before. Although industrialization may be but one of several determinants influencing the functional and structural breakdown of corporate descent groups and extended family systems, it is still a powerful determinant in some cultural situations. What has not been theoretically considered is that in a society *without* descent groups, industrialization may, under very special circumstances, help provide the organizational and technological factors facilitating the emergence of a new type of descent group. The ethnographic evidence for such a descent group is the subject of this monograph. This is a descent group with voluntary, not ascribed, membership; where lineality is ambilineal, not unilineal, and affiliation may be plural, not prescriptively singular; whose primary function is to organize members into social activities, not economic and political ones, where the kin tie is primarily affective, not instrumental; and whose solidarity bond is conjugal, not filial. Furthermore, its segregation from the occupational system is thorough-going; it does not interfere with geographic or occupational mobility, and in some instances it is actually facilitative, and, finally, its authority structure is that of a formal organization. As a descent group system, its fit with the American industrial system is an excellent one. Although industrialization may contribute to the fragmentation of descent group systems in some societies, the findings of this study document that, under special circumstances, it can contribute to their formation as well.

Appendices

A. Studying family clubs
Methods and problems

To carry out this anthropological study of family clubs, I used several methods and related techniques to collect data that would be broad as well as deep, statistical as well as intimate. To accomplish this, I relied primarily on intensive informant interviews, participant observation and respondent questionnnaires. Each has contributed to my understanding of Jewish family clubs. These methods are discussed both substantively and in terms of some of the problems – mostly unanticipated – incurred during the research.[1]

INFORMANT INTERVIEWS

The interview data on 31 family clubs – 20 family circles and 11 cousins' clubs – were given by 29 informants (two informants each gave data on two clubs). All of the informants were interviewed by me with the exception of three interviewed by my colleague, Hope Jensen Leichter.

Thirteen of the informants, all women, were clients of the Jewish Family Service; the other 16 became informants by a variety of ways. Five were students to whom I had lectured on Jewish kinship at Brooklyn College and at the Cooper Union for the Advancement of Science and Art. Two were employees of the Jewish Family Service and two were personal friends. Four of the informants I met through intermediaries. These were a relative of a Jewish Family Service employee; the business associate of a friend; the wife of a friend; and a relative of a friend of my wife's. Of the remaining three informants, I met one at a cousins' club party I attended (the informant also belonged to a family circle), another I met at a professional gathering, and one I contacted when I discovered his name in a family circle newsletter on file in the Jewish Division of the New York City Public Library.

Most of my informants were women; only nine were men. All were married with the exception of four in their early twenties. The men's ages varied from 20 to 28 and their occupations were college student, teacher, small merchant, advertising executive, lawyer, and physician. The women's ages varied from 24 to 53 and they were housewives with the exception of a secretary, a clerical worker, and a small merchant. From the foregoing description it is obvious that no attempt was made to interview a random sample of informants on their family clubs. I simply found informants in a variety of social categories where and how I could and then hoped that they were reasonably well informed and verbal. Fortunately, they were.

Interviews on 18 of the clubs were held in one of the several New York City offices of the Jewish Family Service. Interviews on eight clubs were held in the informant's home and on five clubs at the informant's office or place of business. The home interviews were the most satisfying in that the permissiveness of a home atmosphere made it possible for the informant to be more discursive than was possible in the office interviews where either the informant or I was bound to a stricter schedule. The home interviews, however, were time consuming. Traveling to the informant's home could involve a long subway ride, a bus ride, and then a walk of several blocks — sometimes in the wrong direction — and take up to almost two hours each way. It usually required at least two interviews of from one hour to two hours each to obtain both the genealogical and organizational data, but occasionally a single interview would last three or four hours.

The principal kinds of data collected in the interviews were genealogical and organizational. For each club I tried to get a complete genealogy showing the relationships among both the members and nonmembers from the apical ancestors to the newest-born baby. The information collected on each living individual included his age, full name, present and past marriages, occupation, place of residence, comparative wealth, nature of his relationships with other family members, membership status in the club, and if eligible but not a member, why. Comparable data were collected for deceased individuals plus their age at death and number of years dead. Of course, it was inevitable that I should learn a great deal more about some individuals than about others. Those persons who were pivotal in the organization of the club in terms of affection, animosity, or familial deviance were the ones about whom I learned the most.

The genealogies were prepared in pencil using special symbols and long-hand notes on large pieces of heavy brown wrapping paper about a foot and a half high and sometimes over 3 feet in length. Because of the size of the paper, we usually worked on a dining table, desk or store counter. One of the important functions of the genealogical work was its success in building up positive rapport with the informant. Watching me graphically plot the history of his family from his own information, he was openly involved in establishing an accurate record.

I was particularly struck with the candor of informants when talking about family members, many of whom were of low socio-economic status and could certainly not enhance the status of the informant. The general straightforwardness and lack of evasiveness during the informant interviews made my work easier than among a sub-culture where an individual might distort social data perceived to reflect discredit on his family. There was one instance, however, in which a woman informant called apologetically requesting me to remove the name of an in-marrying Gentile from the genealogy. She had told her father about helping with my research and when he discovered that there was a genealogical record involved, demanded that the Gentile be removed from the record. This was but one of numerous instances indicating a strong Jewish endogamy among some Jews and an attitude of denial when the ideal marriage pattern is not followed.

The interviews that specifically discussed the organization and history of a family club were tape recorded and transcribed verbatim except for five clubs. Generally I did not tape the genealogical interviews because of their highly structured factual nature. Although my informants did not know prior to the interview that I wished to tape it, none objected or appeared suspicious or concerned. However, before we began to record I explained my rationale for using the recorder. First, it freed me from taking notes and did not slow us down. Second, the data were more accurate if I could take my notes from the actual interview at my convenience. I also stressed the confidentiality of the data and that it was the standard operating procedure of our research group to remove all identifying names and to substitute code numbers when data were written up. Finally, I explained that the tapes were usually used repeatedly and that we recorded over old interviews once the data were extracted. Most informants were curious to hear how they sounded and at the end of the interview I would play back short sections for their amusement.

During both the genealogical and organization interviews, I tried to learn as much about my informant's life as feasible while essentially focusing on his family club. The kinds of questions I asked in the organizational interview included those on officers, their duties and the present incumbents, frequency and kind of elections, where and how often meetings are held, records maintained, financial affairs, description of the last meeting attended, relationship to other kinship clubs, criteria for affiliation, the group's origins and history, conflict within the group, source of the club's name, and impressions about the club's future. Such topics formed the core of the interview. But I also was asking many implicit questions as I attempted to learn how the club influenced the life of the informant or, for example, to understand the kinds of informal sanctions the club could impose on its members and what were the cementing factors in the group's cohesiveness.

THE INTERVIEW RELATIONSHIP

I already have indicated how each of the participants in the study came to be my informant but have not described, except incidentally, my relationship to them. Although there were unique features in my role relationship to each informant, here I am concerned with describing its prescriptive aspects.

In making contact with a prospective informant it was explained that I was an anthropologist working on a research project studying the Jewish family under the sponsorship of the Jewish Family Service and the Russell Sage Foundation. Most of the informants were familiar with the agency, if not the foundation, although both helped to give me a firm institutional tie. It was further explained that I was especially interested in the family circles and cousins' clubs of New York City and doing a separate but related study on these institutions. This explanation was repeated when I began an actual interview with an informant. Many wondered why I should want to study these organizations and especially theirs. Some protested that there wasn't much to tell, that it was just an "ordinary" family circle. A few initially seemed suspicious of my motives, especially those contacted from outside the agency.

I think all of the informants wondered whether I were Jewish or not. A few asked me outright during the first interview, but others asked in the context of our conversations, especially if we touched on Jewish customs. I volunteered to most of them that I was not Jewish so they would not assume I had cultural knowledge I did not have. My informants seemed very interested in who I was in other ways, and I found it helped our rapport if I gave them information on my origins, where I lived, or any other fact that helped them to see me in a fuller and deeper social perspective. So instead of waiting to be pumped for data, I could always count on an amused expression, for example, when I volunteered that I had been born and raised on the Kansas plains.

Some of my younger informants and my own Jewish friends seemed particularly amused that I was a Gentile and studying these very Jewish family organizations. At first this joking attitude rather puzzled me until I learned more about the culture, for the Jewish family is a closed group that looks inward, not outward. In a sense it was ludicrous and perhaps a little irritating for a *goy*, especially one as obviously Gentile in appearance and background as I, to be so deeply involved with, and taking so seriously, the family circle and cousins' club.[2]

Before I began to interview informants I consulted two Jewish friends who were sophisticated about the anthropological role and asked for advice on interviewing New York Jews of Eastern European background. I was told that I would make my informants nervous if I sat too still or was too quiet and aloof. I was instructed to gesture more, to look "bright-eyed" and "act lively". I don't know how successful or convincing I was in developing these expressive behavioral features, but when I moved to northern Vermont at the end of the study, I was admonished by my wife, a Vermonter, to modify my interaction style. There it was the "village idiot", not the successful man, who cultivated verbal and behavioral expressiveness.

My informants were uniformly frank and open, and showed no

hesitation in disagreeing with me or correcting me if they thought I misunderstood a point. This avidly outspoken and expressive style of interaction, while initially vexing because I felt "put down" and embarrassed by their abruptness, greatly facilitated my research as I never had to "pull" information out of informants. They were often there with the data in detail before I had the presence of mind to ask for it.

Regardless of the methods I undertook to accommodate myself to the Jewish subculture, I feel that my not being Jewish was sometimes a limiting factor in my investigatory role. When an anthropologist's own ethnic group, on the basis of sound historical data, is perceived as discriminatory and potentially dangerous by the group he is studying, parts of the research undoubtedly will be influenced by these intergroup hostilities. Regardless of the goodwill and intent of the investigator, he will at times be treated in terms of the negative cultural stereotype. When this does occur, it is personally very disconcerting, and only ingenuity and luck can break this kind of stranglehold on the research.

It was during this study that I first became acutely conscious of being a Gentile and, like my informants, began to see the world in a Jewish-Gentile dichotomy. This happened early in my research at a meeting of a club I was studying and the circumstances and my reaction are recorded in my notebook:

This family circle meeting was the first time I was accosted with a Jewish-Gentile dichotomy. It was presented to me in several quite personal ways. Some pleasant and some joking; others that were to me of a negative tinge. Aunt Edith, who is 50, kept coming up to me and telling me how fine the Jews were, that the Jews and Gentiles should learn to get together, that the Jews want to get along with the Gentiles, that most Jews are fine people like here at the family circle; all they want to do is be friends with the Gentiles, isn't it a shame the way the Jews are sometimes treated, etc. I was quite amazed by all of this talk and even more at a loss at how to handle the indomitable interaction entrances. It all seemed quite irrelevant and annoyed me that I was being accepted — provisionally — as a "good" Gentile rather than as a fellow human being.

Much more fun was Leo's joking about the *goyim* and especially in reference to me as a *goy*. This came up one time when he was trying to find someone to draft as the new president . . ..and he looked at me and said that I could be the next one! That, after all, I knew more about these organizations than anyone else in the world and that I could help save the club. All this with much laughter. "So what if you're a *goy*; at least you would know how to run the damn thing!"

But I was always as keenly aware of the pejorative connotation of the term *goy* as were my informants. Only male informants who also became my friends used the term jokingly in reference to me. It became humorous when an informant with whom I had a warm peer relationship could refer to me by the traditionally correct but negative linguistic category for the "unclean" outsider.

Because of my own idealism regarding intergroup interaction and because I was an "integrated" member of a Jewish social agency, at first I unwittingly tended to discount Jewish-Gentile animosities in my research. I especially underestimated the deep impact that the annihilation of European Jews by the Germans in WWII had upon my informants' perceptions of Gentiles. Throughout the study I was aware that I might be perceived as a *strange* Gentile, but that I might be perceived as a potentially *dangerous* Gentile did not become obvious to me until the last week of the New York City interviews.

The point first struck me, but only obliquely, when an informant wisecracked that I was collecting Jewish genealogies for "a giant Manhattan concentration camp". I laughed, but the fear and suspicion within the joke somewhat unsettled me, and I noted the incident in my notebook. Mostly I was surprised that a man of my own age and American-born could bring such a macabre association to my genealogies. Undoubtedly I would have dismissed the incident as an idiosyncracy of my informant, but three days later during the second interview with another informant, the "concentration camp" image reappeared in connection with my research. I wrote in my notebook:

[My informant] said that he had asked his uncle, who is president of the Katz Family Circle, for the documents and explained what I was doing. The uncle was skeptical and joked about my collecting all of the family names for a concentration camp. [My informant] said it was doubtful if he could get the documents for me.

This time I did not laugh but with a shudder I thought I realized why some of my informants were initially so suspicious of my research and why it was almost impossible to obtain access to club documents. Viewing myself from the cultural perspective of my informants and their families, I must admit that as a strange Gentile, I was also a potentially dangerous one. The families I worked with all had living members who were reared in Eastern European communities where the fear and distrust the Jews felt for the politically and numerically dominant Gentiles was well founded.[3] When this basic cultural perception of the Gentile is reinforced by the atrocities of the Nazis and the discriminatory practices in our society, a skeptical attitude towards the Gentile stranger may be regarded as prudent behavior.[4]

It is also relevant that many of my informants lived in an almost entirely Jewish world in terms of significant relationships in their neighborhoods, at work, and in their friendships. This is possible in a city with two and one half million Jews where large sections of the city and even certain industries have become predominatly Jewish in composition. For persons who have spent most of their lives in an almost totally Jewish milieu, social relations with Gentiles are obviously unusual and when they do occur, are touched with apprehensiveness. After a pleasant visit with a Jewish family accompanied by an informant, I learned that I was the first Protestant Gentile to enter the home. My informant's comment about our hostess was, "I bet she sighed a sigh of relief when you went out the door!"

However, this was a social visit. In my home visits that were work-oriented, the situation was usually more relaxed. In each instance after an initial hesitation the family brought me completely into their lives. I might be treated for a few minutes in the first interview as an intruding stranger when suddenly I felt I was a friend of the family. A refreshing beverage with some cookies or cake was offered, and we settled to work at the kitchen table. But I was never treated as a professional person the way, for example, New York Chinese families had treated me in an earlier study. There was no deference, no ceremonial politeness. Informants felt free, even constrained, to disagree with me or to instruct me. Our relationships were always informal, open, and free-wheeling. It was exciting research because I could get so much data in depth in such a short time.

In those interviews at the end of the study where I mostly saw informants in my office, I never achieved the same free-wheeling rapport as when I was in their own homes or places of business. In rereading these last interviews, my imagery is a blank. I can hear the voices, but the setting is wholly mine. Divorced from the informant's milieu, the voices remain voices. Nor did these interviews exhilarate me with the immense input of a rich sensory field. My office's vapid green walls and their maps spoke only about the agency and me.

PARTICIPANT OBSERVATION

The most vexing and disappointing part of the research was that, partly for reasons already discussed, I found it very difficult to get permission to attend meetings of the clubs I was studying. My informants who were clients of the Jewish Family Service could not invite me because many of their relatives did not know about their being in casework treatment, and their tie to me might be a give-away. But this constraint did not exist in my relations with the rest of my informants. Still I was able to attend business and social meetings of only four groups, two family circles and two cousins' clubs.

When I asked an informant whether I could attend a meeting, it put him in a very embarrassing and difficult position. Since the group meetings are exclusive and closed to nonmembers except by special invitation, it meant that at the next meeting he had to explain my project and why I wanted to come. This then had to be put into the form of a motion and voted on by the group. He was in effect putting his personal prestige within the group on the line, and apparently most did not feel that they wanted to risk being put down by the group. I also knew how it made one informant feel whose group voted the motion down. Consequently, I was in an unenviable situation of placing my informant, who had gone considerably out of his way to help me, in the position of being rebutted by his family for my presumptuousness. Still, I had to ask because obtaining observational data was important to my research design. It was always rather awkward for us both when I did. A few said it would be too difficult to arrange, and one hinted that my not being Jewish was a special problem. Some gave excuses that they didn't know when they would be attending another meeting, but most indicated without enthusiasm that they would try to arrange it. Among those that I checked back with, nothing had been done.

I imagine that by stronger pressure and persistence on my part, I might have visited several other groups. But I could not in good conscience push my informants into an awkward position within their families. As it was, I maintained good relations with all of my informants and was able to call on them for additional data when it was necessary.

Of the four groups whose meetings I did succeed in attending, I visited a single gathering of three groups and two gatherings of the fourth group. But I never felt completely comfortable or totally accepted at any of the gatherings — I was being watched too closely. It is easy, however, to understand why some members could not fathom why I wanted to come to watch *them*. From some of the jokes I was made clearly aware that the popular image of the anthropologist is someone who goes to study "savages," and my presence apparently wasn't one that particularly enhanced their image of themselves.[5] And why should I want to travel on a cold night from Manhattan to Queens, Brooklyn, or the Bronx just to study their family group?

Among the more informal cousins' clubs, there was the added problem of the relaxed and intimate nature of their behaviour at gatherings. It was not the place to include a stranger. Here are my notes on one informant and her cousins' club:

> When Janice asked some of the members if I could attend, they said, "No, give him the minutes, but don't let him come." This was because they felt that they acted very foolish at the meetings and didn't want an outsider to see them. Janice said they felt that I would think they were all crazy.

Janice, however, was a particularly enterprising informant and very interested in my study. This is how she finally arranged for my wife and me to attend an actual meeting.

One Sunday all of the relatives came together to visit with a cousin who had just arrived from California and Janice used the occasion to collect additional social data I wanted for the genealogy. Taking the members aside individually to get her data, she also asked each if it was all right if my wife and I attended one meeting. When asked separately, each gave his assent as Janice had predicted. Then she announced to the gathering that there was a favorable consensus among the members and she would invite us to the club's next meeting. Her husband, who first told me this story, said he was "astounded and amazed" that his wife had accomplished the impossible because the club had been adamant about not inviting us.

My wife accompanied me to each of the club meetings and her presence helped to alter the research aspect of my presence to make it more legitimately social. We did not take notes — it would have been rudely inappropriate — but wrote up our observations on the long subway rides back to Manhattan.

The officers of the clubs we visited were very cordial to us and I was always asked to give a short talk about my research. Others went out of their way to make us feel welcome, but there were always some who remained pointedly aloof and uninterested in us. At one meeting my wife was left to sit alone on the sofa for a time while the men talked about cars in the kitchen and the women visited in small groups about their children and homes. But in another group she was warmly accepted by the hostess, introduced to a number of the other women and included in all of their conversations. At another meeting we attended just before Thanksgiving the hostess, who became very friendly with my wife during the evening, insisted that we must return for Thanksgiving dinner as we were alone in the city without relatives.

CLUB DOCUMENTS

The closed and exclusive nature of these clubs is again indicated by the troublesome resistance I met when trying to gain access to group-held documents, e.g., minutes of meetings or financial records. None of the groups allowed me complete access to their financial records. Some of the groups that I visited did allow me to look over their bank book and Treasurer's reports at meetings. But whenever I suggested that I would like a closer perusal, I could feel the individual involved — usually the treasurer whom I had just met — begin to draw away from me, and permission was not volunteered. As an outsider I apparently was moving in too close and expecting too much. Interestingly, this restriction on my working directly with financial records did not extend to discussing the group's financial affairs with informants. All of my informants freely answered my questions on group finances within the extent of their knowledge. Some also volunteered considerable financial data, particularly in the context of discussing intragroup conflicts.

There was a similar reticence to let me examine the minutes of meetings. Again most informants said they must see whether the group would permit me to study the minutes, but I rarely heard from them again on the matter. Although I was able to examine the minutes of the four groups that I visited, I was given total access by only two. I had no better luck in gaining total access to club constitutions.

These documents are the common ones I systematically tried to see. However, a number of other types of group documents, e.g., a family history, a club newsletter, and a family genealogy were brought to me by various informants including, those that were agency clients. These were documents distributed by the club and, as the informant had his personal copy, he was willing to show it to me.

QUESTIONNAIRE SAMPLES

Two questionnaires administered to clients of the Jewish Family Service, the Assigned Service Questionnaire (N = 441 adults) and the Family Research Questionnaire (N = 448 adults) contained specific items on Jewish family clubs. These items are given in Appendix B.

The *Assigned service questionnaire* is completed by all new clients of the agency. It is concerned primarily with background data on the client and his family and includes questions on the presence of family circles and cousins' clubs among the husband's and wife's relatives. Questionnaires returned during the ten-month period of January 1, 1960, through October 31, 1960, were coded and then transferred to IBM cards. During this period, 542 questionnaires should have been returned by new clients to Jewish Family Service offices; 441 or 81 per cent actually were.

The *Family research questionnaire* was specifically developed by our research group for the study of the kinship relations of Jewish Family Service clients. The sampling process was as follows. The total universe of cases at the time the sample was drawn on September 30, 1960, was 1,457. But the actual sample was drawn from a sub-universe of 1,226 clients with intact marriages living in the same home with their spouses. This sub-universe was 84 per cent of the total universe. The size of the sample drawn was 300, but two could not be used leaving the sample at a total of 298 families, or 24 per cent of the sub-universe and 21 per cent of the total universe.

Each family received two questionnaires, one for the husband and one for the wife. The husband's form and the wife's form were modified versions of the same questionnaire, and the differences between the forms were designed to avoid duplication of data where possible. The questionnaires were mailed from the Research Department with covering letters from the agency administrators and from the director of research. Addressed, stamped envelopes were included for returning the questionnaires directly to the Department; thus, the caseworker and the casework process were not involved.

The questionnaires were returned by one or both individuals in 210 families, or 71 per cent of the sample drawn. In 24 of the families returning questionnaires, the husband did not return the form, and in one case the wife did not; the total number of individuals returning the questionnaires was, therefore, 395.

Questionnaires were also sent to an additional group of clients from the agency's special Service to the Aged in order to make possible comparisons with a group at a later stage of the life cycle. At the time there were only 128 cases in this service, and of those only 55 were intact marriages. Questionnaires were then sent to all of these intact families because a further sample would have made the number too small. In the Service to the Aged universe, questionnaires were returned by 28 families, or 51 per cent of the sample drawn. Of these families, two husbands and one wife did not return the forms, making the total number of individuals returning the form 53.

To summarize information on the *Family research questionnaire* samples we have family club data on 210 couples from 395 respondents in the regular client sample, and on 28 couples from 53 respondents in the Service to the Aged sample. The two samples combined give us family club data on 238 couples from 448 respondents. Within this combined sample, data were collected on 42 active cousins' clubs and 48 active family circles, a total of 90 family clubs in all.

Items for the questionnaires, including those on Jewish family clubs, were developed mainly from material collected in open-ended interviews with nine client families. These families were selected through discussion with caseworkers. The items were then pretested on 13 families who were administered the questionnaires in interviews. These families were also selected on the basis of data obtained in interviews with caseworkers.

The questionnaires provided two levels of data: responses to closed- and open-ended questions. Not all clients, of course, answered all items completely or clearly so that the number of responses for some items are fewer than the questionnaires returned. Questions on several aspects of the family clubs were included, among them the respondents' values regarding these organizations, opportunities to affiliate and actual affiliation, membership status, age of the organization, and if a group was defunct, why it broke up. Data on these items, as on all of the others, were transferred to IBM decks for analysis.

Excluding the Service to the Aged sample, the majority of married couples returning the *Family research questionnaire* were between the ages of 35 and 50. Most had school-age children in the home. Respondents also usually were born in the United States although their parents or grandparents were born in Eastern Europe. The wives tended to have more formal schooling than their husbands. Over half the wives completed high school, but only a few of the wives and husbands completed college.

About half of the respondents indicated that in terms of religion, they were "just Jewish", the others indicating affiliation with a formal branch of Jewish religion, e.g., Chassidic, Orthodox, Conservative, or Reform. About 75 per cent of the husbands were employed, the others being disabled, retired, or out of a job. There were more husbands in white collar jobs than blue collar ones. About one-third of the wives also worked but almost exclusively in white collar jobs. In terms of the wives' style of cooking, only one-fourth said that it was "strictly kosher". The other wives indicated in rank order that their cooking style was somewhat Jewish but not kosher, that they kept some of the dietary laws but not all, or that their cooking was not at all Jewish style. As might be expected, the Service to the Aged respondents were much older, retired, more frequently immigrants, less well educated, and with stronger traditional religious ties than the regular client sample.

For a detailed discussion of the sampling procedures and background data on the questionnaire respondents see Leichter and Mitchell (1967).

PUBLISHED MATERIALS

Other than those originated by the present research, there are no published studies of Jewish family circles and cousins' clubs in the anthropological or sociological literature and only a few early references to their existence. Slotkin (1950:466) in a discussion of the "kindred" in America gives an informant's brief description of a kin group that certainly must be a Jewish family circle although it is not indentified as such. Brav (1940:72—73), in a study of Jewish family solidarity in a Southern community, includes an informant's description of his family circle in New York City as "a sample of this interesting institution", but the organization was not a part of the community he studied, and no analysis was attempted. Ackerman (1938), in a psychosocial paper on the units of the family, describes a conflict over a family circle cemetery.

The only published analytical work that includes data on Jewish family clubs is the study in Yiddish by the Yiddish Writers' Group of the Federal Writers' Project (Rontch, 1939), a WPA project that also produced a volume on *landsmanshaft fareynen*. The Rontch book is not a sociological study in terms of its theoretical orientation but more of a historical study of Eastern European Jewish immigration to New York City and immigrant family life. It is an uneven book and in surveying its 206 pages, much of the content was not germane to the present inquiry. But parts of the chapters on a study of 112 family circles of New York City (54 more were contacted but did not participate) are extremely relevant. The data on the 112 family circles were collected by questionnaire, but interesting descriptive data of family circles are also included. This study, while it lacks a dynamic approach to the organizations as systems, has added greatly to the historical depth of my findings. Also, a very few family circles have privately printed books about their family organization and are referred to in the text.

B. Questionnaire items

Assigned service questionnaire

4. (a) Does husband's family have a family circle or cousins' club?

   ____ Yes, a family circle ____ Yes, a cousins' club ____ No

   (b) Does wife's family have a family circle or cousins' club?

   ____ Yes, a family circle ____ Yes, a cousins' club ____ No

Family research questionnaire

[The following data were collected from both the husband and wife]

160. (a) At present, are there any cousins' clubs or family circles among your *mother's* relatives?

   ____ No ____ Yes, a cousins' club ____ Yes, a family circle ____ Yes, both

   (b) If yes:
   (1) How old is the organization? _____
   (2) Are you a member?   ___ Yes ___ No
   (3) Do you attend some meetings
       each year?   ___ Yes ___ No
   (4) Have you ever held office? ___ Yes ___ No

161. [The above questions were also asked for the *father's* relatives]

162. (a) In the past, have there ever been any cousins' clubs or family circles among either your mother's or father's relatives that no longer exist?

   ____ Yes ___ No

C. Examples of club documents

CONSTITUTIONS AND BY-LAWS

In this section the constitutions of two family circles are recorded in their entirety. The first is quite short; the second is long and detailed. The difference in length relates partly to the difference in the extensiveness of their service functions for members.

The Sussman Cousins' Club did not have a formal constitution but did have a document that was referred to by members as the "by-laws", although its official title was "Sussman Cousins' Club Laws, Statutes, Amendments". This document was compiled by club officers from a review of the club's minutes for policy decisions and is recorded here in full. All documents were typewritten unless otherwise indicated.

1. *Constitution of the Marcus Family Circle*

PREAMBLE

This organization was founded in 1920 by [names of members]. In appreciation of their efforts, and to perpetuate their work, we now adopt this constitution.

1. Name. The name of the organization shall be the Marcus Family Circle.

2. Purpose. The purpose and principles of the Association are best expressed in the verse from the Psalms: "Behold how good and pleasant it is for brothers to dwell together in harmony."

3. Eligibility for Membership. All Marcus relatives by blood or marriage shall be eligible for membership.

4. Officers. The officers shall be a President, not less than two and not more than five Vice-Presidents, a Recording Secretary, a Corresponding Secretary, and a Treasurer. Their duties shall be the usual ones implied by their titles.

5. Executive Board. The business of the Association shall be conducted by an Executive Board consisting of nine trustees in addition to the officers. The Board shall have the power to establish standing and sub-committees from the membership at large.

6. Elections. The first election of officers and trustees shall be held on [a specific date]. At that meeting a Nominating Committee of nine shall be appointed by the Chairman to prepare and recommend for election a list of candidates. Additional nominations may be made from the floor. The officers and trustees then elected shall serve until the Spring meeting of [next year], or until their successors are elected. Thereafter, elections shall be held at every Spring meeting, and such a Nominating Committee shall be appointed by the Executive Board at least 30 days in advance of such meeting. The recommendations of the Nominating Committee shall be mailed to the membership at least ten days before the Spring meeting.

7. Meetings. There shall be at least three general meetings a year, at times and places to be fixed by the Executive Board.

8. Voting. All members over the age of 13 shall have the right to vote.

9. Dues. $1.00 per year per member shall be the minimum dues.

10. Amendments. This Constitution may be amended by a two-thirds vote of the membership voting at any regular or special meeting. A draft of the proposed amendment shall be submitted in writing to the Corresponding Secretary, who shall mail a copy thereof to the membership at least ten days before the meeting.

2. *Constitution of the Weinstock Family Circle*

ARTICLE 1

Name:

The name of the organization shall be the Weinstock Family Circle.

ARTICLE ll

Object:

The object of the organization is to create a closer relationship between the members and to carry into effect programs that will mutually benefit the entire family.

ARTICLE lll

Membership:

Any person is eligible for membership who is a descendant of Chaim and Reba Weinstock according to the Family Tree on file with this Constitution, their offspring, and their spouses.

ARTICLE lV

Dues:

1. Dues shall be paid by all members over 21 years of age, or if married, prior to that age.

2. Dues shall be as follows: $8.50 per year for a single member; $12.00 per year for a married couple.

3. Dues shall be waived for any member in military service during the term of such service, but in no event longer than two (2) enlistments.

ARTICLE V

Voting:

Each member shall be entitled to one vote in any motion or proposition at a meeting of the membership. Non-dues paying members are ineligible to vote.

ARTICLE Vl

Meetings:

1. Regular meetings of the Weinstock Family Circle shall be held once each month except during the months of June, July, and August, on such dates as shall be decided by the membership.

2. Special meetings shall be held at the call of the President.

3. Meetings shall be held at a place previously designated by the membership.

ARTICLE VII

Officers:

1. The officers shall be President, Vice-President, Recording Secretary, Social Secretary, Treasurer, and a Four-Year Trustee.

2. *Election of Officers*: First nominations shall be made at the regular March meeting. Further nominations and election shall be held at the April meeting. All officers shall be elected by a majority vote of those cast at the April meeting of the membership and shall hold office for two years with the exception of the Trustee, who shall hold office for four years, and all shall hold office until their successors have been elected and installed. In the event of a tie, a second or more ballots shall be taken until a candidate is elected. Installation of officers shall take place at the May meeting. No officer may be elected for a period longer than two successive terms.

3. *Vacancies*: Should vacancies occur in any office, nominations and elections for the unexpired term shall take place at the next or subsequent meeting. Notice of election for such vacancies must be mailed to all members.

ARTICLE VIII

Duties of Officers:

1. *President*: The President shall be the Chief Executive Officer of the Family Circle. He shall preside at meetings and appoint all committees. He shall be ex-officio a member of all committees.

2. *Vice-President*: The Vice-President shall assist the President in the discharge of his duties, and shall help to maintain order and decorum at meetings. He shall as such officer also preside and assume the duties of President during the absence of the President.

3. *Recording Secretary*: The Recording Secretary shall keep an accurate record of all meetings of the Family Circle.

4. *Corresponding Secretary*: The Corresponding Secretary shall send out all notices.

5. *Social Secretary*: The Social Secretary shall send out

greeting cards and shall perform such other duties as shall be required of her by the President.

6. *Treasurer*: The Treasurer shall be the fiscal officer of the Family Circle; shall be the custodian of all monies and securities of the Family Circle and shall keep full and accurate accounts of all receipts and disbursements. He shall deposit all monies and securities in the name of the Weinstock Family Circle in such depositories as may be designated for that purpose by the Family Circle. He shall report on the condition of the finances at each regular meeting.

7. *Trustee*: The Trustee shall be the custodian of all valuable papers, documents, deeds and bonds of the Family Circle. He shall serve for a period of four years.

ARTICLE IX

Quorum:

The presence of seven (7) members at a duly called meeting shall constitute a quorum.

Meetings need not be conducted by the rules of parliamentary procedure. The President, however, is under a duty to maintain order.

ARTICLE X

Withdrawals:

All withdrawals from the account of the Family Circle shall be made upon the joint signatures of the President or Vice-President and the Treasurer.

The President shall have the authority to obligate the Family Circle up to twenty-five ($25.00) dollars without calling a special meeting therefor.

ARTICLE XI

Audit:

The financial records of the Family Circle are to be audited every two years by a committee of three (3) members appointed by the President; within thirty (30) days from the expiration of the Auditing Committee.

Any change required to be made in the bank as to the names of the persons authorized to withdraw funds, shall be completed between June 1st and August 1st following the election of officers.

ARTICLE XII

Executive Committee:

1. The Executive Committee shall consist of all the officers of the Family Circle.

2. Duties:

       (a)   To manage the affairs of the Family Circle.

       (b)   To adopt such rules, regulations, or by-laws as may be consistent with the constitution and designed to carry out the objects of the Family Circle.

ARTICLE XIII

Committees:

1. *Entertainment Committee*: The Entertainment Committee shall have charge of all affairs, social events and similar occasions, and shall have authority to formulate plans therefor, subject to the approval of the Family Circle.

2. *Membership Committee*: The Membership Committee shall investigate all new applicants for membership and interview said applicants; shall maintain the membership of the Family Circle and shall have such other duties as the President shall impose.

3. *Cemetery Committee*: The Cemetery Committee shall have charge of the Family Circle burial grounds; shall attend funerals and unveiling of monuments, and shall visit the families of the bereaved during the period of mourning.

ARTICLE XIV

Burial:

The Family Circle shall at all times contract for, lease or own a cemetery for the burial of its deceased members or those of their families entitled thereto, as herein provided.

In the event . . . [the] Cemetery or any other cemetery in which the Family Circle owns a family plot refuses to allow the interment of a deceased member or such member's children for any reason whatsoever, then the surviving spouse of the deceased member or the person legally entitled to the estate of the deceased member, shall be paid by the Family Circle the sum of fifty ($50.00) dollars less any indebtedness due to the organization by the deceased member for dues or otherwise, and such payment shall release the Weinstock Family and its members from any further claims.

ARTICLE XV

Resignation:

Any member resigning, withdrawing, expelled or suspended, or severing his or her connection with the Family Circle organization for any cause whatsoever, shall not be entitled to refund of any monies paid into the organization during the term of such membership, nor to any of the assets of the organization.

ARTICLE XVl

Members Attaining Majority:

The children of members in good standing shall have the privilege of becoming dues-paying, voting members upon reaching 21 years of age in addition to the method as herein otherwise provided, and shall be admitted to membership without initiation fee in the event they apply before their twenty-second birthdays. In the event such child or any member shall be called to Military Service after his twenty-first birthday and before his twenty-second birthday, then, in that event, such person shall have one year from the date of discharge from Military Service to apply for membership without initiation fee. Upon the failure to exercise the right or privilege afforded by this paragraph, upon subsequent application by such person for membership he shall be obligated to pay an initiation fee in an amount recommended by the Membership Committee. Such amount shall be voted upon by the membership.

ARTICLE XVll

Privileges:

In order to be eligible for benefits in the organization, a member shall not be in arrears more than one (1) year in the payment of dues, assessments or other indebtedness. Such member in arrears shall be automatically suspended from all benefits and same shall apply to his family deriving benefits undker [sic] him. Reinstatement and restoration to good standing in the Family Circle may be effectuated without initiation fee within two years from date of suspension upon the payment of all arrears. This Article shall be effective and apply to any members so in arrears on and after March 1, 1957. Reinstatement and restoration to good standing thereafter may be effectuated by payment of initiation fee.

ARTICLE XVIII

Amendments:

No part of this Constitution shall be suspended, repealed, altered, amended or annulled except by amendment in writing, proposed and signed by at least three (3) members in good standing. Such amendment shall be read in two successive meetings and acted upon at the second meeting. A notice of the fact that such amendment will then be acted upon shall be contained in the usual notice of such meeting. It shall require the votes of a majority of the members in good standing present at such meeting to adopt such amendment, and at least twelve (12) members shall have voted.

ARTICLE XIX

This Constitution shall be read aloud at the first meeting following installation of new officers.

3. *By-Laws of the Sussman Cousins' Club*

1. The dues are $1.00 per person monthly payable even if absent from meeting.
2. Dues for members in school are $.50 per month, until working.
3. Checking account for club monies in the name of treasurer and one other member as co-signer.
4. Birthdays and anniversary and condolence cards to members and flowers, candies, cake and other items, when deemed necessary, are to come out of treasury funds.
5. No entertaining expense is to come out of club funds until there is a treasury balance of $100.00. There must be a minimum balance of $50.00 at all times.
6. No meeting shall be held if there are less than 50% of the members present.
7. Aunt [Rachel] voted Honorary Member, and is to come to all meetings and get all benefits as the rest of members.

8. Any cousin dropping out of club will have to pay $5.00 fee when deciding to return to club, if after 6 months absence.

9. Absence of less than 6 months permits re-instatement after payment of back dues.

10. Subject to change voted by members later, allowances for expenditures will be $5.00 High School graduation; $10.00 for College Graduation; Congratulation card for Grammar School graduation; $5.00 or $10.00 for other graduation at discretion of members; $5.00 for births; $10.00 wedding gifts for members.

11. Meetings held on first Saturday of each month.

12. Any cousin joining prior to their 18th birthday does not pay initiation fee. If over 18, then initiation fee must be paid.

13. In case of illness to hostess, at whose home the meeting is to be held, or illness in her family, the meeting is automatically postponed to the following week.

14. Members over 18 years of age, missing three consecutive meetings, will be notified that the next meeting will take place at their home.

15. Birthday cards to be sent to all Aunts and Uncles. (Void)

16. A permanent picture album will be kept and added to by the club.

17. Members not attending any function which the treasury applies financial allowance towards, such as paying for tickets, is to receive the monies from treasury.

18. Expenses in taking pictures, equipment, etc. will be paid for by the club.

19. If new members join and the club has tickets for a show, the new members are not included. (Void)

20. A nominee for office, when nominated by two people, cannot refuse the nomination.

21. Two candidates, at least, must be nominated for each office.

22. Dues will not be paid in the months of July & August.

23. No member is entitled to theatre ticket allowances if more than one month delinquent in payment of dues. (Void)

24. Any member missing two consecutive meetings, excluding illness, without providing advance notification one week prior to next meeting will be fined $1.00.

25. All present officers will remain in office for another two years.
26. Elections will be held once every three years.
27. An officer cannot be elected for two consecutive terms to the same office.
28. The people being honored at an affair (including the Rosenstein affair and any other future affair) should not pay anything for the affair or receive any returns. [added in script]
29. Future affairs should be limited to members, honored guests, the guests' children, in-laws and their brothers and sisters. [added in script]

MEETING MINUTES

Following are selections from the minutes of four family clubs including two family circles and two cousins' clubs. The minutes of the Horowitz and Margareten Family Association were found printed in a 1921 newsletter in the Jewish Division of the New York City Library. The other excerpts of minutes were made available to me for study by informants with the permission of their clubs.

Each selection is written by a different club secretary. Spelling and punctuation are as in the original. Months, but not the year of the meeting reported, are omitted. Unless otherwise indicated, the original minutes are typed.

1. *Meeting Minutes of the Horowitz and Margareten Family Association*

On June 5th The Horowitz-Margareten Family Association held its second meeting since its birth, at the home of Father, Grandfather, Uncle, Cousin, or Machuton Ignatz Margareten (depending on one's point of view). Those most intimately related to this newborn infant immediately set to work to provide it with a proper name, choose proper guardians to look after its welfare and to lay down special rules to govern its habits and conduct.

The family tree was well represented by branches, offshoots and budding blossoms of the coming harvest. A stranger could have easily recognized the characteristic family traits in all those present, for, 'tis said that acorns do not fall far from the tree.

After the preliminary handshaking and kissing the family sat down to the business of the evening.

Never did one dream that such wealth of oratory lay dormant in the deadlier members of the species.

Shades of Webster, Clay and Ingersoll! When various clauses of the constitution during the discussion met with their disfavor, they argued so convincingly, that even the most rabid were appeased; that is they were convinced that this person as a last resort could fall back on the heritage of her sex to win the day; either the hypnotic eye, or, if one is made of sterner stuff, to keep on talking till one tires.

Joe Goldstein as temporary chairman proved to be quite a capable politician and the smoothness with which some clauses of the constitution were steam-rollered through made one feel that Jack Horowitz and the chairman had previously rehearsed them.

All in all, the constitution is a credit to, and a reflection on the capabilities of the family lawyers.

Under new business, election of officers was the first thing in order. Like a charm the lagging spirit of the House of Representatives took a new lease of life. The youngsters no longer discussed the latest Shimmy, nor the women Paris styles, or the latest scandal of the Stillman Case!

Despite his determined stand that the younger generation should rule, Uncle Joseph Horowitz's extreme modesty was finally overcome, and by a unanimous vote he was designated to steer our ship through the Seas of Uncertainty for the coming year.

The election of Uncle Joseph initiated such a babble and commotion that our correspondent could not very well, despite his recognized ability, disentangle the construction of the rest of the ticket. It appeared to him that Advocate Julius Weiss was assigned a seat to the left of Uncle Joseph, while the sharpened quill became the temporary heritage of the ex-Chairman, Joe Goldstein.

The multitude made no mistake in their choice for treasurer, for, who can better take care of the family purse than our Uncle Ignatz. So, wisely too, was the designation of Ben Landau and

Mary Margareten to inculcate the "Silence of Gold" dictum on the masses.

However, the choicest plum of the evening fell to the lot of the one who drew up our Declaration of Independence, namely Jack Horowitz. His pen and that of his confreres on the committee will be the medium through which fountains of family knowledge will be sprayed over forgotten and neglected sprouts in the family garden.

The House Committee provided plenty of home-made cakes so as to provide the men with an excuse for evading the Volstead Law.

The meeting finally ended as it started — with handshakes and kisses and wishes that this child will thrive under proper nourishment during the summer so that at its next presentation in the fall it will have gained in body and spirit.

2. Meeting Minutes of a Family Circle

[month] 1956

Minutes read and accepted as corrected.

Old Business

Ben Maksik's plan presented — decided to attend last show on Saturday night, and to have chicken dinner.

Entertainment fund discussed — whether enough money existed for each member attending, etc. Discussion to be individual with each member and treasurer.

New Business

It was decided that no meetings are to be postponed no matter what the situation. If a scheduled member cannot have the meeting said member is to notify the next one on the list to take over the secretary. Meetings are to be held on the first Saturday of each month.

Clarification of rules for joining made to Bertha Winer. No incoming member must pay retroactive, but simply from the date of joining.

Meeting closed in good order.

Respectfully submitted

[Secretary's name]

[month] 1959

The meeting was called to order BY THE President, and the minutes were read and accepted as read.

The money report:

	in bank	218.55
	Collections	164.95
		383.50
	Money out	57.00
		326.50

A motion was made by Frieda and seconded by Bertha to make it compulsory for each member to save a minimum of $1.00 per week. The motion was carried unanimously.

A clarification of the interest on loans was made. Loans are charged interest at the rate of 6% per year, payable in advance. This means that at the end of one year period, the unpaid balance must be charged an additional 6% interest.

The entertainment fund will definitely remain a separate fund. The treasurer has found that this method works easily enough to maintain.

The Workman's Circle invites groups to join. The secretary was assigned to find out more information.

The Entertainment Committee has suggested joining the Lodge function at the Elegante April 19th. Sam Kalb will tentatively reserve 16 tickets for us.

Sam will secure tickets for March 13th for Three Penny Opera or Hamlet of Stepney Green.

The meeting was closed by the President in good order. Next meeting at . . . Street, Brooklyn.

Respectfully, submitted,
[Secretary's name]

3. *Meeting Minutes of a Cousins' Club*

[month] 1954

Meeting at Ruth and Leslie's.

Everyone was present except David. We had guests. Cousins Peggy and Larry were among us and we enjoyed having them. Dora got a hold of Uncle Frank and he served as her back scratcher this month — who is next?

Linda's baby was sent his gift from us. Sammie raised a discussion, that Linda had a right to let the club know she was home but it was ruled out — as we are cousins and we don't stand on ceremonies.

Harold our new Pres. really has pep to run our meetings fast and furious. We brought everyone up to date on our anniversary. Bang up affair to take place Nov. 1954 — Our 10th Anniversary. We are going to live it up and celebrate big and loud.

Instead of having a meeting in March maybe we will get together and go someplace. Someone suggested seeing a Burlesque show bowling or skating. We took a vote on it — bowling won out. [Next month] we skip meeting and go out.

Foster Alley - Foster and Remsen Ave.

8 p.m.

Meeting Closed, Dues Collected

Bank bal. 97.31 [signed by secretary]

[month] 1960

Meeting at Sue & Sammie's. All present except Marie & Joe, Leo, Fred, Murray, & Evelyn. Ruth & Avon sent a note thanking the cousins for their 25th anniversary party at the Golden Slipper Nightclub & also for the lovely set of dishes.

Treasury Report: Financial Status $183.63 (Before evening out) Total cost of party $347.35. Dues were collected & it was said that each couple's share was $30. Of this the club would allow $20 a couple & each couple would pay $10 cash.

New Business

Motion: The people being honored at an affair (including the Ross party or any future party) should not pay anything for the affair or receive any returns. This motion was passed & this amended into our club laws.

Motion: Future affairs should be limited to members, honored guests & the honored guests' brothers — sisters — inlaws or children. This motion was passed and amended into the laws of the club.

Joel suggested that a vote of thanks be given to Dora & Sue for planning a very entertaining & lovely affair. All members agreed & a cheer was given.

Linda suggested we remember the original idea of this club which is togetherness & happinness.

Joel made a motion that a committee be appointed to approach Aunt Roslyn to obtain from her the family tree so we might be able to add to it. Sue volunteered to speak with Aunt Roslyn. All agreed.

Sharon then told us that a study of Jewish Culture was being made by the Federation of Jewish Philanthropists.* They are interested in the idea of Cousins Clubs by people of Jewish faith. Since our club is fifteen years old & a second generation club this organization is interested in reading our minutes. All cousins then agreed to lend the minutes to this group for the purpose of studying them.

Table: Members to do constructive work in the future such as in the field of charity work.

Meeting adjourned at 12:00.

Next meeting given by Betty & Roger.

4. *Meeting Minutes of a Cousins' Club*

The last meeting was held on Sunday . . . at the home of Danny and Bess Berman.

John Zimmerman, president, announced the dates for the next 5 meetings of the year as follows. . . .

Raffle tickets were sold at $1 each and a total of $14 was collected. The prize for this meeting will be presented to raffle winner Max Zimmerman at the next meeting to be held at the home of Abe and Sarah Wohl.

A motion was made and passed that we sell raffles at $1 each at every meeting. A prize will be obtained by the board of directors (the cost of the item not to exceed $2.50) for the winning raffle. The balance of this raffle money will be used to establish a welfare fund.

The meeting was then adjourned.

[Written with ink in longhand.]

*This was our study. The Jewish Family Service is one of the member agencies of the Federation of Jewish Philanthropies.

D. Examples of genealogies

GENEALOGY OF A LARGE FAMILY CIRCLE

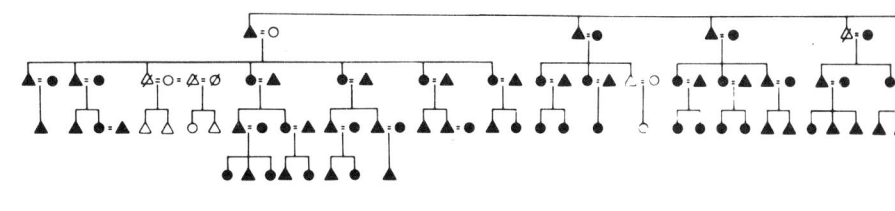

GENEALOGY OF A SMALL FAMILY CIRCLE

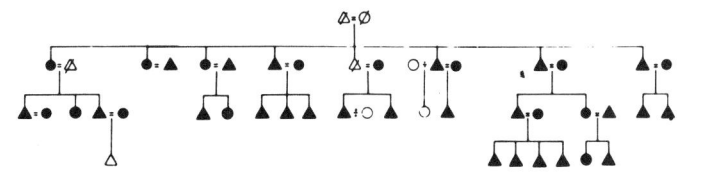

GENEALOGY OF A LARGE COUSINS' CLUB

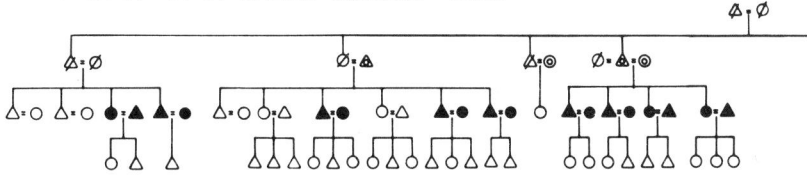

GENEALOGY OF A SMALL COUSINS' CLUB

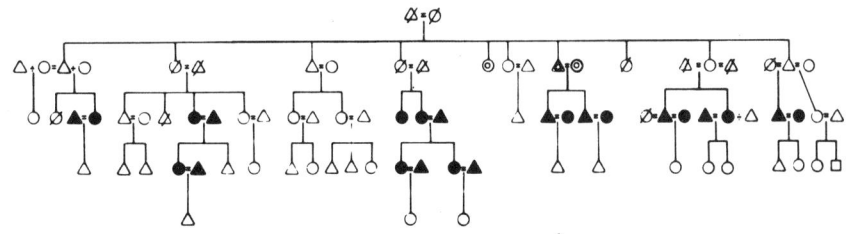

Fig. 2 *Four family club genealogies*

The four family club genealogies below are for two family circles and two cousins' clubs. They were collected according to the methods discussed in Appendix A. For reasons of confidentiality, I have not included data on occupations, residence, or other social placement data beyond sex, marital status, decedence, generation, and club membership.

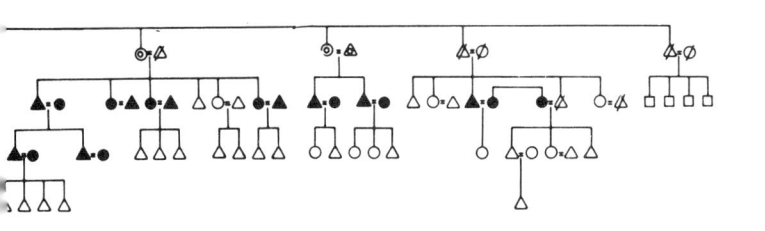

△-Male	= -Marital Tie
○-Female	+ -Divorce
⚠-Deceased	▲- Member
□-Sex Unknown	▲-Honorary Member
to Informant	

Notes

NOTES TO CHAPTER 1

1. Physically speaking, it is scientifically incorrect to refer to Jews as the "Jewish race". Race is a biological concept and the tremendous variation of physical characteristics among Jews disqualifies them from being a "race". See Shapiro (1960) and Newman (1965:21–30).
2. In the following discussion of the immigration and settlement patterns of New York City Jews, I have found Grinstein (1945) most helpful on the earlier migrations and Rischin (1962) on the Eastern European immigration. Some of the other works important for my orientation to the patterns and problems of Jewish immigration and settlement are Baron (1937, 1942, 1964), Bernheimer (1905), Birmingham (1967), Dubnow (1916–20), Fishman (1973), Ginsberg (1956), Glazer (1957, 1958), Gordon (1959), Goren (1970), Hapgood (1967), Jones (1960), Katz (1973), Kramer and Leventman (1961), Kranzler (1961), Landes and Zborowski (1950), Landesman (1969), Poll (1962), Roseman (1974), Rosenthal (1954), Sanders (1969), Vetulani (1962), Wagley and Harris (1958), Weinryb (1958), Wirth (1956), and Zborowski and Herzog (1952). For a recent and vivid historical account of New York's Eastern European Jews see Howe (1976).
   The best social science oriented introduction to contemporary American Jewry is by Sklare (1971); also see his notable collections of articles on the American Jew (Sklare 1958, 1974a, 1974b).
3. For two studies of the Jews of England see Freedman (1955) and Gartner (1960).
4. Torah is the Hebrew name for the five books of Moses also referred to as the Law of Moses or the Pentateuch. The Torah is believed by Orthodox Jews to have been handed down to Moses on Mt. Sinai and then transmitted by him to all Jews. It laid down the fundamental laws of moral and physical conduct. Through the centuries a large theological commentary on the original law has accumulated and the term Torah is also sometimes used to refer to the entire Jewish religious literature. For an extended discussion of the social implications of the Torah for the Eastern European Jews, see Zborowski and Herzog (1952:105–123) and Zborowski (1949).
5. The Nazis' virtual extermination of the Eastern European Jews is told by Hilberg (1967) and Dawidowicz (1975). For two historical discussions of discrimination against Jews, see Higham (1957) and Wagley and Harris (1958:230). There is also a voluminous philosophical and political litera-

ture on anti-Semitism. For one famous example see Sartre (1946).

6. See Slater (1969) for a critical discussion of factors facilitating Jewish upward mobility in the United States.

NOTES TO CHAPTER 2

1. There are data (Rontch 1939) indicating that at least one American family circle was derived from a family synagogue in Eastern Europe. This appears, however, to be an isolated occurrence.
2. See Appendix A for information about the research questionnaires and Appendex B for specific question items.
3. "Old home" refers to the immigrating ancestor's place of residence in Europe where other relatives still may live.
4. The data presented are not complete enough to judge with certainty whether the Unser Cousins' Family Circle organized in 1934 is a classical family circle, a cousins' club or a "mixed" transitional type. It met twice a month, had 150 members and a written constitution. Because of the large number of members, my guess is that it was a family circle and I have classified it as such.
5. The two exceptional groups state their purpose is to honor a dead ancestor.
6. This is the only club I know of that has incorporated friends into its organization. Another group considered this innovation hoping to make the organization more attractive to young couples but when some of the older members threatened to resign, the proposal was withdrawn.
7. For a complete listing of the names of family clubs studied by the WPA Yiddish Writers' Group, see Rontch (1939:204—206).

NOTES TO CHAPTER 3

1. Although it was Parsons (1943) who first focused theoretical interest on the importance of the conjugal tie in the kinship system of Western urban industrial societies, his point has been amply demonstrated by subsequent research, e.g., Bott (1957), Firth (1956), Firth, Hubert and Forge (1970), Garigue (1956), Leichter and Mitchell (1967), Mogey (1956), Rosenberg and Anspach (1973), Schneider (1968), Schneider and Smith (1973), Sussman (1959), Townsend (1957), and Winch and Greer (1967). Thus the fact that a person's mate, an affine, may be included in a family club is not surprising. This is very different from the organization of unilineal descent groups where full membership is usually *exclusively* cognatic with affines excluded. For a summary of the controversy over the alleged "isolation" of the American family from its relatives see Winch (1968).
2. "INF" is an abbreviation for "informant"; "WM" are the interviewer's initials.
3. Such acts of benefice by high-status relatives to those of lower status is in complete accord with the custom of giving in the now vanished Eastern European Jewish communities. According to Joffe (1949:239), "In this culture the two main characteristics of giving are that it is downward and is not returned in kind. . . . For help or gifts of any kind to flow upward is rare." While this is still true when the status of giver and recipient are widely separated, a very pronounced pattern of symmetrical giving has

developed in America especially around life cycle occasions such as births, Bar Mitzvahs, and weddings. Here gift giving among those of similar means is expected to be reciprocal. Although not a major pattern of giving before immigration, it still has its roots in the *shtetl*. For example, Joffe (1949:246) tells us that when women exchanged holiday sweetmeats, "The offerings are not identical but are carefully calculated to be equivalent, and if one fails to match the gift of her opposite number in such an exchange, the effect is apt to be unpleasant."

4. See Schneider and Smith (1973) for a recent discussion of class differences in American kinship.

5. But as Schneider (1968:70—71) notes, it is not at all the same as being biologically dead. The "ex-child" is more analogous to the status of an "ex-spouse" than to a deceased child.

6. This number includes children as well as adults. I was told that there are about 100 families who could be members but have been dropped because of nonpayment of dues. Besides the Greater New York area, members live in Alabama, California, District of Columbia, Florida, Iowa, Georgia, New Jersey, Massachusetts, Minnesota, New Mexico, Ohio, Oklahoma, Pennyslvania, Tennessee, Texas, Utah, Virginia, and West Virginia. A minority of the members reside in the following foreign countries: Argentina, Canada, Czechoslovakia, England, France, Hungary, Italy, Mexico, and Switzerland. The large executive committee meets monthly, but the principal meeting is the annual "convention" held at a resort hotel near New York City. Because the only service provided by this family circle is a monthly newsletter of family events, the dues are only one dollar a year. Members who wish to help to sponsor a newsletter may contribute $20 to the club's treasury.

7. This analytical distinction is obviously related to Parsons' and Bales' (1955:47) concepts of "instrumental" and "expressive" roles but is more behaviorally circumscribed.

8. Firth and Djamour in the study of English kinship edited by Firth (1956:39) introduce the concept of "pivotal kin" to denote ". . . relatives who act as linking points in the kinship structure by their interest in, and knowledge of, genealogical ramifications". In my usage of the concept I am emphasizing the social centrality of the pivotal kin's kinship role, not his genealogical knowledge.

9. A single exception is a cousins' club without a president but with a volunteer secretary and treasurer. The club does collect dues so one of the women members volunteered to assume this task, and she is now called the treasurer. There is also a self-appointed secretary to keep track of decisions made at the meetings. This is a small group with under 20 members. The host or hostess at whose home the meeting is held, I was told, is supposed to conduct the meeting. But as the host couple is often busy preparing the refreshments to be served following the meeting, the treasurer and secretary usually conduct the informal meeting.

NOTES TO CHAPTER 4

1. For examples of documents see Appendix C.

2. Two of the clubs I visited were interested in my genealogical chart of family members and I responded to their request for duplicate copies.

NOTES TO CHAPTER 5

1. One study (Matz 1961) on the meaning of the Christmas tree to the American Jew indicates, not surprisingly, that the third generation is more likely to think favorably about the Christmas tree than the second generation. Among Orthodox Jews, however, the Christmas tree is one of the most contentious symbols of Christian culture. One non-religious informant told me of her panic when an old Orthodox relative dropped by unexpectedly and she had to stash the "children's" Christmas tree in a closet before opening the door. For a discussion of "role strain" among Jews at Christmas time see Gerson (1969). For a recent study of ambivalence among American Jews see Liebman (1973).

NOTES TO CHAPTER 6

1. Joint businesses with several relatives are not uncommon among New York City Jews of Eastern European background. In one sample, 30 per cent of the husbands were at present or had at some time been in a business with kin outside their present nuclear family. In our society we have no clear way of structuring relationships when occupational and kinship roles overlap, and most of the husbands reported negative feelings about the experience of working with kin. For details of this research see Leichter and Mitchell (1967:135—145).

NOTES TO CHAPTER 7

1. In Radcliffe-Brown's (1958) use of the contrasting methodological terms "ethnology" and "social anthropology", my usage of historical and cultural factors relates to ethnology and its concern with historical connections among social phenomena; the set of factors I have called socioeconomic relates to the methodology of social anthropology and its concern with functional relationships among social phenomena. The two methodologies are complementary, not competing.
2. Westerman (1967) is critical, however, of Balswick's global approach to the American-Jewish family and of his failure to define exactly his referent for "closeness".
3. The historical data for this section are primarily from Grinstein (1945) and Rischin (1962).
4. According to Schmidt and Babchuk (1973:146) fraternal orders date to 1717 when Freemasonry was established in England. By 1730 Masonry was present in America as well. Also see Vondracek (1972).
5. There were, of course, other types of associations of a more purely social nature such as the literary societies that were popular for a time. These social groups, mostly of young people, did not play an important part as a model for the early family circles although they may have been forerunners of the later "social" clubs that the cousins' clubs are patterned after.
6. Firth (1963) defines a cognatic stock as "the descendants of a married pair reckoned through both male and female offspring. This is a theoretical category, not necessarily a group". Also see Radcliffe-Brown (1950:22) and Freeman (1961:199).

7. For further discussion on this point and data on telephone interaction with kin, see Leichter and Mitchell (1967:103—114) and Mitchell (1965b).

NOTES TO CHAPTER 8

1. Other papers in which I have dealt with aspects of this problem include Leichter and Mitchell (1967), Mitchell (1961a, 1961b, 1963, 1965a, 1965b), and Mitchell and Leichter (1961).
2. In an interesting article, De Vos (1975) reminds us that the urge to classify is to a great extent culturally determined. Discussing Mary Douglas' (1966) study of Jewish concepts of pollution De Vos (1975:91) finds her ". . . focus on fear of pollution as it reflects the Jewish dislike for anomaly and hybrid monsters is an outgrowth of her own society's need to control conceptually by classifying the totality of human experience" and in marked contrast to the toleration in Japanese folk culture for diffused and blurred distinctions *except* in the differentiation of social status.
3. Scheffler's (1966) discussion of these conflicting referents for descent group attributes, among others, the first usage to Goody (1959, 1961), Fortes (1959), and Leach (1962) and the second usage to Davenport (1959), Firth (1957, 1963), Goodenough (1955, 1961), Murdock (1960), and Peranio (1961). The debate is continued in Fortes (1969) and Scheffler (1973).
4. Nadel (1951:147—150) also stresses the importance of names for groups in that "they make groups visible" and "that they express the awareness of 'belonging'."
5. Although a family club has, from time to time, refused membership to a member's spouse who was not "Jewish" by descent, this is not to what I am referring here.
6. Cumming and Schneider (1961) in a paper on American kinship make the general observation that ours is an age-graded society. They see this reflected in American kinship as "sibling solidarity".
7. Firth (1963:24), however, does indicate awareness of this problem by wondering to what extent descent groups exist in an industrialized society like Britain.
8. Sociologists have elaborated the study of formal organizations with two distinct approaches, viz., the "rational model" or organizational analysis exemplified by the pioneer work of Weber, and the "natural-system model" derived from Compte with Selznick and Parsons major contemporary exponents. For an enlightening discussion of these two models see Gouldner (1959:404—487). Sociologists have devised numerous typologies of formal organizations, e.g., Blau and Scott (1962:40—58), Hughes (1952), Katz and Kahn (1966:110—148), Parsons (1960:40—58), and Thompson and Tuden (1959). For recent summaries and discussion of these and other typologies see Hall (1972:39—78) and Hass and Drabek (1973:362—374).
9. Lowie's book *Primitive Society*, published in 1920, was the first to give a general treatment of associations along with systems of kinship and marriage. His initial definition (1947:257) of associations is a global one including ". . . the social units not based on the kinship factor". In a later discussion (1948:12—14) he abandons the concept of association as the generic term in favor of *sodality*, a concept that includes both voluntary and involuntary ". . . associations not primarily connected with kin-

ship or coresidence". But the term never won favor (Service [1962] is an exception), and anthropologists write variously about "cults" (Barth 1975:24, Mitchell 1963, Worsely 1957), "societies" (Ottenberg 1971: 113—131, Stewart 1973:302—304, White 1962:136—182), "fraternities" (Aceves 1974:150—152, Hoebel 1949:303—308), and "brotherhoods" (Drucker 1958), but most frequently about "associations" (Anderson 1971, Banton 1968, Coombs 1973, Freedman 1957:92—95, Haviland 1974:406—409, Little 1965, Plotnicov 1967:66—73, Spradley and McCurdy 1975:207—217, Warner and Lunt 1941:301—335 and Wu 1975).

10. The term "cognatic descent group" seems to have won out over "non-unilineal descent group" and I am adopting the former as defined by Firth (1963:23) although it is different from the referent I once proposed (Mitchell 1961a:127). The term "sept" (Davenport 1959:562, Ember 1959:573) was proposed for cognatic descent groups whose members acknowledge a common descent line but cannot trace actual genealogical connections, and "ambilineage" (Mitchell 1961a:127) for a cognatic descent group whose members *can* trace genealogical connections to a common ancestor.

11. The organization of Leyton's (1965:107—110) Jewish-Canadian "composite descent group" is fundamentally different from these. Members are recruited from two intermarried cognatic stocks, the integrating force is a family business instead of a club, and the organization is not culturally stereotyped.

12. Some groups, however, are land-owning. See Young and Geertz' (1961: 135) discussion of the Kellinger Family Association, Inc., a formal organization of the descendants of John and Sarah Kellinger, who lived in Connecticut in 1641. This group publishes a magazine and owns the homestead of the apical ancestors.

NOTES TO APPENDIX A

1. See Hubert, Forge, and Firth (1968) for an interesting discussion of research methods in the study of kinship among middle-class Londoners and Lancaster's (1961) paper for a more theoretical discussion of conceptual and methodological problems in studying British kinship. Leichter and Mitchell (1967:293—306) survey some of the special problems of studying urban Jewish kinship within a social casework agency. Adams' (1968) survey study of kinship in Greensboro, North Carolina, includes a helpful copy of his interview instrument.

2. As Mayer (1973:152) notes, it is unusual for a Gentile to study Jewish society: "the sociology of Jews has been written almost exclusively by Jews".

3. See Zborowski and Herzog (1952:61) for more data on this Eastern European perception of Gentiles.

4. The inverse of this point is made by two Jewish sociologists (Kramer and Leventman 1961:xxii) who in studying a Jewish community in the midwest found that "So important was a shared universe of discourse to many informants that they demanded assurance of the interviewers' Jewish background before volunteering certain responses (especially those reflecting their less public attitudes about the dominant [i.e. Gentile] group)."

5. Morton Fried (1959:351) has described a similar response to his 1947 field work in east-central China when "... he was summoned to appear at once at the office of the county magistrate. The magistrate was polite but cold: an anthropological study of his country was an affront; anthropologists, said the magistrate, studied only savages and barbarians".

References

Aceves, Joseph B. (1974), *Identity, Survival and Change.* Morris-
town, N. J.: General Learning Press.

Ackerman, Nathan W. (1938), *The Unity of the Family.* Archives
of Pediatrics 55:51—56.

Adams, Bert N. (1968), *Kinship in an Urban Setting.* Chicago:
Markham.

Anderson, Robert T. (1971), Voluntary Associations in History.
American Anthropologist 73:209—222.

Arensberg, Conrad M. (1955), American Communities. *American
Anthropologist* 57:1143—1162.

— (1957), Anthropology as History. In: *Trade and Market in the
Early Empires.* Karl Polanyi, Conrad M. Arensberg and Harry
W. Pearson, Eds. Glencoe: Free Press.

Ayoub, Millicent R. (1966), The Family Reunion. *Ethnology*
5:415—433.

Balswick, Jack (1966), Are American-Jewish Families Closely
Knit? *Journal of Jewish Social Studies* 26:157—167.

Banton, Michael (1968), Voluntary Associations: Anthropological
Aspects. In: *International Encyclopedia of the Social Sciences*
16:357—362.

Baron, Salo Wittmayer (1937), *A Social and Religious History of
the Jews.* 3 Vols. New York: Columbia University Press.

— (1942), *The Jewish Community: Its History and Structure to
the American Revolution.* 3 Vols. Philadelphia: Jewish Publication Society of America.

— (1964), *The Russian Jew under Tsars and Soviets.* New York:
Macmillan.

Barth, Fredrik (1975), *Ritual and Knowledge among the Bakta-*

man of New Guinea. New Haven: Yale University Press.

Beidelman, Thomas O. (1970), Umwano and Ukaguru Students' Association: Two Tribalistic Movements in a Tanganyika Chiefdom. In: *Black Africa: Its Peoples and their Cultures Today*. John Middleton, Ed. New York: Macmillan.

Berheimer, Charles S., Ed. (1905), *The Russian Jew in the United States*. Philadelphia: John C. Winston.

Birmingham, Stephen (1967), *"Our Crowd": The Great Jewish Families of New York*. New York: Harper and Row.

Blau, Peter M. and Scott, W. Richard (1962), *Formal Organizations: A Comparative Approach*. San Francisco: Chandler.

Bott, Elizabeth (1957), *Family and Social Network*. London: Tavistock.

Bowers, Alfred W. (1965), *Hidatsa Social and Ceremonial Organization*. Smithsonian Institution Bureau of American Ethnology, Bulletin 194.

Brav, Stanley R. (1940), *Jewish Family Solidarity: Myth or Fact?* Vicksburg: Nogales Press.

Bressler, Marvin (1952), Selected Family Patterns in W. I. Thomas' Unfinished Study of the *Bintl Brief*. *American Sociological Review* 17:563–571.

Brown, Robert (1963), *Explanation in Social Science*. Chicago: Aldine.

Buckley, Walter (1967), *Sociology and Modern Systems Theory*. Englewood Cliffs, N. J.: Prentice-Hall.

Coombs, Gary (1973), Networks and Exchange: The Role of Social Relationships in a Small Voluntary Association. *Journal of Anthropological Research* 29:96–112.

Cumming, Elaine and Schneider, David M. (1961), Sibling Solidarity: A Property of American Kinship. *American Anthropologist* 63:498–507.

Davenport, William (1959), Nonunilinear Descent and Descent Groups. *American Anthropologist* 61:557–572.

Dawidowicz, Lucy (1975), *The War Against the Jews*, 1933–1945. New York: Holt, Rinehart and Winston.

De Vos, George (1975), The Dangers of Pure Theory in Social Anthropology. *Ethos* 3:77–91.

Douglas, Mary (1966), *Purity and Danger: An Analysis of Concepts of Pollution and Taboo*. New York: Praeger.

Drucker, Philip (1958), *The Native Brotherhoods: Modern Inter-tribal Organizations on the Northwest Coast.* Smithsonian Institute Bureau of American Ethnology, Bulletin 168.
Dubnow, S. N. (1916–20), *History of the Jews in Russia and Poland.* 3 Vols. Philadelphia: Jewish Publication Society of America.

Ember, Melvin (1959), The Nonunilinear Descent Groups of Samoa. *American Anthropologist* 61:573–577.
Etzioni, Amitai (1964), *Modern Organizations.* Englewood Cliffs, N. J.: Prentice-Hall.

Fine, Morris and Himmelfarb, Milton, Eds. (1961), *American Jewish Yearbook.* Vol. 62, Philadelphia: The Jewish Publication Society of America.
Firth, Raymond (1956), *Two Studies of Kinship in London.* London: The Athlone Press.
— (1957), A Note on Descent Groups in Polynesia. *Man* 57:4–8.
— (1963), Bilateral Descent Groups: An Operational Viewpoint. In: *Studies in Kinship and Marriage.* I. Schapera, Ed. Royal Anthropological Occasional Paper No. 16.
Firth, Raymond, Hubert, Jane and Forge, Anthony (1970), *Families and their Relatives: Kinship in a Middle-class Sector of London.* New York: Humanities Press.
Fishman, Priscilla, Ed. (1973), *The Jews of the United States.* New York: Quadrangle.
Fortes, Meyer, (1959), Descent, Filiation and Affinity: A Rejoinder to Dr. Leach. *Man* 59:193–197, 206–212.
— (1969), *Kinship and the Social Order.* Chicago: Aldine.
Freedman, Maurice (1955), *A Minority in Britain: Social Studies of the Anglo-Jewish Community.* London: Vallentine Mitchell.
— (1957), *Chinese Family and Marriage in Singapore.* London: Her Majesty's Stationery Office.
Freeman, J. D. (1961), On the Concept of Kindred. *The Journal of the Royal Anthropological Institute* 91:192–220.
Fried, Morton H., Ed. (1959), *Readings in Anthropology*, Vol. 2, New York: Thomas Y. Crowell.
— (1967), *The Evolution of Political Society.* New York:Random House.

Fromenson, A. H. (1905), Amusements and Social Life: New York. In: *The Russian Jew in the United States*. Charles S. Bernheimer, Ed. Philadelphia: John C. Winston.

Gans, Herbert J. (1958), The Origin and Growth of a Jewish Community in the Suburbs: A Study of the Jews of Park Forest. In: *The Jews: Social Patterns of an American Group*. Marshall Sklare, Ed. Glencoe: Free Press.

Garigue, Philip (1956), French Canadian Kinship and Urban Life. *American Anthropologist* 58:1090—1101.

Gartner, Lloyd P. (1960), *The Jewish Immigrant in England, 1870—1914*. London: George Allen and Unwin.

Gerson, Walter M. (1969), Jews at Christmas Time: Role-Strain and Strain-Reducing Mechanisms. In: *Social Problems in a Changing World*. Walter M. Gerson, Ed. New York: Crowell.

Ginsberg, Morris (1956), *The Jewish People Today: A Survey*. London: World Jewish Congress.

Glanz, Rudolf (1947), *Jews in Relation to the Cultural Milieu of the Germans in America up to the Eighteen Eighties*. New York: Yivo.

Glazer, Nathan (1957), *American Judaism*. Chicago: University of Chicago Press.

— (1958), The American Jew and the Attainment of Middle-Class Rank: Some Trends and Explanations. In: *The Jews: Social Patterns of an American Group*. Marshall Sklare, Ed. Glencoe: Free Press.

Goldberg, David and Sharp, Harry (1958), Some Characteristics of Detroit Area Jewish and Non-Jewish Adults. In: *The Jews: Social Patterns of an American Group*. Marshall Sklare, Ed. Glencoe: Free Press.

Goode, William J. (1963a), Industrialization and Family Change. In: *Industrialization and Society*. Bert F. Hoselitz and Wilbert E. Moore, Eds. Paris—The Hague: Mouton Publishers and Paris: Unesco.

— (1963b), *World Revolution and Family Patterns*. New York: The Free Press of Glencoe.

Goodenough, Ward H. (1955), A Problem in Malayo-Polynesian Social Organization. *American Anthropologist* 57:71—83.

— (1961), Review of Social Structure in Southeast Asia, G. P. Murdock, Ed. *American Anthropologist* 63:1341—1347.

Goody, Jack (1959), The Mother's Brother and the Sister's Son in

West Africa. *Journal of the Royal Anthropological Institute* 89: 61–88.

— (1961), The Classification of Double Descent Systems. *Current Anthropology* 2:3–25.

Gordon, Albert I. (1959), *Jews in Suburbia*. Boston: Beacon Press.

Goren, A. A. (1970), *New York Jews and the Quest for Community: The Kehillah Experiment, 1908–1922*. New York: Columbia University Press.

Gouldner, Alvin W. (1959), Organizational Analysis. In: *Sociology Today*. Robert Merton, Leonard Broom and Leonard Cottrell, Eds. New York: Basic Books.

Greenfield, Sidney M. (1961), Industrialization and the Family in Sociological Theory. *American Journal of Sociology* 67:312–322.

Grinstein, Hyman Bogomolny (1945), *The Rise of the Jewish Community of New York 1654–1860*. Philadelphia: Jewish Publication Society of America.

Hall, Richard H. (1972), *Organizations: Structure and Process*. Englewood Cliffs, N. J.: Prentice Hall.

Hammel, E. A. and Yarbrough, Charles (1973), Social Mobility and the Durability of Family Ties. *Journal of Anthropological Research* 29:145–163.

Hapgood, Hutchins (1967), *The Spirit of the Ghetto*. Cambridge: Harvard University Press.

Haas, J. Eugene and Drabek, Thomas E. (1973), *Complex Organizations: A Sociological Perspective*. New York: Macmillan.

Haviland, William A. (1974), *Anthropology*. New York: Holt, Rinehart and Winston.

Higham, John (1957), Social Discrimination Against Jews in America. *American Jewish Historical Society* 47:1–33.

Hilberg, Raul (1967), *The Destruction of the European Jews*. Chicago: Quadrangle Books.

Hoebel, E. Adamson (1949), *Man in the Primitive World*. New York: McGraw-Hill.

Homans, George, and Schneider, David M. (1955), *Marriage, Authority, and Final Causes: A Study of Unilateral Cross-Cousin Marriage*. Glencoe: Free Press.

Howe, Irving (1976), *World of Our Fathers*. New York: Simon and Schuster.

Hubert, Jane, Forge, Anthony, and Firth, Raymond (1968), *Methods of Study of Middle-class Kinship in London: A Working Paper on the History of an Anthropological Project 1960–65.* London: Occasional Papers of the Department of Anthropology, London School of Economics and Political Science.

Hughes, Everett C. (1952), Memorandum on Going Concerns. Unpublished paper read at the 1952 Annual Meeting of the Society for Applied Anthropology.

Joffe, Natalie (1949) The Dynamics of Benefice among Eastern European Jews. *Social Forces* 27:238–247.

Jones, Maldwyn Allen (1960), *American Immigration.* Chicago: University of Chicago Press.

Josephy, Marcia Reines (1967), The Social Structure of a Jewish Family Organization. Unpublished Master's Thesis, Department of Anthropology, Columbia University.

Katz, Daniel and Kahn, Robert L. (1966), *The Social Psychology of Organizations.* New York: John Wiley.

Katz, Jacob (1973), *Out of the Ghetto: The Social Background of Jewish Emancipation, 1770–1870.* Cambridge: Harvard University Press.

Kramer, Judith R. and Leventman, Seymour (1961), *Children of the Gilded Ghetto.* New Haven: Yale University Press.

Kranzler, George (1961), *Williamsburg: A Jewish Community in Transition.* New York: Philipp Feldheim.

Lancaster, Lorraine (1961), Some Conceptual Problems in the Study of Family and Kin Ties in the British Isles. *British Journal of Sociology* 12:317–333.

Landes, Ruth and Zborowski, Mark (1950), Hypothesis Concerning the Eastern European Jewish Family. *Psychiatry* 13:447–464.

Landesman, A. F. (1969), *Brownsville: The Birth, Development and Passing of a Jewish Community in New York.* New York: Bloch Publishing Co.

Leach, E. R. (1961), *Rethinking Anthropology.* London: The Athlone Press.

– (1962), On Certain Unconsidered Aspects of Double Descent Systems. *Man* 62:130–134.

Leichter, Hope Jensen and Mitchell, William E. (1967) *Kinship and Casework.* New York: Russell Sage Foundation.

Leyton, Elliott (1965), Composite Descent Groups in Canada. *Man* 65:107—110.

Liebman, Charles S. (1973), *The Ambivilent American Jew: Politics, Religion and Family in American Jewish Life*. Philadelphia: Jewish Publication Society of America.

Little, Kenneth (1965), *West African Urbanization: A Study of Voluntary Associations in Social Change*. Cambridge: Cambridge University Press.

Litwak, Eugene (1960a), Occupational Mobility and Extended Family Cohesion. *American Sociological Review* 25:9—21.

— (1960b), Geographic Mobility and Extended Family Cohesion. *American Sociological Review* 25:385—394.

Loudon, J. B. (1961), Kinship and Crisis in South Wales. *British Journal of Sociology* 12:333—350.

Lowie, Robert H. (1947) *Primitive Society*. New York: Liverwright. (original 1920).

— (1948), *Social Organization*. New York: Rinehart.

Margareten, Joel *et al.* (1955), *Directory and Genealogy of the Horowitz-Margareten Family*. Los Angeles and New York: Horowitz-Margareten Family Association.

Marris, Peter (1961), *Family and Social Change in an African City: A Study of Rehousing in Lagos*. London: Routledge and Kegan Paul.

Matz, Milton (1961), The Meaning of the Christmas Tree to the American Jew. *Jewish Journal of Sociology* 3:129—137.

Mayer, Egon (1973), Jewish Orthodoxy in America: Towards the Sociology of a Residual Category. *Jewish Journal of Sociology* 15:151—165.

Mead, Margaret (1947), *The Mountain Arapesh*. Anthropological Papers of the American Museum of Natural History, Vol. 40.

— (1964), *Continuities in Cultural Evolution*. New Haven: Yale University Press.

Meillassoux, Claude (1968), *Urbanization of an African Community: Voluntary Associations in Bamako*. Seattle: University of Washington Press.

Merton, Robert K. (1957), *Social Theory and Social Structure*. Glencoe: Free Press.

Miller, J. Martin (1903), The Twentieth Century Atlas of the Commercial Geographical and Historical World. n.p.: L. G. Stahl.

Mitchell, William E. (1961a), Descent Groups Among New York City Jews. *Jewish Journal of Sociology* 3:121–128.

– (1961b), Lineality and Laterality in Urban Jewish Ambilineages. Read at the 60th Annual Meeting of the American Anthropological Association, Philadelphia.

– (1963), Theoretical Problems in the Concept of Kindred. *American Anthropologist* 65:343–354.

– (1965a), The Kindred and Baby Bathing in Academe. *American Anthropologist* 67:977–985.

– (1965b), Proximity Patterns of the Urban Jewish Kindred. *Man* 65:137–140.

– (1973), A New Weapon Stirs up Old Ghosts. *Natural History* 82:74–84.

Mitchell, William E. and Leichter, Hope Jensen (1961), Urban Ambilineages and Social Mobility. Read at the 31st Annual Meeting of the Eastern Sociological Society, New York City.

Mogey, John M. (1956), *Family and Neighborhood: Two Studies in Oxford.* London: Oxford University Press.

Murdock, George Peter (1960), Cognatic Forms of Social Organization. In: *Social Structure in Southeast Asia.* G. P. Murdock, Ed. Viking Fund Publication in Anthropology No. 20.

Nadel, S. F. (1951), *The Foundations of Social Anthropology.* Glencoe: Free Press.

Nagel, Ernest (1961), *The Structure of Science: Problems in the Logic of Scientific Explanation.* New York: Harcourt, Brace and World.

Newman, Louis I. (1965), *The Jewish People, Faith and Life.* New York: Bloch Publishing Co.

Norbeck, Edward (1962), Common-Interest Associations in Rural Japan. In: *Japanese Culture: Its Development and Characteristics.* Robert J. Smith and Richard K. Beardsley, Eds. Viking Fund Publications in Anthropology No. 34.

Ottenberg, Simon (1971), *Leadership and Authority in an African Society.* Seattle: University of Washington Press.

Parsons, Talcott (1943), The Kinship System of the Contemporary United States. *American Anthropologist* 45:22–38.

– (1954), *Essays in Sociological Theory.* Glencoe: Free Press.

— (1955), The American Family: Its Relations to Personality and to the Social Structure. In: *Family, Socialization and Interaction Processes*. Talcott Parsons and Robert F. Bales, Eds. Glencoe: Free Press.

— (1960), *Structure and Process in Modern Societies*. New York: Free Press of Glencoe.

Parsons, Talcott and Bales, Robert F., Eds. (1955), *Family, Socialization and Interaction Process*. Glencoe: Free Press.

Paudling, J. K. (1905), Educational Influences: New York. In: *The Russian Jew in the United States*. Charles S. Bernheimer, Ed. Philadelphia: John C. Winston.

Peranio, Roger (1961), Descent, Descent Line and Descent Group in Cognatic Social Systems. Proceedings of the 1961 Meeting of the American Ethnological Society.

Plotnicov, Leonard (1967), *Strangers to the City: Urban Man in Jos, Nigeria*. Pittsburgh: University of Pittsburgh Press.

Poll, Solomon (1962), *The Hasidic Community of Williamsburg*. New York: Free Press of Glencoe.

Radcliffe-Brown, A. R. (1950), Introduction. In: *African systems of Kinship and Marriage*. A. R. Radcliffe-Brown and Daryll Forde, Eds. London: Oxford University Press for the International African Institute.

— (1958), *Method in Social Anthropology*. Chicago: University of Chicago Press.

Reizenstein, Milton (1905), General Aspects of the Population: New York. In: *The Russian Jew in the United States*. Charles S. Bernheimer, Ed. Philadelphia: John C. Winston.

Rew, Alan (1974), *Social Images and Process in Urban New Guinea: A Study of Port Moresby*. American Ethnological Society Monograph No. 57. St. Paul: West Publishing Co.

Rischin, Moses (1962), *The Promised City: New York's Jews 1870–1914*. Cambridge: Harvard University Press.

Rontch, I. E., Ed. (1939), *Jewish Families and Family Circles of New York*. New York: Yiddish Writers' Union. (In Yiddish).

Roseman, Kenneth D. (1974), American Jewish Community Institutions in their Historical Context. *Jewish Journal of Sociology* 16:25–38.

Rosenberg, George S. and Anspach, Donald F. (1973), *Working Class Kinship*. Lexington, MA: D. C. Heath.

Rosenthal, Celia (1954), Deviation and Social Change in the Jewish Community of a Small Polish Town. *American Journal of Sociology* 60:177–181.

Sartre, Jean Paul (1946), *Réflexions sur la question juive*. Paris: Paul Morihien.

Sanders, Ronald (1969), *The Downtown Jews: Portraits of an Immigrant Generation*. New York: Harper and Row.

Scheffler, Harold W. (1966), Ancestor Worship in Anthropology: Or, Observations on Descent and Descent Groups. *Current Anthropology* 7:541–551.

– (1973), Kinship, Descent and Alliance. In: *Handbook of Social and Cultural Anthropology*. John J. Honigmann, Ed. Chicago: Rand McNally.

Schmidt, Alvin and Babchuk, Nicholas (1973), Trends in U.S. Fraternal Associations in the Twentieth Century. In: *Voluntary Action Research: 1973*. David Horton Smith, Ed. Lexington, MA: D. C. Heath.

Schneider, David M. (1965), Some Muddles in the Models: Or, How the System Really Works. In: *The Relevance of Models for Social Anthropology*. ASA Monographs No. 1. London: Tavistock.

– (1968), *American Kinship: A Cultural Account*. Englewood Cliffs, N. J.: Prentice-Hall.

Schneider, David M. and Homans, George C. (1955), Kinship Terminology and the American Kinship System. *American Anthropologist* 57:1194–1208.

Schneider, David M. and Smith, Raymond T. (1973), *Class Differences and Sex Roles in American Kinship and Family Structure*. Englewood Cliffs, N. J.: Prentice-Hall.

Schurtz, Heinrich (1902), *Altersklassen und Männerbünde: Eine Darstellung der Grundformen der Gesellschaft*. Berlin: Reimer.

Seligman, Ben B. (1958), Some Aspects of Jewish Demography. In: *The Jews: Social Patterns of an American Group*. Marshall Sklare, Ed., Glencoe: Free Press.

Service, Elman (1962), *Primitive Social Organization*. New York: Random House.

Shapiro, Harry I. (1960), *The Jewish People: A Biological History*. Paris: Unesco.

Sills, David L. (1968), Voluntary Associations: Sociological

Aspects. In: *International Encyclopedia of the Social Sciences* 16:362—379.

Sklare, Marshall, Ed. (1958), *The Jews: Social Patterns of An American Group*. New York: Free Press.

— (1971), *America's Jews*. New York: Random House.

— Ed. (1974a), *The Jew in American Society*. New York: Behrman House.

— Ed. (1974b), *The Jewish Community in America*. New York: Behrman House.

Slater, Mariam K. (1969), My Son the Doctor: Aspects of Mobility Among American Jews. *American Sociological Review* 34:359—373.

Slotkin, James Sydney (1950), *Social Anthropology*. New York: Macmillan.

Stewart, Elbert W. (1973), *Evolving Life Styles*. New York: McGraw Hill.

Spradley, James P. and McCurdy, David W. (1975), *Anthropology: A Cultural Perspective*. New York: John Wiley and Sons.

Strodtbeck, Fred L. (1958), Family Interaction, Values, and Achievement. In: *The Jews: Social Patterns of an American Group*. Marshall Sklare, Ed. Glencoe: Free Press.

Sussman, Marvin B. (1959), The Isolated Nuclear Family: Fact or Fiction. *Social Problems* 6:333—340.

Sutherland, John W. (1973), *A General Systems Philosophy for the Social and Behavioral Sciences*. New York: George Braziller.

Sutker, Solomon (1958), The Role of Social Clubs in the Atlanta Jewish Community. In: *The Jews: Social Patterns of an American Group*. Marshall Sklare, Ed. Glencoe: Free Press.

Szold, Henrietta (1905), Elements of the Jewish Population in the United States. In: *The Russian Jew in the United States*. Charles S. Bernheimer, Ed. Philadelphia: John C. Winston.

Thompson, James D. and Tuden, Arthur (1959), Strategies, Structures, and Processes of Organizational Decision. In: *Comparative Studies in Administration*. James D. Thompson *et al.*, Eds. Pittsburgh: University of Pittsburgh Press.

T'ien Ju-K'ang (1953), *The Chinese of Sarawak*. The London School of Economics and Political Science Monographs on Social Anthropology No. 12.

Townsend, Peter (1957), *The Family Life of Old People: An Inquiry in East London*. London: Routledge and Kegan Paul.

Vetulani, Adam (1962), The Jews in Medieval Poland. *Jewish Journal of Sociology* 4:274–294.

Vondracek, Felix John (1972), The Rise of Fraternal Organizations in the United States, 1868–1900. *Social Science* 47:26–33.

Wagley, Charles and Harris, Marvin (1958), *Minorities in the New World*. New York: Columbia University Press.

Warner, W. Lloyd and Lunt, Paul S. (1941), *The Social Life of a Modern Community*. New Haven: Yale University Press.

Weinryb, Bernard D. (1958), Jewish Immigration and Accommodation to America. In: *The Jews: Social Patterns of an American Group*. Marshall Sklare, Ed. Glencoe: Free Press.

Westerman, Jacqueline (1967), Note on Balswick's Article – A Response. *Jewish Social Studies* 28:241–244.

White, Leslie A. (1962), *The Pueblo of Sia, New Mexico*. Smithsonian Institute Bureau of American Ethnology, Bulletin No. 184.

Winch, Robert F. (1968), Some Observations on Extended Familism in the United States. In: *Selected Studies in Marriage and the Family*. Robert F. Winch and Louis Wolf Goodman, Eds. New York: Holt, Rinehart and Winston.

Winch, Robert F., Greer, Scott and Blumberg, Rae Lesser (1967), Ethnicity and Extended Familism in an Upper-Middle-Class Suburb. *American Sociological Review* 32:265–272.

Wirth, Louis (1956), *The Ghetto*. University of Chicago Press.

Worsley, Peter (1957), *The Trumpet Shall Sound: A Study of "Cargo" Cults in Melanesia*. London: MacGibbon and Kee.

Wright, Charles R. and Hyman, Herbert H. (1958), Voluntary Association Memberships of American Adults: Evidence from National Sample Surveys. *American Sociological Review* 23:284–294.

Wu, David H. (1975), To Kill Three Birds with one Stone: The Rotating Credit Associations of the Papua New Guinea Chinese. *American Ethnologist* 3:565–584.

Young, Michael and Geertz, Hildred (1961), Old Age in London and San Francisco: Some Families Compared. *British Journal of Sociology* 12:124-141.

Zborowski, Mark (1949), The Place of Book-Learning in Traditional Jewish Culture. *Harvard Educational Review* 19:97—109.

Zborowski, Mark and Herzog, Elizabeth (1952), *Life is with People: The Jewish Little-Town of Eastern Europe*. New York: International Universities Press.

Zelditch, Morris, Jr. (1955), Role Differentiation in the Nuclear Family: A Comparative Study. In: *Family Socialization and Interaction Process*. Talcott Parsons and Robert Bales, Eds. Chicago: Rand McNally.

— (1964a), Family, Marriage, and Kinship. In: *Handbook of Modern Sociology*. Robert E. L. Faris, Ed. Chicago: Rand McNally.

— (1964b), Cross-Cultural Analyses of Family Structure In: *Handbook of Marriage and the Family*. Harold T. Christensen, Ed. Chicago: Rand McNally.

Index